Beginning Programming For Dummies®

Cheat Sheet

Tips for writing programs

- Use descriptive variable names.
- Use appropriate data types.
- Write programs that are easy to read and understand.
- Use simple algorithms and data structures whenever possible.
- Comment your program liberally.
- Write modular programs by dividing a large program into several smaller programs that are isolated from one another.
- Test boundary conditions by giving your program extremely high and extremely low numbers.
- Choose the right algorithm and data structure for your program.
- Eliminate all unnecessary instructions or variables.
- Make your program work first; then worry about optimizing the program to make it smaller and faster. Remember that a slow, bloated program that works is preferable to a small, fast program that doesn't work.

Shortcut keys for QBASIC

Key	What It Does
F1	Display context-sensitive help
Shift+F1	Display instructions for using QBASIC's help file
F2	View a different subprogram
F3	Repeat last find
F4	View the output screen
F5	Continue running a program after temporarily pausing
Shift+F5	Start running a program
F8	Step through a program line by line
F9	Toggle a breakpoint
F10	Step through a program line by line, skipping over subprograms
Shift+Del	Cut
Ctrl+Ins	Copy
Shift+Ins	Paste
Del	Clear

QBASIC type declaration characters

Data Type	Character	Example	Equivalent To
Double	#	DIM Fraction#	DIM Fraction AS DOUBLE
Integer	%	DIM Count%	DIM Count AS INTEGER
Long	&	DIM BigNum&	DIM BigNum AS LONG
Single	!	DIM SmallNum!	DIM SmallNum AS SINGLE
String	$	DIM MyString$	DIM MyString AS STRING

...For Dummies®: Bestselling Book Series for Beginners

Beginning Programming For Dummies®

Cheat Sheet

QBASIC loop structures

```
DO WHILE Condition
    Instructions
Loop

DO
    Instructions
LOOP WHILE Condition

DO UNTIL Condition
    Instructions
LOOP

DO
    Instructions
LOOP UNTIL Condition

FOR Counter = Start TO End
    Instructions
NEXT Counter

FOR Counter = Start TO End STEP
Increment
    Instructions
NEXT Counter
```

Common filename extensions

Extension	Description
ASM	Assembly language source code
BAS	QBASIC or Visual Basic source code
C	C language source code
CPP	C++ language source code
CLA	Java class file (byte code format, short for CLASS)
EXE	Executable file (machine code format)
HTM	HyperText Markup Language file (short for HTML)
JAV	Java source code (short for JAVA)
JS	JavaScript source code
PAS	Pascal language source code
TXT	Text or ASCII file

QBASIC control structures

```
IF Condition THEN
Instructions

IF Condition THEN
    Instructions1
    Instructions2
END IF

IF Condition THEN
    Instructions1
ELSE
    Instructons2
END IF

IF Condition1 THEN
    Instructions1
ELSEIF Condition2 THEN
    Instructions2
END IF

SELECT CASE VariableName
CASE X
    Instructions1
CASE Y
    Instructions2
CASE Z
    Instructions3
END SELECT

SELECT CASE VariableName
CASE X
  Instructions1
CASE Y
    Instructions2
CASE Z
    Instructions3
CASE ELSE
    InstructionsDefault
END SELECT
```

BEGINNING PROGRAMMING

FOR DUMMIES®

IDG
BOOKS
WORLDWIDE

IDG Books Worldwide, Inc.
An International Data Group Company

Foster City, CA ◆ Chicago, IL ◆ Indianapolis, IN ◆ New York, NY

Beginning Programming For Dummies®

Published by
IDG Books Worldwide, Inc.
An International Data Group Company
919 E. Hillsdale Blvd.
Suite 400
Foster City, CA 94404
www.idgbooks.com (IDG Books Worldwide Web site)
www.dummies.com (Dummies Press Web site)

Library of Congress Catalog Card No.: 99-64910

ISBN: 0-7645-0596-3

Printed in the United States of America

10 9 8 7 6 5 4 3 2 1

1B/RW/QY/ZZ/IN

Distributed in the United States by IDG Books Worldwide, Inc.

Distributed by CDG Books Canada Inc. for Canada; by Transworld Publishers Limited in the United Kingdom; by IDG Norge Books for Norway; by IDG Sweden Books for Sweden; by IDG Books Australia Publishing Corporation Pty. Ltd. for Australia and New Zealand; by TransQuest Publishers Pte Ltd. for Singapore, Malaysia, Thailand, Indonesia, and Hong Kong; by Gotop Information Inc. for Taiwan; by ICG Muse, Inc. for Japan; by Norma Comunicaciones S.A. for Colombia; by Intersoft for South Africa; by Eyrolles for France; by International Thomson Publishing for Germany, Austria and Switzerland; by Distribuidora Cuspide for Argentina; by LR International for Brazil; by Galileo Libros for Chile; by Ediciones ZETA S.C.R. Ltda. for Peru; by WS Computer Publishing Corporation, Inc., for the Philippines; by Contemporanea de Ediciones for Venezuela; by Express Computer Distributors for the Caribbean and West Indies; by Micronesia Media Distributor, Inc. for Micronesia; by Grupo Editorial Norma S.A. for Guatemala; by Chips Computadoras S.A. de C.V. for Mexico; by Editorial Norma de Panama S.A. for Panama; by American Bookshops for Finland. Authorized Sales Agent: Anthony Rudkin Associates for the Middle East and North Africa.

For general information on IDG Books Worldwide's books in the U.S., please call our Consumer Customer Service department at 800-762-2974. For reseller information, including discounts and premium sales, please call our Reseller Customer Service department at 800-434-3422.

For information on where to purchase IDG Books Worldwide's books outside the U.S., please contact our International Sales department at 317-596-5530 or fax 317-596-5692.

For consumer information on foreign language translations, please contact our Customer Service department at 1-800-434-3422, fax 317-596-5692, or e-mail rights@idgbooks.com.

For information on licensing foreign or domestic rights, please phone +1-650-655-3109.

For sales inquiries and special prices for bulk quantities, please contact our Sales department at 650-655-3200 or write to the address above.

For information on using IDG Books Worldwide's books in the classroom or for ordering examination copies, please contact our Educational Sales department at 800-434-2086 or fax 317-596-5499.

For press review copies, author interviews, or other publicity information, please contact our Public Relations department at 650-655-3000 or fax 650-655-3299.

For authorization to photocopy items for corporate, personal, or educational use, please contact Copyright Clearance Center, 222 Rosewood Drive, Danvers, MA 01923, or fax 978-750-4470.

About the Author

After spending his first two post-college years working for a dead-end corporation that encouraged its employees to use euphemisms to disguise the fact that they were manufacturing weapons with the potential to wipe out most forms of life on the planet, **Wallace Wang** decided that his life was meant to be spent doing something more exciting than existing in a corporate culture that stifled freedom and democracy while building missiles ostensibly to protect freedom and democracy. With the thought of escape in his mind, he bought one of the first IBM personal computers on the market — and quickly realized that the accompanying computer manuals were completely incomprehensible.

Upon deciphering the manuals and learning to master the arcane commands of the ancient MS-DOS version 1.25 operating system, he decided to publish fragments of his notes in a local computer magazine for the amusement of others and to provide an alternative source of income for his eventual departure from the mentally suffocating environment of the military-industrial complex.

When people began responding favorably to his introductory computer magazine articles, he continued writing more, eventually turning to writing full-time. For the first time, he managed to earn a living in a job that didn't involve developing something that could blow up people who happen to live in another part of the world.

Today, the author is happily pursuing a dual career in the book publishing industry and the stand-up comedy industry. His eventual goal is to convince people that it's all right to enjoy yourself while learning. In the meantime, he'll continue making fun of any idiots and morons who happen to get in his way.

ABOUT IDG BOOKS WORLDWIDE

Welcome to the world of IDG Books Worldwide.

IDG Books Worldwide, Inc., is a subsidiary of International Data Group, the world's largest publisher of computer-related information and the leading global provider of information services on information technology. IDG was founded more than 30 years ago by Patrick J. McGovern and now employs more than 9,000 people worldwide. IDG publishes more than 290 computer publications in over 75 countries. More than 90 million people read one or more IDG publications each month.

Launched in 1990, IDG Books Worldwide is today the #1 publisher of best-selling computer books in the United States. We are proud to have received eight awards from the Computer Press Association in recognition of editorial excellence and three from Computer Currents' First Annual Readers' Choice Awards. Our best-selling ...*For Dummies*® series has more than 50 million copies in print with translations in 31 languages. IDG Books Worldwide, through a joint venture with IDG's Hi-Tech Beijing, became the first U.S. publisher to publish a computer book in the People's Republic of China. In record time, IDG Books Worldwide has become the first choice for millions of readers around the world who want to learn how to better manage their businesses.

Our mission is simple: Every one of our books is designed to bring extra value and skill-building instructions to the reader. Our books are written by experts who understand and care about our readers. The knowledge base of our editorial staff comes from years of experience in publishing, education, and journalism — experience we use to produce books to carry us into the new millennium. In short, we care about books, so we attract the best people. We devote special attention to details such as audience, interior design, use of icons, and illustrations. And because we use an efficient process of authoring, editing, and desktop publishing our books electronically, we can spend more time ensuring superior content and less time on the technicalities of making books.

You can count on our commitment to deliver high-quality books at competitive prices on topics you want to read about. At IDG Books Worldwide, we continue in the IDG tradition of delivering quality for more than 30 years. You'll find no better book on a subject than one from IDG Books Worldwide.

John Kilcullen
Chairman and CEO
IDG Books Worldwide, Inc.

Steven Berkowitz
President and Publisher
IDG Books Worldwide, Inc.

Eighth Annual Computer Press Awards ≥1992

Ninth Annual Computer Press Awards ≥1993

Tenth Annual Computer Press Awards ≥1994

Eleventh Annual Computer Press Awards ≥1995

Dedication

This book is dedicated to all the wonderful people I've met along the path of life, including:

Cassandra (my wife) and her cats (Bo, Scraps, Tasha, and Nuit).

Lily Carnie, the only person I know who can truly see both sides of the story.

Budd Friedman, for putting me on his show, "A&E's Evening at the Improv."

Pat Buckles, for putting me on the show, "Extreme Gong."

All the friendly folks I've met while performing at the Riviera Comedy Club, located at the Riviera Hotel & Casino in Las Vegas: Steve Schirripa, Don Learned, Bob Zany, Gerry Bednob, Steve Seagren, Tony Vicich, and George Hirschmann. The next time you're visiting Las Vegas, drop by the Riviera and watch a comedy show. Then dump some money in a slot machine on the way out to ensure that the Riviera Hotel & Casino continues making enough money to keep its comedy club open.

Patrick DeGuire and Dat Phan, who helped me form Top Bananas (www. topbananas.com), our company devoted to providing clean, quality stand-up comedy to the wonderful people in San Diego. Thanks must also go to Leo (the man, the myth, the legend) Fontaine, Dante, Chris (the Zooman) Clobber, and Karen Rontowski (who gets excited just to see her name in a book).

Author's Acknowledgments

If it wasn't for Matt Wagner and Bill Gladstone at Waterside Productions, this book might never have been written (at least by me). That's why I don't mind paying these guys 15 percent of the book royalties so that they can afford to buy their groceries.

Some other people who deserve thanks include Ryan Rader, Gwenette Gaddis, Greg Croy, Rev Mengle, and the rest of the happy gang of editors, managers, and workers who make IDG Books Worldwide, Inc. a great company to work for, because they're the complete opposite of their competition across town.

Additional thanks go to Allen Wyatt (the technical reviewer) for making sure that everything in this book is accurate, and to Cassandra (my wife) for putting up with multiple computers that (from her point of view) seem to spontaneously appear and disappear from the house at random. Each time a computer disappears, a more advanced model appears that promises more speed and hard disk space, but still never seems to have more speed or as much room as the previous computer model that it replaced.

A final note of thanks must go to the Chinese and Russians who have translated my other books, *Microsoft Office For Dummies* and *Visual Basic For Dummies*. The Chinese and Russian editions are the only foreign translations of my books ever to include my previously published references to General Dynamics as a "bomb factory." Whether translators in other countries purposely omitted this humorous reference or whether it's just a coincidence that only the Chinese and Russian editions included this reference is unknown.

Still, this fact alone provides an endless source of amusement to think that Chinese and Russian readers are privy to an American joking about his country's nuclear missile factories, while readers in other countries are not. For that reason alone, the Chinese and Russian translators of my books have my eternal gratitude and blessing, not because they happen to be Chinese or Russian, but because they appear to be able to understand a joke.

Publisher's Acknowledgments

We're proud of this book; please register your comments through our IDG Books Worldwide Online Registration Form located at http://my2cents.dummies.com.

Some of the people who helped bring this book to market include the following:

Acquisitions, Editorial, and Media Development

Project Editor: Ryan Rader

Acquisitions Editor: Greg Croy

Copy Editor: Gwenette Gaddis

Technical Editor: Allen Wyatt

Editorial Manager: Leah P. Cameron

Editorial Assistant: Beth Parlon

Production

Project Coordinator: Maridee V. Ennis

Layout and Graphics: Amy Adrian, Angela F. Hunckler, Kate Jenkins, Dave McKelvey, Brent Savage, Jacque Schneider, Janet Seib, Michael Sullivan, Brian Torwelle, Mary Jo Weis, Dan Whetstine,

Proofreaders: Arielle Carole Mennelle, Nancy Price, Marianne Santy

Indexer: Sherry Massey

Special Help
William Barton; James Russell

General and Administrative

IDG Books Worldwide, Inc.: John Kilcullen, CEO; Steven Berkowitz, President and Publisher

IDG Books Technology Publishing Group: Richard Swadley, Senior Vice President and Publisher; Walter Bruce III, Vice President and Associate Publisher; Steven Sayre, Associate Publisher; Joseph Wikert, Associate Publisher; Mary Bednarek, Branded Product Development Director; Mary Corder, Editorial Director

IDG Books Consumer Publishing Group: Roland Elgey, Senior Vice President and Publisher; Kathleen A. Welton, Vice President and Publisher; Kevin Thornton, Acquisitions Manager; Kristin A. Cocks, Editorial Director

IDG Books Internet Publishing Group: Brenda McLaughlin, Senior Vice President and Publisher; Diane Graves Steele, Vice President and Associate Publisher; Sofia Marchant, Online Marketing Manager

IDG Books Production for Dummies Press: Michael R. Britton, Vice President of Production; Debbie Stailey, Associate Director of Production; Cindy L. Phipps, Manager of Project Coordination, Production Proofreading, and Indexing; Shelley Lea, Supervisor of Graphics and Design; Debbie J. Gates, Production Systems Specialist; Robert Springer, Supervisor of Proofreading; Laura Carpenter, Production Control Manager; Tony Augsburger, Supervisor of Reprints and Bluelines

◆

The publisher would like to give special thanks to Patrick J. McGovern, without whom this book would not have been possible.

◆

Contents at a Glance

Cartoons at a Glance

By Rich Tennant

page 7

page 147

page 205

page 339

page 59

page 291

page 251

Fax: 978-546-7747 • E-mail: the5wave@tiac.net

Table of Contents

Introduction

First, let's get one thing out of the way: Anyone can learn to program a computer. Computer programming doesn't require a high IQ and an innate proficiency in advanced mathematics. Computer programming just requires a desire to learn and the patience to never give up.

Programming is a skill like swimming, dancing, and juggling. Some people are naturally better than others, but anyone can get better with constant practice. That's why so many kids become programming wizards at such an early age. The kids aren't necessarily brilliant; they're just willing to put in the time to learn a new skill, and they're not afraid of failing.

If you've ever dreamed about writing your own programs, rest assured that you can. Programming can be lots of fun, but it can also be frustrating, annoying, and time-consuming. That's why IDG Books Worldwide published this particular book — to help you learn how to program a computer with the minimum amount of inconvenience and the maximum amount of enjoyment.

Whether you want to learn computer programming for fun, to start a new career, or to help make your current job easier, consider this book your personal guide through the sometimes scary, and initially intimidating, world of computer programming.

By the time you finish this book, you'll be able to choose the best programming language to accomplish a particular task, understand the tools that programmers use, and even write your own programs for personal use or for sale to others.

After you read *Beginning Programming For Dummies*, you can get more detailed information about specific languages by reading *Visual Basic 6 For Windows For Dummies*, by Wallace Wang; *C For Dummies*, by Dan Gookin; *Visual C++ 6 For Dummies*, by Michael Hyman and Bob Arnson; *Access Programming For Dummies*, by Rob Krumm; *C++ For Dummies*, by Stephen R. Davis; *Java Programming For Dummies*, by Donald J. Koosis and David Koosis; *Windows 98 Programming For Dummies*, by Stephen R. Davis and Richard J. Simon; and *Borland C++ Builder 3 For Dummies*, by Jason Vokes (all published by IDG Books Worldwide, Inc.).

Who Should Buy This Book

You should buy this book right now, because you know the importance of stimulating the economy by spending as much money as possible. But you should especially buy this book if you want to know the following:

- How to write a computer program.
- The best programming languages to use and why.
- Shortcuts for programming a computer as simply and quickly as possible.
- The evolution of computer programming languages.
- How to program a Macintosh, PalmPilot, Linux, Windows 95/98/NT/2000, or Windows CE computer.
- Whether to write your next computer program using Visual Basic, C++, Delphi, or some other programming language.

To help you get started right away, this book shows you how to use a programming language called QBASIC, which comes free with every copy of MS-DOS 5.0 or later and Windows 95 or later. Using this book and QBASIC, you can start programming right away and later graduate to the other programming books in the popular ...*For Dummies* series.

How This Book Is Organized

This book follows the tradition of the printing industry by organizing consecutively numbered pages one after the other to form a book. To help you find what you need quickly, this book is divided into seven parts, with each part covering a certain topic about programming a computer. Whenever you need help, just flip through the book, find the part that covers the topic you're looking for, and then keep the book at your side as you get back to work.

Part I: Programming a Computer

If computer programming seems a mysterious arcane science, relax. This part of the book demystifies all the common myths about computer programming, shows you exactly how computer programs work, and explains why programming isn't as difficult as many people think.

To help you better understand programming, this part also shows you how programming has evolved, why so many different programming languages exist, and how programming follows easy-to-remember principles. It helps you get started programming your own computer right away.

Part II: Learning Programming with QBASIC

Trying to learn programming from a book is like trying to learn judo by reading a pamphlet. In both cases, you may have a theoretical understanding of the subject, but until you actually practice your skill, you don't know how much you've really picked up.

To give you practical, hands-on experience using an honest-to-goodness programming language, this part of the book explains how to install and use QBASIC, which enables you to write computer programs using the BASIC programming language. Writing programs in QBASIC helps you to better understand how programming really works as you work with programs and see the results right on your own computer.

Part III: Advanced QBASIC Programming

QBASIC provides plenty of advanced features for displaying graphics, making sound, and debugging your programs. This part of the book shows you how to take advantage of these special features and shows you the principles behind writing programs in other languages at the same time.

Part IV: Dealing with Data Structures

As do people, computers need a place to store information. People usually dump their information in wallets, purses, filing cabinets, or garages, but computers don't have that luxury.

Instead, computers must store information in something called a data structure. Every computer program uses data structures, and programmers have invented all sorts of different data structures for various uses.

Part V: Algorithms: Telling the Computer What to Do

Algorithms are a fancy way of telling a computer how to accomplish a specific task, step-by-step. Think of an algorithm as a recipe that the computer blindly follows without question.

One perfect algorithm doesn't exist for writing all computer programs, just as one perfect recipe doesn't exist for making dinners. To make programming easier, programmers have invented common algorithms for accomplishing certain tasks. This part of the book explains how those algorithms work and why you would want to use them.

Part VI: Internet Programming

The Internet is fast becoming an integral part of the computer world, so this part of the book introduces you to the basics of various Internet languages, ranging from HTML (which designs the appearance of Web pages) to JavaScript and Java.

In this part, you also see how other people create cool Web pages that look good and can display forms and respond to users. You can use this information to create Web sites that interact with users.

Part VII: The Part of Tens

This book gently guides you toward writing your own programs, so this part of the book provides information that you may find useful to take your programming education a step further.

This part shows you many of the opportunities that a career in programming can afford you. In this part, you also discover where to find and use various free or commercial programming languages, with common names such as C++ and BASIC or bizarre names such as LISP, Modula-3, and Python.

How to Use This Book

Most people use this book to read, although a few have been known to line their bookshelves with copies to give the room a more literary appearance. You're most likely to use this book as a reference, a tutorial, or a weapon (if you can throw it really hard at somebody you don't like).

Ideally, you should use this book along with your computer. Read some of the book and then try what you just read on your computer so that you can see with your own eyes how programming works.

Foolish assumptions

I assume that you have access to a computer (because trying to understand computer programming is tough if you can't get near a computer). To take full advantage of this book, you should have a computer running Microsoft Windows 95, Windows 98, Windows NT, or Windows 2000.

If you don't feel comfortable with Windows 95 or Windows 98, buy *Windows 95 For Dummies* or *Windows 98 For Dummies,* by Andy Rathbone (published by IDG Books Worldwide, Inc.). For more information about Windows NT, pick up a copy of *Windows NT 4 For Dummies,* by Andy Rathbone and Sharon Crawford (published by IDG Books Worldwide, Inc.).

If you have a Macintosh or any computer that doesn't run MS-DOS or Windows, don't worry. This book focuses on programming in general, so you can apply the programming principles from this book to use on your specific computer.

Icons used in this book

Icons highlight useful tips, important information to remember, or technical explanations that can amuse you for a moment before you forget all about them. Keep an eye open for the following icons throughout the book:

This icon highlights useful information that can save you time (as long as you remember it, of course).

This icon reminds you to do something or emphasizes an important point that you don't want to forget.

Watch out! This icon tells you how to avoid headaches and trouble.

This icon points out step-by-step explanations that show how the computer follows the instructions in a typical program.

This icon highlights information that's nice to know but that you can safely ignore if you choose. (If you want to become a real programmer, though, you should cram your brain with as much technical information as possible so that you can fit in with the rest of the programmers in the world.)

Part I
Programming a Computer

The 5th Wave   By Rich Tennant

IF BOB DYLAN HAD PURSUED A CAREER IN COMPUTERS

"PUT HIM IN FRONT OF A TERMINAL AND HE'S A GENIUS, BUT OTHER-WISE THE GUY IS SUCH A BROODING, GLOOMY GUS HE'LL NEVER BREAK INTO MANAGEMENT."

In this part . . .

Figuring out how to program a computer may seem intimidating, so this part of the book gently guides you through the wonderful world of computer programming. First, you see exactly what programs do and how professionals write programs.

Next, you find out why so many different programming languages exist for you to choose from and why some are more popular than others. You get to know the different tools that programmers use to create, edit, and distribute a program from start to finish.

Finally, this part shows you what to consider when you decide to write a program. You see the pros and cons of using different programming languages and understand how people can write programs even though they may have very little programming experience.

By the time you finish this part of the book, you'll have a better idea of how to write a program, what steps to follow, and how to convert your idea for a program into an actual working product that you can sell or give away for others to use.

Chapter 1

Learning Computer Programming for the First Time

*D*espite what you may have heard, learning to program a computer isn't difficult. Computer programming is a skill that anyone can pick up, given enough practice and patience.

Although computers may seem like tremendously complex electronic beasts, relax. Few people know how an internal-combustion engine works, yet people still learn how to drive a car. Similarly, anyone can learn programming without worrying about the specific details that make a computer work.

Why Learn Computer Programming?

The first question that you (or your friends, co-workers, and relatives) may ask is, "Why should I bother learning to program a computer?" The answer depends on your ultimate goals, but here are some stock answers to consider:

✔ **For fun:** People learn skiing, dancing, gardening, scuba diving, and flower arranging because they enjoy the experience. They may never become professionals or experts in their chosen hobby, but they enjoy fiddling around with it nevertheless. Likewise, programming a computer can be fun because you can make simple programs that can display your boss's ugly face on the computer. More complex programs can make you a million dollars so that you never need to work for a boss who has an ugly face. Figure 1-1 shows a program called Comedy Writer, which prods users into creating funny ideas. A stand-up comedian wrote the program in BASIC for his own amusement, using a program called CA-Realizer. Then he decided to sell the program to others.

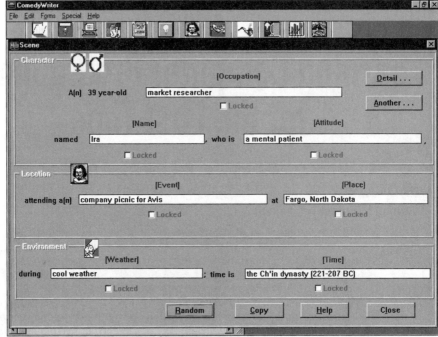

Figure 1-1:
The Comedy
Writer
program is
an example
of fun
computer
program-
ming.

✔ **To fill a need:** Many people learn programming with no intention of
becoming a full-time, professional programmer. They just want a program that solves a particular problem, but they can't find a program that
does it, so they write the program themselves. For example, a man once
needed a program to help him file his taxes, but he couldn't find one, so
he taught himself programming and wound up creating one of the very
first tax-preparation programs. Similarly, a psychologist, who specialized
in dream interpretation, used his knowledge and a program called
ToolBook to create and sell DreamScape, a program that interprets the
meaning of dreams (as shown in Figure 1-2). Whatever your interests,
you can write a program to solve a specific problem that others may find
useful as well.

✔ **For a new or second career:** With computers taking over the world, you
will never be unemployed for long if you know how to program a computer. Companies are always looking to create new programs, but you'll
also find a growing market for programmers who can maintain and

modify the millions of existing programs that do everything from storing hotel reservations to transferring bank deposits electronically. If you know how to program a computer, you're in a much better position to earn a lot of money and live wherever you want. You may still want to keep your current job, but programming gives you a new way to expand and share your knowledge. For example, a group of alternative care practitioners wrote IBIS (as shown in Figure 1-3), a program that provides information for treating a variety of ailments by using acupuncture, massage, diet, and homeopathy. They wrote IBIS by using MetaCard, a program similar to Apple Computer's HyperCard.

Although you can make a decent living programming computers, you can also make a decent living selling paper clips, fixing leaky toilets, or raising farm animals. If you aren't doing what you truly enjoy, all the money in the world isn't going to make your life better. Choose to learn programming because you want to, not because you think it's going to make you rich.

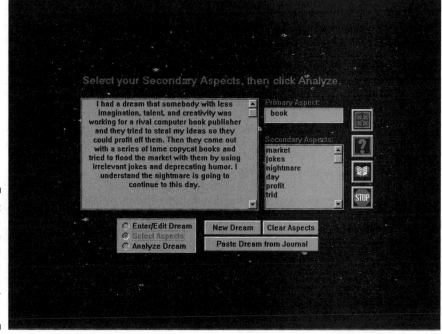

Figure 1-2:
DreamScape
can help
you
interpret the
meaning
of your
dreams.

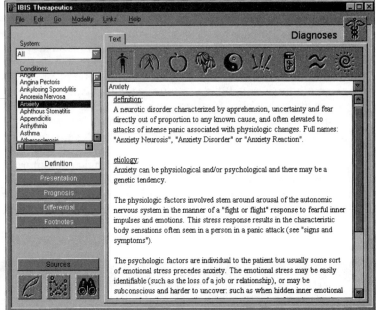

Figure 1-3:
The IBIS
program
gives
medical
treatment
information.

How Does a Computer Program Work?

Computers don't do anything without being told what to do, much like the average teenager. To make the computer do something useful, you must give it instructions.

You can give a computer instructions in two ways: One, you write a program, which tells a computer what to do, step-by-step, much like you write out a recipe. Two, you can buy a program that someone else has already written that tells the computer what to do. Ultimately, to get a computer to do something useful, you (or somebody else) must write a program.

A program does nothing more than tell the computer how to accept some type of input, manipulate that input, and spit it back out again in some form that humans find useful. Table 1-1 lists some common types of programs, the type of input they accept, and the output they produce.

Table 1-1	Input and Output for Various Programs		
Type of Program	*Input*	*What the Program Does*	*Output*
Word processor	Characters typed from the keyboard	Formats the text, corrects spelling	Displays and prints neatly organized text
Game	Keystrokes or joystick movements	Calculates how fast and far to move a cartoon figure on-screen	Moves a cartoon figure on-screen
Stock-market predictor	Current and past prices for stocks	Tries to recognize trends in a stock's price fluctuations	Predicts the future price of a stock
Missile guidance program	Current location of the missile and the target	Calculates how to make the missile's location and the target's location coincide	Corrects the missile's trajectory so that it stays aimed at the target
Optical character recognition (OCR)	Text from a scanner	Recognizes shapes of characters	Converts scanned text into a text file that can be edited by a word processor
Web browser	Hypertext Markup Language (HTML) codes stored on other computers	Converts the HTML codes into text and graphics	Displays Web pages on the computer screen

Programming is problem solving

Essentially, a program tells the computer how to solve a specific problem. Because the world is full of problems, the number and variety of programs that people can write for computers is practically endless.

But to tell a computer how to solve one big problem, you usually must tell the computer how to solve a bunch of little problems that make up the bigger problem. For example, if you want to make your own video game, you need to solve some of the following problems:

✔ Determine how far to move a cartoon figure on-screen (such as a car, a spaceship, or a man) as the user moves a joystick.

✔ Detect whether the cartoon figure bumps into a wall, falls off a cliff, or runs into another cartoon figure on-screen.

✔ Make sure that the cartoon figure doesn't make any illegal moves, such as walking through a wall.

✔ Draw the terrain surrounding the cartoon figure and make sure that, if the cartoon figure walks behind an object such as a tree, the tree realistically blocks the figure from sight.

✔ Determine whether bullets fired by another cartoon figure are hitting the player's cartoon figure. If so, determine the amount of damage, how it affects the movement of the damaged cartoon figure, and how the damage appears on-screen.

The simpler the problem is that you need to solve, the more easily you can write a program that tells the computer how to work. A program that displays a simple Ping-Pong game with two stick paddles and a ball is much easier to write than a program that displays World War II fighter airplanes firing machine guns and dropping bombs on moving tanks, while dodging anti-aircraft fire.

Programming isn't difficult; it's just time-consuming

Programming really isn't that difficult or mysterious. If you can write step-by-step instructions directing someone to your house, you can write a program.

The hardest part about programming is identifying all the little problems that make up the big problem you're trying to solve. Because computers are completely stupid, you need to tell them how to do everything.

For example, if you were giving a friend instructions to get to your house, you may write down the following:

✔ Go south on Highway I-5.

✔ Get off at the Sweetwater Road exit.

✔ Turn right at the light.

✔ Turn into the second driveway on the left.

Of course, if you tried giving these instructions to a computer, the computer would get confused and want to know the following:

Sometimes programs never work

After spending years writing a program, sometimes people find that throwing away the whole thing and starting over is easier (and cheaper) than trying to figure out why the current program isn't working and how to make it work.

For example, back in the mid-1980s, the United States government had the bright idea to develop a self-propelled, anti-aircraft weapon nicknamed the Sergeant York. The purpose of the Sergeant York weapon was simple: Find an enemy aircraft and shoot it down.

Unfortunately, the program controlling the Sergeant York never quite worked correctly. After spending millions of dollars and countless hours rewriting the program, testing it, and rewriting it again, the programmers thought they had finally gotten the program to work right.

To celebrate their achievement, the company that made the Sergeant York weapon staged a demonstration for the top Pentagon generals and officials. They put the Sergeant York in a field, sat all the people from the Pentagon in a

nearby grandstand, and flew a remote-controlled drone overhead to demonstrate the Sergeant York's ability to track and shoot down an enemy airplane.

But instead of aiming at the overhead target, rumor has it that the Sergeant York leveled its twin 40mm cannons toward the ground and swiveled its guns until they pointed directly at the grandstand where all the Pentagon officials were sitting.

Needless to say, the Pentagon officials created quite a commotion as they scrambled to get out of the line of fire. Fortunately, the Sergeant York didn't fire its cannons into the grandstand, but after this disastrous demonstration, the Pentagon cancelled further development and scrapped the entire Sergeant York project.

So if you ever start writing a program and feel like giving up before it ever works, you'll be in good company with the Pentagon, military contractors, Fortune 500 corporations, and practically everyone else in the world.

> ✔ Where do I start and exactly how far south do I drive down Highway I-5?
>
> ✔ How do I recognize the Sweetwater Road exit, and how do I get off at this exit?
>
> ✔ After I turn right at the light, how far to the right should I turn, and do you mean the traffic light or the street light on the corner?
>
> ✔ After I turn into the second driveway on the left, what do I do next? Park the car? Honk the horn? Gun the engine and accelerate through your garage door?

Computers need to be told how to do everything, which can make giving them instructions as aggravating and frustrating as telling children what to do. Unless you specify everything you want the computer to do and exactly how to do it, the computer doesn't do what you want it to do.

What Do I Need to Know to Program a Computer?

If you're the type who finds the idea of making a program (such as a video game) more exciting than actually using it, you already have everything you need to program a computer. If you want to learn computer programming, it helps to have a healthy dose of these three qualities:

- ✔ **Desire:** If you want something badly enough, you tend to get it (although you may have to serve time in prison afterward if you do something illegal to get it). If you have the desire to learn how to program a computer, your desire helps you learn programming, no matter what obstacles may get in your way.

- ✔ **Curiosity:** A healthy dose of curiosity can encourage you to experiment and continue learning about programming long after you finish reading this book. With curiosity behind you, learning to program seems less like a chore and more like fun. And as long as you're having fun, you tend to learn and retain more information than does someone without any curiosity whatsoever (such as your boss).

- ✔ **Imagination:** Computer programming is a skill, but imagination can give your skill direction and guidance. A mediocre programmer with lots of imagination always creates more interesting and useful programs than a great programmer with no imagination does. If you don't know what to do with your programming skill, your talent will go to waste without imagination prodding you onward.

Desire, curiosity, and imagination are three crucial ingredients that every programmer needs. If you have these qualities, you can worry about trivial details such as learning a specific programming language (such as C++), studying advanced math, or attending a university where you can buy a college degree that you could have made with your computer and a desktop-publishing program instead.

Learning to program a computer may (initially) seem an impossible task, but don't worry. Just remember that, back in the 1960s, teams of highly paid professional programmers were responsible for creating the well-publicized Y2K Millennium Bug because they failed to anticipate that the year 2000 would actually arrive. Computer programming is relatively simple to understand; everything tends to fall apart whenever you try to put a program into practical use.

Chapter 2

All About Programming Languages

*P*rogramming is nothing more than writing step-by-step instructions telling the computer exactly what you want it to do. Because computers are stupid, they require exact instructions, and this limitation is what makes programming so time-consuming.

Computers don't understand English (or French, Chinese, Arabic, Spanish, or any other language used by human beings). Because computers are functionally illiterate, people must write instructions for a computer by using a language that the computer can understand. Hence, we have the term *programming language*.

A collection of instructions that tell the computer what to do is called *source code*, which defines how a program works.

Why So Many Different Programming Languages?

You have so many programming languages to choose from because each language serves a specific purpose, and people are always creating new languages to solve different types of problems.

Of course, computers really understand only one language, which consists of zeroes and ones, also known as *machine language*. A typical program, written in machine language, may look something like this:

```
0010 1010 0001 1101
0011 1100 1010 1111
0101 0110 1101 0101
1101 1111 0010 1001
```

Machine language has two major drawbacks:

- ✔ You can easily mistype a 0 or 1 by mistake, thereby preventing you from giving the computer the correct instructions.
- ✔ Machine language takes a long time to write (and an even longer time to understand what the language is actually telling the computer to do).

Because of these two huge problems, few people program computers in machine language. To make writing a program easier, programmers quickly invented a simpler programming language called *assembly language*.

The joy of assembly language

The whole purpose of assembly language is to enable you to program more easily than you can by using machine language. So rather than force programmers to write cryptic programs using 0s and 1s, assembly language uses short, easy-to-remember phrases such as JMP, MOV, and ADD, which represent specific machine-language instructions.

Not only does this convention make assembly language source code shorter and easier to write, but it also makes it easier to read and modify later. The following is what a typical assembly language program looks like:

```
title Nap Program
; This program displays "Take a nap!" on the screen
dosseg
.model small
.stack 100h
.data
my_message db 'Take a nap!',0dh,0ah,'$'
.code
main    proc
        mov ax,@data
        mov ds,ax
        mov ah,9
        mov dx,offset my_message
        int 21h
        mov ax,4C00h
        int 21h
        main endp
end main
```

Making programs easy to read and modify is crucial because most programs never work right the first time you use them. Even worse, when you may want to add new features to a program later, you need to understand how the current program works so that you know how to modify it.

Programmers created assembly language for their convenience only. As far as the computer is concerned, it has no idea how to read or use any instructions written in assembly language.

Because computers can't read assembly language instructions, programmers created special programs that translate assembly language into machine language. These special programs are called *assemblers*.

Assemblers convert assembly language programs (which the computer doesn't understand) into machine code (which the computer does understand).

Assembly language offers two distinct advantages over machine language:

- ✔ Assembly language programs are easier to read than machine language programs.
- ✔ Assembly language programs are easier to write (and modify) than machine language programs.

Of course, assembly language has the following disadvantages:

- ✔ Programs created by using assembly language run slower and are larger than equivalent programs created by using machine language.
- ✔ A program written in assembly language for one computer can't be easily transferred (or to use programming lingo, *ported*) to another computer.
- ✔ Writing a program in assembly language can be extremely tedious, time-consuming, and complicated. That's why few people bother to write large programs in assembly language.

In general, the easier the programming language is to read and write, the slower and larger are the programs it creates. The Holy Grail of computer programming is to create programs that run as fast as possible while taking up as little space as possible.

C: The portable assembler

Writing assembly language programs can be difficult and time-consuming (not to mention that the programs are complicated to modify and impossible to port from one computer to another). So programmers created a wide variety of different programming languages, such as COBOL and FORTRAN. But some programmers felt that they needed a language that would combine the power to access hardware (like assembly language) but would be easier to read, write, and modify (like COBOL and FORTRAN). Eventually, they invented a programming language called *C*.

The C programming language is based on an early programming language called B, even though no programming language called A ever existed.

Programmers wanted to make programming as easy as possible for themselves, so they made the C programming language look more like actual words that people can understand, like this:

```
main()
{
    printf ("Take a nap!\n");
}
```

Why entire programs aren't written in assembly language anymore

In the mid-1980s, the most popular word processor on the market was called WordStar. To maximize program speed while keeping the program size small enough to fit on a single floppy disk (because this was before the days of hard disks), the programmers wrote WordStar using assembly language.

Unfortunately, the WordStar Corporation made a fatal mistake. Rather than update WordStar (version 3.3), the company chose to create an entirely new word processing program dubbed WordStar 2000. For some strange reason, WordStar 2000 looked and acted completely different from the original WordStar program, even to the point that documents saved in WordStar couldn't be edited in WordStar 2000.

Sensing that they no longer had a future working for the WordStar Corporation, many of the original WordStar programmers left the company and formed a rival word processing company called NewStar, which essentially sold an enhanced version of WordStar 3.3 called NewStar.

As sales of WordStar 2000 languished and competitors such as WordPerfect and Microsoft

Word ate away at the market share of WordStar 3.3, the WordStar Corporation decided that it needed to update WordStar 3.3 to remain competitive. Unfortunately, all the programmers who understood how the WordStar 3.3 assembly language source code worked had already defected to work for the NewStar Corporation.

Because understanding the source code for WordStar 3.3 would be time-consuming for new programmers, the WordStar Corporation simply bought out the NewStar Corporation and hired back all the original programmers who understood how to modify the assembly language source code for WordStar 3.3.

By this time, though, WordStar had already lost its lead in the word processing market and would never again play a major role in the computer industry. The lesson learned was that source code is useless if nobody can understand and modify it later.

Because of the difficulty in understanding and modifying assembly language source code, few large programs, such as word processors or databases, are written entirely in assembly language anymore.

This C program is equivalent to the assembly language program printed in the previous section of this chapter that displays "Take a nap!" on-screen. Comparing the two, you can see that the C language program is smaller and easier to read than the equivalent assembly language program.

Programmers sacrificed readability for speed and size. A program written in C runs slower and creates larger programs than an equivalent assembly language program. However, C is much easier to read, write, and modify than assembly language (and far easier to read, write, and modify than an equivalent machine-language program).

The C programming language had three main goals:

- ✔ To be easier to read and write than assembly language.

- ✔ To offer programmers the capability to access all the parts of the computer like assembly language.

- ✔ To provide a small, simple language that can be easily ported from one computer to another. Programs written in C can run on different computers without massive rewriting, which is the main drawback with assembly- and machine-language programs.

This third goal may look strange, so here's the rationale behind it. Computers don't understand C any better than they understand assembly language. (Computers are notorious for not understanding much of anything, which is why programming must be so precise.) If you write an entire program using C, your computer doesn't have the slightest clue how to read your instructions.

To make a computer read and understand instructions written in C, you must convert your C program into equivalent machine-language instructions. Programmers created special programs, called *compilers*, to do this for them. A compiler takes your C program and converts it into machine language, which is like translating a Jules Verne novel from French into English.

As is true of translations between human languages, the simpler the language, the easier the translation. Translating a children's book from French into Japanese is much easier than translating a mathematics dissertation from French into Japanese, mainly because a children's book uses simple words, while a mathematics dissertation uses more complicated words.

So the only way you can run a C program on another computer is if someone has already written a C compiler for that other computer. Because C is a simple language, writing C compilers for different computers is relatively easy, especially compared to other programming languages such as Ada or LISP.

C compilers are fairly easy to write; you can find C compilers for almost every computer in the world. Theoretically, you can write a C program for the Macintosh, copy it to a computer running Windows 98, and run the program with little or no modification.

Although C programs are supposed to run on different computers without modification, the reality is that you almost always must modify a C program slightly or drastically to get it to run on a different computer. However, modifying a C program is still much easier than modifying an assembly- or machine-language program.

Given C's power and portability, C has quickly become one of the most popular programming languages in the world. The majority of all programs are written in C, including operating systems such as Windows 95/98/NT/2000, UNIX, and Linux, and major commercial programs such as Quicken, Netscape Navigator, and Microsoft Word.

Although C is popular, it has its share of flaws:

- ✔ C creates larger and slower programs than equivalent assembly- or machine-language programs.

- ✔ The C language gives programmers access to all parts of a computer, including the capability to manipulate the computer's memory. Unfortunately, all this power can be as dangerous as giving a hyperactive monkey a chainsaw and a hand grenade. If you don't write your C programs carefully, they can accidentally wreck your computer's memory, causing your program to crash your computer.

In a desperate attempt to make C programming more reliable, programmers developed two languages based on C, called C++ and Java. C++ adds a special feature called object-orientation, which encourages programmers to write small programs that can be easily reused and modified. Java protects programmers from writing programs that can mess up the computer's memory, as C programs can do, while providing greater portability between different types of computers.

High-level programming languages

Because writing machine- or assembly-language programs was so difficult and confusing, people developed additional languages that look more like human languages, with names such as FORTRAN, COBOL, BASIC, Pascal, and Ada. By making programming languages look more like ordinary human languages, the creators of these high-level languages hoped to make programs easier to write and modify later on.

One of the first high-level languages was FORTRAN (which stands for FORmula TRANslator). FORTRAN was designed specifically for mathematical calculations. Another early high-level language was COBOL (COmmon Business-Oriented Language), which was designed for business data processing. Because each language has a specialized purpose, most people aren't going to use FORTRAN or COBOL to write video games, operating systems, or word processors (although you can still do so).

Because programming was still too difficult for many people, computer scientists soon created both Pascal and BASIC to teach people programming. BASIC, which stands for Beginner's All-purpose Symbolic Instruction Code, was designed to teach complete novices how to program. Beginners could start learning to program by using C, but the complexities of C can discourage people too soon — sort of like trying to teach a three-year-old how to ride a bicycle by putting him on a motorcycle in the middle of rush-hour traffic.

The main advantage of BASIC is its simplicity. To print the words "Take a nap!" on-screen, you need only one command:

```
PRINT "Take a nap!"
```

When compared to the equivalent C or assembly language program, BASIC enables you to focus on the task that you want to accomplish instead of worrying about the cryptic commands of a specific programming language.

Pascal (named after the French philosopher, Blaise Pascal) is another language designed to help beginners learn how to program. The main difference between BASIC and Pascal is that Pascal encourages you to write well-structured programs that can be easily read, understood, and modified at a later date. The following is a Pascal program that displays "Take a nap!" on-screen:

```
Program Message (Input, Output);
Begin
   Writeln ('Take a nap!');
End.
```

Compared to Pascal, BASIC is much less structured, which makes writing a BASIC program easy but makes reading and understanding large BASIC programs much more difficult. Pascal is more structured and forces you to plan your program before you write, as you do when you create an outline before you write a term paper. This planning may take longer, but your program and your term paper are more organized than if you rush into the writing. On the other hand, BASIC enables you to start writing your term paper (program) right away, which more than likely leads to a more disorganized term paper (program).

BASIC is such a popular language that programmers have tried to combine the structured features of Pascal with the simplicity of BASIC to create various dialects of BASIC. QBASIC (see Chapter 5) is one example of a structured version of BASIC.

As usual, high-level programming languages such as Pascal, BASIC, FORTRAN, Ada, and COBOL have their own share of problems:

✔ High-level programming languages create larger and slower programs than equivalent C, assembly-language, or machine-language programs.

✔ High-level programming languages shield you from accessing all the parts of the computer, preventing you from using the power available in C, assembly-language, or machine-language programs. As a result, it is more difficult (but not impossible) to write certain types of programs, such as operating systems or disk utility programs (such as the Norton Utilities), in high-level languages.

✔ High-level programming languages more closely resemble human languages, so writing a compiler for a high-level language is more difficult. If your computer doesn't have a compiler for your favorite high-level language (such as Ada), you can't write a program for your computer in that particular programming language.

Ada is a complicated high-level programming language, so it took years for programmers to write Ada compilers for different computers. Because so few Ada compilers were initially available, few people bothered to learn or write programs in Ada. Ultimately, this meant that Ada never became as popular as C, COBOL, FORTRAN, BASIC, or Pascal.

Of course, nobody would use high-level programming languages such as Pascal, BASIC, FORTRAN, Ada, and COBOL unless they offered some advantages over C, assembly language, or machine language. Here are several reasons for using a high-level programming language:

✔ You can write programs much faster with a high-level programming language than with assembly language or machine language. (You can write a program in C in roughly the same amount of time as in a high-level language such as Pascal.)

✔ It takes less time to learn and master a high-level programming language.

✔ Because high-level programming languages shield you from accessing all parts of a computer, they protect you from writing programs that accidentally mess up the computer, causing it to crash.

✔ Reading and modifying a program written in a high-level language is much easier than reading and modifying an equivalent program written in C, assembly language, or machine language.

✔ Programs written in high-level languages can run on a variety of computers. If you write a program in a high-level language, you can (theoretically) port that program to run on a different computer.

Rapid Application Development (RAD) programming languages

Most programming languages were designed back in the days when computer screens displayed nothing but text. The screen didn't show graphics, mouse pointers, buttons, or windows.

Because computer screens could display only text, languages such as C++, BASIC, and Pascal just had simple commands to display information, such as the following BASIC command:

```
PRINT "This sentence appears on the screen."
```

After computers developed fancy graphical user interfaces with windows, scroll bars, and toolbars, people began demanding programs that included all these fancy graphical features as well. To help programmers create programs with fancy user interfaces, many companies developed special dialects of existing languages, dubbed *rapid application development* (RAD) languages.

RAD languages enable programmers to design the way they want their program to look (the user interface) and then write source code to make that user interface actually do something useful, such as display information in a window. Figure 2-1 shows an interface created in Visual Basic.

Three popular RAD languages are Visual Basic (derived from the BASIC language), Delphi (based on Pascal), and C++ Builder (based on C++).

RAD languages offer the following benefits:

✔ You can write programs with graphical user interfaces much faster by using RAD than you can by using ordinary C++, BASIC, or Pascal. Figure 2-2 shows StoryCraft, a story-creating program developed by two professional fiction writers to help people create original stories for novels, short stories, plays, or screenplays.

✔ RAD languages simplify the process of creating user interfaces so that you can focus on getting the rest of your program to work. Without a RAD language, you would need to write instructions to make the user interface work and then write additional instructions to make the rest of the program work as well, essentially doubling your work and the chance of making a mistake.

✔ Because RAD languages are based on existing high-level languages (C++, BASIC, and Pascal), you can learn and start programming in a RAD language right away if you already know C++, BASIC, or Pascal.

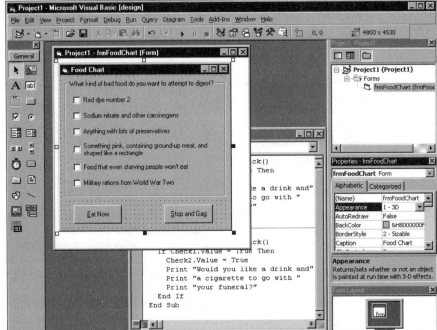

Figure 2-1:
Visual Basic
enables you
to draw
your user
interface
and then
write BASIC
commands
to make
your
program do
something
useful.

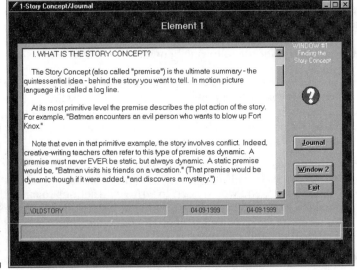

Figure 2-2:
A story-
creating
program
with a
graphical
user
interface.

Not surprisingly, RAD languages have a few major drawbacks, which shouldn't surprise you, because nothing involving computers is ever perfect:

✔ Programs written in RAD languages are not portable between different computers. For example, Visual Basic runs only on Microsoft Windows 95/98/NT/2000, so if you write a program in Visual Basic, you can never run it on a Macintosh, Linux, or other computer operating system without extensive modification.

✔ RAD languages create larger and slower programs than equivalent programs written in pure C++, BASIC, or Pascal. A RAD language may help you create programs faster, but you sacrifice speed and program size.

Database programming languages

Programming languages such as C++, BASIC, and Pascal were designed as general-purpose languages, which means that you can use them to write a flight simulator, an accounting program, a voice-recognition program, or a word processor.

However, one of the most popular uses for computers is storing and retrieving information, such as names, addresses, phone numbers, prison records, credit history, and past job experience. Such information is stored in a database.

Almost every business relies on databases to store information about customers, inventories, and employees, so nearly every company uses a database program.

Unfortunately, most people don't want to know the strange and often bizarre commands needed to store, retrieve, or print information from a database. To make databases easier to use, most databases include a programming language.

If you write programs using a database's programming language, you can create custom databases for different companies. Best of all, database programming languages enable you to create custom databases much faster than using a general-purpose language such as C++ or BASIC. When you use a database programming language, you write instructions only to manipulate the database information. When you use a general-purpose language such as C++, you must write instructions to store information and then write additional instructions to manipulate that information, essentially doubling the amount of work to accomplish the same task.

Most popular database programs, such as dBASE, FileMaker, FoxPro, and Microsoft Access, offer their own special programming language. For manipulating large amounts of data such as on big mainframe computers, database programs tend to use a language called *SQL* (which stands for Structured Query Language). The following dBASE code displays the message "Take a nap!":

```
row = 15
column = 15
clear
@ row, column SAY "Take a nap!"
```

Database programming languages can fill specific needs:

- ✔ If you're writing a program that stores huge chunks of information, you can write a program much faster by using a database programming language than by using a general-purpose language such as C++ or Pascal.

- ✔ Database programming is a lucrative field. If you know how to create customized databases, you almost never need to worry about being unemployed or not making enough money.

Of course, database programming languages aren't for everybody. They have several crucial limitations:

- ✔ Database programs are often tied to a specific database language. For example, if you write a custom database using dBASE, you can run your program only on a computer that can also run the dBASE program. Because dBASE is currently limited to the MS-DOS and Windows operating systems, you can't run a dBASE program on a Macintosh or a computer that uses Linux.

- ✔ Database programming languages are great at making custom databases but lousy at making anything else, such as video games, word processors, or utility programs (such as anti-virus utilities). If you need to create a variety of programs, you can't rely on a database programming language by itself.

Scripting programming languages

Writing a program from scratch gives you the most flexibility but can take a really long time and drive you nuts in the process. For example, suppose that you wanted to write a word processor specifically for creating screenplays.

If you decided to use a general-purpose language such as C++ or Pascal, you'd first need to write instructions that create a simple word processor; then you'd need to write additional instructions to give the word processor the features needed to create and format screenplays.

As an alternative to going mad by writing everything yourself, many programs offer their own scripting languages. Rather than write an entire word processor from scratch, you could buy an existing word processor (such as WordPro, WordPerfect, or Microsoft Word) and then use that word processor's scripting language to make the word processor do what you want it to do (such as create and format screenplays). A scripting language enables you to focus on the task that you want to accomplish without worrying about irrelevant details.

Most Microsoft programs, such as Word, Excel, PowerPoint, and Access, offer a scripting language called Visual Basic for Applications (VBA), which is nearly identical to Visual Basic. The Macintosh operating system also includes a scripting language called AppleScript, so you can write programs to automate your Mac, to a limited extent. The following code shows how to use AppleScript to display the message, "Take a nap!" on-screen:

```
on DisplayMessage()
  display dialog "Take a nap!" buttons {"OK"}
end DisplayMessage

DisplayMessage()
```

Scripting programming languages can come in handy in many ways:

- A scripting language enables you to modify an existing program, such as a word processor or spreadsheet. That way, you can create sophisticated programs quickly with very little programming.

- Scripting languages are generally easier to learn than more powerful programming languages, such as C++. As a result, you can learn and start writing programs faster.

But before you jump wholeheartedly into learning and using a scripting language, beware of these problems:

- Scripting languages are tied to a specific program. If you customize a word processor using a scripting language, your program runs only on computers that run that particular word processor. If you customize Microsoft Word, your program works only on computers that can run Microsoft Word, such as Windows and Macintosh computers.

- Selling and distributing your programs is much more difficult. To use your program, people must buy or already own the program (word processor, spreadsheet, and so on) that you customized. So if you create a custom program for WordPerfect, Microsoft Word users can't use it.

- A scripting language provides much less flexibility than a general-purpose programming language such as C++. Make sure that the tradeoff of convenience and ease of programming is worth the limitations of using a scripting language.

Web page programming languages

In the early days of the Internet, people communicated through plain old text without fancy graphics, animation, or forms that make up today's Web pages. Although people have been reading text for years, it can get boring and difficult to read when viewed on a computer screen that requires constant scrolling to view an entire document.

To remedy this problem and spruce up the appearance of text, programmers created HyperText Markup Language (HTML), which defines the graphical appearance of Web pages. Figure 2-3 shows a typical Web page as defined by its HTML code.

HTML codes tell a browser how to display a page. So when you use a browser to view a Web page (such as www.dummies.com), your browser automatically converts the HTML code into the fancy graphics, as shown in Figure 2-4.

After a while, people got tired of plain ol' HTML Web pages that resemble billboards viewed through your computer screen. To make Web pages capable of interacting with the user (for playing games, filling out forms, and so on), programmers created special Web page programming languages such as Java, JavaScript, and VBScript.

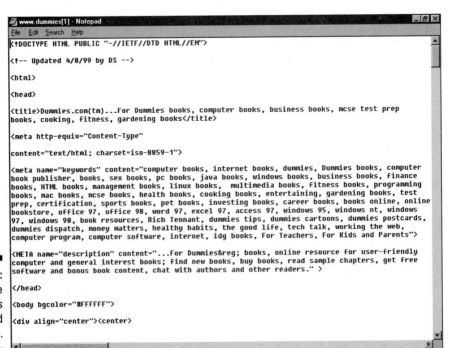

Figure 2-3: HTML code looks messy and unreadable.

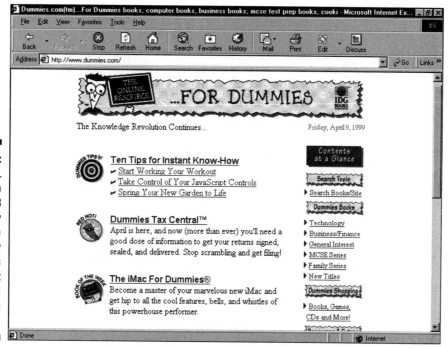

Figure 2-4:
The HTML
code in
Figure 2-3
actually
defines the
pretty
graphics
and text
for the
Dummies
Web site.

Java can create two types of programs: stand-alone applications (such as games or word processors) and smaller applets, which can run off a Web page. The following code shows how a Java application can display the words, "Take a nap!" on-screen:

```
public class DisplayMessage {
  public static void main (String args[]) {
system.out.println ("Take a nap!");
  }
}
```

Web page programming languages enable you to create Web sites that more closely resemble video games rather than scanned images of paper displayed on the computer screen. Such interactive Web pages can increase interest in your Web site and encourage people to return.

Web page programming languages offer the following advantages:

✔ You can create interactive Web pages to make your site more interesting to look at and to encourage viewers to stay on your site longer.

✔ The language is easy to learn and enables you to create programs that can be used by anyone around the world with Internet access.

Then again, Web page programming languages are very limited in their capabilities:

- Not all browsers support all features of Web page languages such as JavaScript or VBScript. As a result, users of older browsers won't be able to run programs created using Web page languages.

- For Internet users saddled with slow access (such as through a 28.8 baud modem), programs created in a Web page language (such as VBScript) can run slowly, discouraging visitors from visiting your Web site.

- Programs created by a Web page language (except for Java) can be run only by people with Internet access. If you want to sell a program to others, you don't want to use a Web page language.

So What's the Best Programming Language to Learn?

No single "best" programming language exists. If you want to write programs professionally, you should learn at least one high-level language (most likely C++ because it's the most popular of the high-level languages) and one database programming language (such as SQL). You can't go wrong learning C++. With so many companies writing programs in C++, people with C++ programming experience can get a job almost anywhere.

But the immense popularity of C++ programming means that competition can be high. To avoid competition, many people are learning COBOL because thousands of older computers still run COBOL programs that need constant updating. With fewer COBOL programmers available, companies often have to pay COBOL programmers a higher salary.

For those planning to work for themselves, one of the most lucrative markets is writing custom databases for other companies. To get into this field, you obviously must learn a database programming language, such as SQL, dBASE, or VBA, which is used in Microsoft Access. If you plan to create Web pages, you want to learn HTML and gain some familiarity with Java, JavaScript, VBScript, and the other Internet programming languages. Ultimately, the best programming language to learn is the one that enables you to accomplish the task you want as quickly and easily as possible, whether that language is C++, BASIC, Java, Delphi, or assembly language.

For a quick introduction to the way different programming languages solve the same problem, visit the Hello World! Web site at www.latech.edu/~acm/HelloWorld.shtml. This Web site provides sample programs, written in a variety of programming languages, that tell the computer to display the words "Hello World!" on-screen.

Chapter 3

How to Write a Program

*A*lthough you could sit down at your computer and start writing a program right now without any planning whatsoever, the result would likely be as messy as trying to bake a cake by throwing all the ingredients together without following a recipe.

If you're writing a simple program that displays your cat's name on the screen, you could write that program without much planning, but for anything more complicated, you should take time to design your program on paper before you even touch a computer. After you're sure that you know what you want your program to do and how it's to look on-screen, you can worry about writing a program that actually accomplishes this task.

Before You Write Your Program

If you design your program before writing it, you don't waste time writing a program that doesn't work or that solves the wrong problem and isn't worth trying to salvage afterward. By planning ahead of time, you increase the odds that your program will actually work and perform the task you want.

The following three items are crucial to consider when designing a program:

✔ **The user:** Who is going to be using your program?

✔ **The target computer:** Which computer do people need to run your program? Is it a Windows 95/98/NT computer, a Macintosh, an Amiga, a mainframe, or a supercomputer?

> ✔ **You:** Are you going to write the whole thing yourself or get help from others? If you're going to have others help you, which parts of the program are they to write?

The program's users

If you're the only person who will use your program, you can pretty much make your program look and act any way you want, just as long as you know how to make it work. But if you plan to give or sell your program to others, you need to know who will be using your program.

Knowing your program's typical user is critical. If users don't like your program for any reason, they won't use it. Whether the program actually works is often irrelevant.

By designing your program with the user in mind, you increase the odds that people will use your program and (you hope) buy a copy for themselves.

Even if you write a program that works perfectly, users still may ignore it because they don't like the way it looks, they don't understand how to give it commands, it doesn't work like the old program they're used to, the colors don't look right to them, and so on. The goal is to make your program meet your users' needs, no matter how weird, bizarre, or illogical they may seem.

The target computer

After you have identified the user, you need to know what type of a computer the user will run the program on. The type of computer that your program will run on can determine which computer languages you can use, the hardware that your program can expect to find, and even the maximum size of your program.

For example, if you're writing a program to run on a Macintosh, your program can take advantage of sound, color graphics, a large hard disk, and plenty of memory. However, that same program needs to be rewritten drastically to run on a PalmPilot, which has limited sound capability, much simpler color graphics, and a limited amount of memory and storage space.

If you can copy and run your program on another computer with little or no modification, your program is considered to be *portable*. The computer language that you use to write your program can determine its portability. That's why so many people use C/C++, because C and C++ programs tend to be more portable than other programming languages if you copy them from one computer to another.

Portability and cross-platform issues

Rather than pick a single computer, many programmers try to write programs that can run on a variety of computers, such as the Macintosh and Windows 95/98/NT/2000. Any program that can run on two or more different types of computers is considered to be *cross-platform*. Microsoft Word is a cross-platform program because you can buy separate versions that run in the Macintosh and Windows environments.

A program that can run on multiple computers increases your number of potential customers, but it also increases the number of potential problems that you must face. Some of the problems include offering customer support for each version of your program and trying to make each program version work the same even though they may be running on completely different

operating systems and computers with different capabilities.

At one time, WordPerfect had versions of its word processor that ran on MS-DOS, Windows, the Macintosh, the Amiga, and the Atari ST. So besides hiring enough programmers to work on each word processor version, the makers of WordPerfect also had to hire technical support people who knew how to answer questions for each computer type. Needless to say, this cost the company a bundle every month.

Developing and supporting so many different versions of WordPerfect cut into the company's profits, so WordPerfect dropped support for the Amiga and Atari ST because it wasn't worth keeping them.

Your own programming skill

When designing any program, consider your own programming skill. You may have a great idea for a program but if you're a beginner with little experience, writing your program may take a long time — if you don't give up out of frustration first.

Your programming skill and experience also determine the programming language you choose. Experienced programmers may think nothing about writing entire programs in C or C++. But novices may need to spend a long time studying C and C++ before writing their program, or they may choose an easier programming language, such as BASIC.

Some novices take the time to learn difficult languages like C/C++ and then go off and write their program. Others take an easier approach and choose a simpler language such as Visual Basic so that they can create (and market) their program right away. Don't be afraid to tackle a heavy-duty language such as C/C++, but don't be afraid to use a simpler language such as Visual Basic either. The important goal is to get your program finished so that you can sell it to others.

Beware of the golden handcuffs

Rather than learn programming themselves, many people hire someone to write programs for them. But be careful! Freelance programmers sometimes live by a rule called the "golden handcuffs," which means that they get the gold and you get the handcuffs.

Here's how the golden handcuffs work: You hire someone to write your program, and they take your money. Then they write a program that doesn't work quite the way you want.

Rather than lose the money you've already invested in developing the program, you pay the programmer more money, and then this programmer develops a new version of your program that doesn't quite work either.

At this point, you're handcuffed. Do you keep paying money to a programmer who never completely finishes the job, or do you give up altogether?

What's worse, you can't hire a new programmer to work on the same program because the original programmer owns your program's source code, so nobody else can modify it. Thus the only way that you can modify the program is to hire the original programmer again and again and again and....

Many programmers create their program by using a language such as Visual Basic and then later hire more experienced programmers to rewrite their programs in a more complicated language such as C/C++, which can make the program faster and more efficient.

The Technical Details of Writing a Program

Few people create a program overnight. Instead, most programs evolve over time. Because the process of actually typing programming commands can be so tedious, time-consuming, and error-prone, programmers try to avoid actually writing their programs until they're absolutely sure that they know what they're doing.

Prototyping

To make sure that they don't spend months (or years) writing a program that doesn't work right, programmers often *prototype* their programs first. Just as architects often build cardboard or plastic models of skyscrapers before a construction crew starts welding I-beams together, programmers create mock-ups (prototypes) of their programs first.

A prototype usually shows the user interface of the program, such as windows, pull-down menus, and dialog boxes. The prototype may look like an actual program, but clicking menus doesn't do anything. The whole idea of the prototype is to show what the program looks like and how it acts, without taking the time to write commands to make the program actually work.

After the programmer is happy with the way the prototype looks, she can proceed, using the prototype as a guideline toward completing the final program.

Visual Basic is popular for creating prototypes. Visual Basic enables you to quickly design the user interface for a program and then add actual commands later to turn your prototype into an honest-to-goodness, working program.

Choosing a programming language

After you refine your prototype until it shows you exactly how your program is supposed to look and act, the next step is choosing a programming language to use.

You can write any program using any programming language. The trick is that some languages make writing certain types of programs easier.

The choice of a programming language to use can pit people against one another in much the same way that religion and politics do. Although you can't find a single "perfect" programming language to use for all occasions, you may want to consider a variety of programming languages. Ultimately, no one cares what language you use as long as your program works.

C/C++

The C and C++ programming language has strong support no matter which computer or operating system you use, so you can't go wrong using C or C++ to write your program. Here are the advantages of writing a program in C/C++:

- ✔ **Efficiency:** C/C++ can create smaller and faster programs than almost any other programming language (with the exception of assembly and machine language).

- ✔ **Portability:** If you write a program in C/C++, you can easily copy it to another computer and run it with a little bit (or a lot) of modifying. This means that you can write a program once and then modify it to work on multiple computers, thereby increasing the market for your program.

- ✔ **Plentiful programmers:** With so many people learning C/C++, you'll have no trouble finding programmers who can modify the program later on.

The majority of commercial programs may be written in C/C++, but many programmers who develop custom software often choose other programming languages because they dislike the following C/C++ drawbacks:

- ✔ **Difficult to master:** C/C++ is one of the more difficult programming languages to master. As a result, by the time you completely learn C/C++, you could have already finished your program if you had chosen another programming language.

- ✔ **Difficult to read and understand:** Programs aren't created as often as they are modified. Because of the cryptic nature of C/C++, understanding how a C/C++ program works so you know how to modify it can be hard.

- ✔ **Complexity:** C/C++ gives you the power and flexibility to manipulate memory and access the computer's hardware directly. Not only does this increase the chance that a bug can keep your program from working right, but it also increases the amount of time that you may need to debug your program to ensure that it works correctly. (See Chapter 14 for more information about computer bugs.)

Many commercial programs for Windows and the Macintosh are written in C/C++ for speed, efficiency, and portability. If these features are important to you, choose C/C++ for your next programming project.

Visual Basic

Visual Basic is one of the most popular languages (after C/C++) for writing programs. Although professional and experienced programmers tend to use C/C++, novice programmers often use Visual Basic for the following reasons:

- ✔ **It's easy to learn:** You can learn Visual Basic and start writing programs much faster than you can with any other programming language. The sooner you can learn any language, the sooner you can write and give away (or sell) your program.

- ✔ **It enables fast prototyping:** You can quickly create prototypes in Visual Basic. Then you can turn the prototype into a real working program. Other programming languages, such as C/C++, are too difficult to use to create a prototype, which means that you must create your prototype and then dump the whole thing to create the actual program from scratch.

But professional programmers often shun Visual Basic as a "toy" language for these reasons:

- ✔ **It's slow:** Visual Basic programs tend to run much slower than equivalent programs written in other languages, such as C/C++. If speed is your program's primary concern, Visual Basic is not the language to use.

- ✔ **It's inefficient:** Visual Basic programs tend to gobble up huge amounts of hard disk space, even for the simplest program. If you need to create a program to squeeze into a small amount of storage space, Visual Basic is never the best language to use.

✔ **It's inflexible:** Visual Basic is easy to learn because it shields you from the technical details of programming a computer. At the same time, it prevents you from taking full control over the computer, which can limit a program's power.

✔ **It limits portability:** Visual Basic runs only on Windows 95/98/NT, which means that any programs you write in Visual Basic can never work on any computer that can't run Windows 95/98/NT. Trying to copy and run a Visual Basic program on a Macintosh can be cumbersome, and the time you spend trying this could have been better spent learning and rewriting your entire program in C/C++.

Visual Basic has been used to create commercial quality programs as well as custom programs by both professionals and novices. If you need to create a program quickly and don't want to spend the time learning C/C++, use Visual Basic.

Delphi

Delphi is similar to Visual Basic, but it uses Pascal as its base language. Although Delphi isn't as popular as Visual Basic or C/C++, it has a loyal following. Essentially, Delphi combines the best (and worst) features of Visual Basic and C/C++. Here are some reasons to consider Delphi:

✔ **It's easy to learn:** Although Delphi isn't as easy to learn as Visual Basic, it is still easier to learn than C/C++, so you can start writing your program right away instead of spending time learning C/C++.

✔ **It offers fast prototyping:** Delphi enables you to create prototypes nearly as quickly as Visual Basic. Then you can turn the prototype into a real working program, just as with Visual Basic.

✔ **It's powerful:** Delphi provides nearly as much power and flexibility as C/C++ without the major drawbacks. Delphi programs run nearly as fast and are nearly as small as C/C++. Delphi shields you from the complexities of the computer (unlike C/C++), so you are less likely to write programs that mess up the computer's memory and cause your program not to work.

Although Delphi is often considered superior to Visual Basic and nearly as good as C/C++, it has its problems:

✔ **It's less popular:** Delphi uses the Pascal programming language, which is less popular than C/C++. So trying to find programmers who can understand and modify a Delphi program later on may be difficult.

✔ **It has limited power:** Delphi shields you from the technical details of the computer, which limits the power you have in controlling the computer. If you need full control over your computer's hardware, use C/C++ instead.

✔ **It has limited portability:** Like Visual Basic, Delphi runs only on Windows 95/98/NT, which means that any programs you write in Delphi will never work on any computer that can't run Windows 95/98/NT. Trying to copy and run a Delphi program on a Macintosh can be extremely difficult, and the time you spend trying to do so can be better spent learning and rewriting your entire program in C/C++.

A skilled Delphi programmer can often create programs faster than a similarly skilled C/C++ programmer. Best of all, Delphi creates programs that run far faster and more efficiently than Visual Basic programs. As a result, Delphi is most often used to create custom programs that don't require portability between different computers.

Java

Java is the latest programming language to gain popular support. With Java, you can create full-blown applications or mini-programs (known as *applets*) that can run over the Internet. Although the language is fairly new, many people have embraced it for the following reasons:

✔ **Write once, run everywhere:** Java is the ultimate portable language, so any program you write in Java can (theoretically) run on all the major computer operating systems (such as Windows, Macintosh, and Linux) without any modification whatsoever.

✔ **Safer than C/C++:** Java took the best of C/C++ and avoided its major drawbacks. As a result, Java programs are less likely to mess up the computer's memory than an equivalent C/C++ program.

✔ **Based on C/C++:** Because Java is derived from C/C++, anyone who knows C/C++ can quickly learn and write programs in Java.

Because Java is still new, Sun Microsystems (the creator of Java) keeps trying to improve the language to make it more appealing. But Java sports a few flaws:

✔ **Slower and less efficient:** Programs written in Java tend to run slower than equivalent programs written in C/C++, but this is changing as Java compilers get better.

✔ **Difficult to learn:** Java looks like C/C++, so it's still just as difficult as C/C++ to learn. If you want to start programming right away, you're better off with Visual Basic or even Delphi.

✔ **Write once, test everywhere:** Theoretically, Java programs can run on different computers without modification. Realistically, you must test your Java programs on different computers to make sure that they work correctly on each type of computer. Because of this drawback, you could spend most of your time making sure that your program works on different computers rather than actually improving and updating your program.

Java is still an evolving language, so many companies are taking a "wait and see" attitude before writing large programs in Java. However, if portability is important, Java is definitely a better choice than Visual Basic, Delphi, and (to a large extent) C/C++.

Specialized programming languages

As an alternative to general-purpose programming languages such as C/C++, Visual Basic, Delphi, and Java, you may consider using a specialized language. For example, two programming languages called LISP and Prolog are used extensively in artificial intelligence research.

If you're creating a program that needs to use a database, taking an existing database (such as Microsoft Access) and using its scripting language to create your own program is much faster and easier.

Depending on your application, a specialized programming language can be useful for the following reasons:

- ✔ **Faster development:** A specialized programming language is designed for solving a narrow range of problems. As a result, writing a program using a specialized language can create a program faster than using any other language, including Visual Basic.

- ✔ **Simpler:** Unlike general-purpose languages, specialized languages are often easier to use for writing specific types of programs. If you find the right specialized language, writing your program is easier than torturing yourself using C/C++ or Visual Basic.

Before you choose a specialized programming language, be aware of the following problems:

- ✔ **Limited portability:** Most specialized languages can't run on different computers without extensive modification. In some cases, programs written in certain specialized languages can't run on other computers at all.

- ✔ **Slow running:** Programs written in specialized languages usually run much slower than equivalent programs written in general purpose languages such as C/C++.

- ✔ **Limited popularity:** Specialized languages are less likely to be known to other programmers, which means finding other people to help you write or modify the program can be difficult (or nearly impossible).

- ✔ **Difficult to market:** If you use a specialized language (for example, a database language such as dBASE or FileMaker Pro), marketing and distributing your program may cost you extra or be simply impossible. For example, if you write a program using Microsoft Access, you must buy a special run-time version of Microsoft Access that you can give away as part of your own program. Unfortunately, this can make your program slower and is likely to require huge amounts of storage, too.

Using multiple programming languages

Instead of writing an entire program using one programming language (such as C++), some compilers can convert source code into a special file called an *object file*. The purpose of object files is that one programmer can write a program in C++, another in assembly language, and still a third in Pascal. Each programmer writes his or her portion of the program in his or her favorite language and stores it in a separate object file. Then the programmers connect (or link) all these object files together to create one big program. The program that converts multiple object files into an executable program is called a *linker*.

In the world of Microsoft Windows, another way to write a program using multiple languages is to use dynamic link libraries (DLLs), which are

special programs that don't have a user interface. One programmer can use C, another can use Java, and a third can use COBOL to create three separate DLL files. Then a fourth programmer can write a program using another language such as Visual Basic, which creates the user interface and uses the commands stored in each separate DLL file.

A third way to write a program is to use your favorite language (such as Pascal) and then write assembly language instructions directly in parts of your program. (Just be aware that not all compilers allow you to switch between different languages within the same program.) By using different programming languages, you can take advantage of each language's strengths, while minimizing its weaknesses.

Depending on your task, specialized programming languages can help you create a program much faster than any other programming language, including Visual Basic or Delphi. Just be careful that the limitations of a specialized programming language don't outweigh its advantages.

If you write a program using a specialized programming language, your program is at the mercy of that language. For example, many people have written programs using Apple's HyperCard. But for the longest time, HyperCard didn't offer color support, which meant that anyone writing programs using HyperCard couldn't use color either. So be careful when choosing a specialized programming language, because your program is limited by its capabilities.

Defining how the program should work

After choosing a specific programming language, don't start typing commands into your computer just yet. Just as programmers create mock-ups (prototypes) of their program's user interface, they often create mock-up instructions that describe exactly how a program works, called *pseudocode*.

For example, if you had to write a program that guides a nuclear missile to another city and wipes out all signs of life within a 100-mile radius, your pseudocode may look like this:

```
1. Get the target's coordinates.
2. Get the missile's current coordinates.
3. Calculate a trajectory so the missile will hit the target.
4. Blow up the nuclear warhead.
```

By using pseudocode, you can detect flaws in your logic before you start writing your program, where the logic behind your program can get buried beneath the complexity of a specific programming language's syntax.

In the preceding example, you can see that each pseudocode instruction needs further refining before you can start writing your program. You can't just tell a computer, "Get the target's coordinates" because the computer wants to know, "Exactly how do I get the target's coordinates?" So rewriting the preceding pseudocode may look like this:

```
1. Get the target's coordinates.
   a. Have a missile technician type the target coordinates.
   b. Make sure that the target coordinates are valid.
   c. Store the target coordinates in memory.
2. Get the missile's current coordinates.
3. Calculate a trajectory so the missile will hit the target.
4. Blow up the nuclear warhead.
```

You can refine the instructions even further to specify how the computer works in more detail, like this:

```
1. Get the target's coordinates.
   a. Have a missile technician type the target coordinates.
   b. Make sure that the target coordinates are valid.
      1) Make sure that the target coordinates are complete.
      2) Check to make sure that the target coordinates are
         within the missile's range.
      3) Make sure that the target coordinates don't acciden-
         tally aim the missile at friendly territories.
   c. Store the target coordinates in memory.
2. Get the missile's current coordinates.
3. Calculate a trajectory so the missile will hit the target.
4. Blow up the nuclear warhead.
```

When programmers define the general tasks that a program needs to accomplish and then refine each step in greater detail, they say they're doing a *top-down design*. In other words, they start at the top (with the general tasks that the program needs to do) and then work their way down, defining each task in greater detail until the pseudocode describes every possible step the computer must go through.

Writing pseudocode can be time-consuming. But the alternative is to start writing a program with no planning whatsoever, which is like hopping in your car and driving north and then wondering why you never seem to wind up in Florida.

Pseudocode is a tool that you can use to outline the structure of your program so that you can see all the possible data that the computer needs to accomplish a given task. The idea is to use English (or whatever language you understand best) to describe the computer's step-by-step actions so that you can use the pseudocode as a map for writing the actual program in whatever language (C/C++, FORTRAN, Pascal, Java, and so on) you choose.

The Life Cycle of a Typical Program

Few programs are written, released, and left alone. Instead, programs tend to go through various cycles where they get updated continuously until they're no longer useful. (That's why many people buy a new word processor every few years even though the alphabet hasn't changed in centuries.)

Generally, a typical program goes through a development cycle (where it's first created and released), a maintenance cycle (where any glaring bugs are eliminated as quickly as possible), and an upgrade cycle (where the program gets new features to justify selling the same thing all over again).

The development cycle

Every program began as a blank screen on somebody's computer. During the development cycle, a program is nurtured from an idea to an actual working program. The following steps make up the development cycle:

1. **Come up with an idea for a program.**
2. **Decide who the typical user of the program may be.**
3. **Decide which computer the program should run on.**
4. **Pick one or more computer languages to use.**
5. **Design the program by using pseudocode or any other tool to outline the structure of the program.**
6. **Write the program.**
7. **Test the program.**

   This step is known as *alpha testing*.
8. **Fix any problems discovered during alpha testing.**

   Repeat Steps 7 and 8 as often as possible.

9. **Give out copies of the program to other people to test.**

   This step is known as *beta testing.*

10. **Fix any problems discovered during beta testing.**

    Repeat Steps 9 and 10 as often as possible.

11. **Release the program to the unsuspecting public and pray that it works as advertised.**

The maintenance cycle

Most programmers would rather create new programs than maintain and modify existing ones, which can be as unappealing as cleaning up somebody else's apartment. But the number of new programs created every year is also less than the number of existing programs, so the chances are good that, at some point in your life, you'll have to maintain and update a program that either you or somebody else wrote.

The following list describes typical steps that you may need to follow to maintain an existing program:

1. **Verify all reports of problems (or *bugs*) and determine what part of the program may be causing the bug to appear.**

2. **Fix the bug.**

3. **Test the program to make sure that the bug is really gone and that the changes you made to the program didn't introduce any new bugs.**

4. **Fix any problems that may have occurred during testing.**

5. **Repeat Steps 1 through 4 for each bug reported in the program.**

   Given the buggy nature of software, these steps could go on continuously for years.

6. **Release a software *patch* that can be added to an existing version of the program, making it incorporate the corrections that have been made to "patch up" the problems.**

The upgrade cycle

Companies don't make money fixing software and making it more stable, reliable, and dependable. Instead, companies make money by selling new versions of their programs that offer additional features and options that most people probably don't use or need in the first place.

Still, because so many programs get modified to take advantage of new hardware or software, you may find yourself occasionally upgrading a program by adding new features to it. The following steps make up the upgrade cycle:

1. **Determine what new feature you want to add to the program.**

2. **Plan how this new feature is to work (by using pseudocode or another tool to help structure your ideas).**

3. **Modify the program to add this new feature.**

4. **Test this new feature (by using alpha testing) to make sure that it works and doesn't introduce new bugs into the program.**

5. **Fix any problems that may have occurred during alpha testing.**

6. **Give out copies of the program to other people to beta test.**

7. **Fix any problems reported by the beta testers.**

8. **Repeat Steps 1 through 7 for each new feature that you need to add to the program.**

9. **Release the program as a new version and wait for the public to start reporting bugs that keep the program from working correctly so that you can start the maintenance cycle all over again.**

Despite all the university courses and such important-sounding titles as "software engineer," programming is still less of a science and more of an art. Writing, modifying, and updating software doesn't require a high IQ or an advanced mathematics degree as much as it requires creativity and plenty of imagination. You can write a program any way you want, but being organized and methodical is the best way to prevent possible problems later on.

Chapter 4

The Tools of a Computer Programmer

*T*o help make computer programming easier, programmers have created a variety of tools. Like a hammer, screwdriver, and hacksaw, each programming tool has a specific purpose. After you know what each tool does and how to use it, you can start writing your own programs in no time.

You need the following two crucial tools to write a program:

✔ An editor (so that you can write your instructions to the computer)

✔ A compiler or an interpreter (which converts your instructions into machine language so that the computer knows what you want it to do)

You may want to use the following additional programs when writing a program:

✔ A debugger (which helps identify problems or bugs in your program)

✔ A Help file authoring program (so that your program can provide Help on-screen instead of supplying the user with a decent manual)

✔ An installation program (to copy your program to the user's computer)

If you buy a specific programming language such as Visual Basic, Delphi, or Visual C++, you usually get an editor, compiler, debugger, and sometimes an installation program as well.

Writing Programs in an Editor

When you write a program, you must type your instructions in a text (or ASCII) file. Although you can use a word processor to create a text file, a word processor offers fancy formatting features (such as changing fonts or underlining text), which you don't need when writing a program.

The magic of source code

Source code acts like a recipe. If you had the recipe to McDonald's hamburgers and fries, you could open up your own restaurant and serve McDonald's-style food without paying McDonald's a single penny.

Likewise, if you had the source code to a program, such as WordPerfect or Windows 2000, you would have the recipe to create and modify WordPerfect or Windows 2000 anytime you wanted. That's why companies jealously guard their source code — to keep competitors from stealing their creations.

In the mid-1980s, when sales of the Macintosh computer were slipping into oblivion, some renegades banded together and called themselves "The Prometheus Project" (named after the mythological character who stole fire from the gods to give to human beings). After seeing sales of their beloved Macintosh plummet, the Prometheus Project members decided to save the Macintosh by encouraging other companies to clone the Macintosh.

Although other companies could buy the same parts that Apple Computer bought and slap together a Macintosh computer, these other companies would still lack the crucial part that made a Macintosh computer behave like a Macintosh — the operating system.

Although the microprocessor (otherwise known as the *central processing unit* or *CPU*) provides the brain of the computer, the operating system (which is nothing more than a program someone wrote) acts like the nervous system that makes all the different parts of the computer work together. Without the crucial Macintosh operating system, even a genuine Macintosh computer wouldn't work or behave like a Macintosh should.

So the Prometheus Project did what they thought was right — they stole the source code to the Macintosh operating system and tried to give it to as many people as possible. They hoped that if the right people got their hands on the Macintosh operating system source code, they would be able to develop a Macintosh clone computer, sell it for a lower price, and flood the world with inexpensive Macintosh computers that everyone could afford to buy. The Prometheus Project hoped to keep the Macintosh alive, despite the bungling management of Apple Computer.

Unfortunately, the Macintosh operating system source code belonged to Apple Computers, and stealing this source code was a crime even worse than breaking into Apple Computer's headquarters and stealing all their desks, filing cabinets, and copying machines.

Ultimately, the Prometheus Project died a quiet death under the scrutiny of the FBI and the Secret Service. No one developed a Macintosh clone using the stolen operating system source code, and sales of Macintosh computers continue their second-fiddle status to Windows computers to this day.

A program consists of one or more instructions that tell the computer what to do. The instructions that make up a program are called the program's *source code.*

Rather than struggle with a word processor, programmers have created special programs for writing, editing, and printing the source code of a program. Almost no one writes a program correctly the first time, so the majority of a programmer's time is spent editing the source code. As a result, the program that enables you to write, edit, and print a program is called an *editor.*

Two types of editors exist: line editors and full-screen editors. Older computers with limited memory and storage space offered only line editors, which can modify only one line at a time. Most programmers use full-screen editors, so they can modify a whole screen full of instructions. Line editors are obsolete, but you may still run into them once in a while. MS-DOS came with a line editor called EDLIN.EXE.

An editor looks like a word processor but may offer special features to make programming easier, such as automatically formatting your source code, offering shortcuts for editing your source code, or providing pop-up Help as you're typing program commands. An example of an editor's pop-up Help is shown in Figure 4-1.

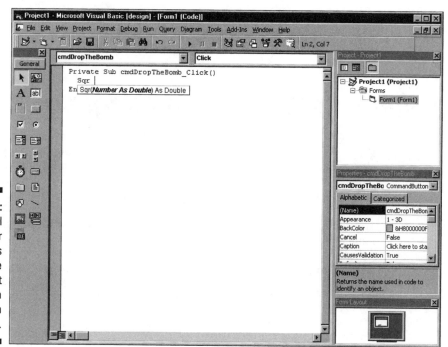

Figure 4-1: The Visual Basic editor displays Help the moment you type a common command.

Linux and the Open Source Movement

In the early days of computers, programmers freely created and shared the source code to their programs. The idea was that if enough people voluntarily worked together on a single program, the chances were good that the program would actually work.

Then programmers decided that they should be paid for their hard work, so they started keeping the source code of their programs to themselves, which helped to spawn the software industry as we know it today (with all its missed deadlines, unreliable programs, and horribly written software manuals).

But now the idea of sharing the source code (often referred to as the *Open Source*

Movement) has resurfaced with the emergence of the Linux operating system. Users can again peek at the source code without paying for it.

Having access to the source code gives you the option of modifying the program if you want or (more likely) hiring someone else to modify it for you. In any event, access to the source code prevents you from being at the mercy of companies that refuse to reveal their source code so that they can force you to pay for program upgrades that still may not fix or add the features you want.

Anytime that you need to write or modify the source code of a program, you must use an editor.

Using a Compiler or an Interpreter

After you type your instructions in an editor by using a programming language such as C++ or Java, guess what? The computer doesn't have the slightest idea what you just created. Computers understand only machine language, so you need to use another special program to convert your source code (the instructions written in C++ or Java) into machine language.

You can use two types of programs to convert source code into machine language:

- ✔ A compiler
- ✔ An interpreter

Compilers

A compiler takes your source code, converts the whole thing into machine language, and then stores these equivalent machine language instructions in a separate file, often called an *executable file*. This is like having a translator study an entire novel written in Spanish and then translate it into Arabic.

When a compiler converts source code into machine language, it is said to be *compiling* a program.

After you compile a program, you can just give away copies of the executable (machine language) version of your program without giving away your source code version. As a result, most commercial programs (such as Microsoft PowerPoint and Lotus 1-2-3) are compiled.

After you use a compiler to convert source code into machine language, you never need to use the compiler again (unless you make changes to your source code).

A compiler creates machine language for a specific microprocessor, such as the PowerPC (used in the Macintosh) or the Intel Pentium family of micro-processors (including clone microprocessors, such as the AMD-K2). If you wrote a program in BASIC and wanted to run it on a Macintosh and a Windows computer, you would need to compile your program twice: once for the Macintosh and once for the Windows environment.

Not all compilers are equal, even though two different compilers may convert the same language into machine language. For example, given identical C++ source code, one C++ compiler may create a program that runs quickly, while a second C++ compiler may create a slower but smaller file.

Interpreters

A second, but less popular, way to convert source code into machine language is to use an interpreter. An interpreter converts each line of your source code into machine language, one at a time. This is like giving a speech in English and having someone translate your sentences, one at a time, into another language (such as French).

Unlike a compiler, an interpreter converts source code into machine language but stores the machine language instructions in the computer's memory. So every time that you turn off the computer, you lose the machine language version of your program. To run the program again, you must feed the source code into the interpreter again.

If anyone wants to run your program, they need both an interpreter and the source code to your program. Because your source code enables everyone to see how you wrote your program (and gives others a chance to copy or modify your program without your permission), very few commercial programs use an interpreter.

Interpreters are now mostly used with Web-page programming languages such as JavaScript and VBScript. Because Web pages can be viewed by different computers, programs written in JavaScript or VBScript can't be compiled into machine language. Instead, your computer's browser uses an interpreter to run a JavaScript or VBScript program.

In the old days, when computers were slow and lacked enough memory and storage space, interpreters were popular because they gave you instant feedback. The moment you typed an instruction into the computer, the interpreter would tell you whether that instruction would work and would even show you the results. With an interpreter, you could write and test your program at the same time. Now, computers are so fast that programmers find using a compiler easier than using an interpreter.

QBASIC is a free BASIC language interpreter that comes with MS-DOS and Windows 95/98. If you want to run a program written in QBASIC, you need a copy of the QBASIC interpreter and the source code to the QBASIC program.

If you want to compile QBASIC programs, you can use a shareware compiler, called FirstBASIC or PowerBASIC, from `www.powerbasic.com`.

P-code: A combination compiler and interpreter

Getting a program to run on different types of computers can be a big pain in the neck. For example, both Macintosh and Windows programs use pull-down menus and dialog boxes. However, you need to write one set of commands to create pull-down menus on the Macintosh and a second set of commands to create the identical pull-down menus in Windows.

Because one program almost never runs on multiple computers without extensive modification, programmers have created a combination compiler and interpreter.

Instead of compiling source code directly into machine language, programmers have created special compilers that compile source code into a special intermediate language called *p-code*. To run a program compiled into p-code, you use an interpreter.

Java is the most popular programming language that uses p-code. After you've compiled a Java program into p-code, you can copy that p-code to a Macintosh, a Windows computer, or a Linux computer. As long as that computer has a Java p-code interpreter, you can run the Java program on that computer without modification.

Best of all, programs compiled into p-code can run without the original source code, which means that you can protect your source code and still give your program away to others.

Naturally, p-code has its disadvantages. Programs created using p-code tend to run much slower than programs compiled directly into machine language. Although p-code programs can run without a copy of the original source code that created them, p-code programs can also be *decompiled*.

Decompiling a p-code program can reveal the original source code that created the program. So if you wrote a program in Java and compiled it into p-code, a rival could decompile your p-code program and see the original Java source code that you wrote. Now your rival has a nearly identical copy of your source code, essentially stealing your program.

You can actually decompile any program, including programs that have been compiled into machine language. But unlike decompiling p-code programs, decompiling a machine language version of a program never gets you the original high-level language source code that was used to write the program. That's because when you compile a program into machine language, the original source code could have been written in C++, COBOL, FORTRAN, BASIC, Ada, LISP, Pascal, or any other programming language in the world. Because the decompiler has no idea what language the original source code was written in, it can only decompile a machine language version of a program into equivalent assembly language.

So what should I use?

If you want to write programs to sell, use a compiler, which protects your original source code. If you want to write a program to run on your Web page, you can use an interpreter or p-code. If you want to write a program that can run on different types of computers, p-code may be your only choice. As a safer but more cumbersome alternative, you could also use multiple compilers and modify your program to run on each different computer.

The language you choose can determine whether you can use a compiler, an interpreter, or p-code. For example, Java programs are often converted into p-code, although they can be compiled directly into machine language. On the other hand, C++ is usually compiled and rarely interpreted or converted into p-code.

Squashing Bugs with a Debugger

No computer program works 100 percent correctly, which explains why computers crash, lose airline reservations, or just act erratically at times. Mathematically, writing a program that works 100 percent correctly every time is impossible because testing a program for all possible types of computers, hardware, and additional software that may interfere with the way your program runs is impossible.

Anytime a program has a problem that keeps it from working correctly, that problem is called a *bug*.

In the early days, computers used mechanical relays and vacuum tubes instead of circuit boards and microprocessors. One day, the computer failed to work correctly. The scientists examined their program; it should have worked. So they next examined the computer itself and found that a moth had gotten smashed in a mechanical relay, preventing it from closing, and thus keeping the computer from working correctly. From that point on, problems in computers have been known as *bugs*, even though real bugs are much less annoying and dangerous than computer bugs.

Because writing a program that works 100 percent correctly all the time is impossible, operating systems (such as Windows 98) unavoidably have bugs that keep them from working right. To convert your source code into machine language, you must use a compiler or interpreter, which is another program that has its share of bugs. Finally, your own program may have bugs of its own. With so many places for bugs to creep in, you shouldn't be surprised that bugs infest computers like cockroaches in a cheap apartment complex.

Although you can do little about bugs in other people's programs (except to not buy the programs), you can reduce (but not completely eliminate) bugs in your own program by using a debugger. A debugger is a special program (which may also have bugs in it) that can help you track down and wipe out bugs in programs that you write.

A debugger provides several ways to track down bugs in your program:

  ✔ **Stepping:** The debugger runs your program, line-by-line, so that you can see exactly which line may be causing the bug. This is like re-reading written instructions to get to another person's house when you're lost. By going over these instructions, one by one, you can find out where you made a wrong turn.

  ✔ **Breakpoints:** Rather than force you to step through an entire program, line-by-line, breakpoints enable you to specify where you want to start examining your program, line-by-line. So if you were lost, rather than re-read the instructions to get to another person's house from start to finish, using a breakpoint would be like skipping those instructions that you know you followed correctly and examining only the remaining instructions that you aren't sure you followed correctly. By using breakpoints, you can selectively examine parts of your program, line-by-line, rather than the whole thing.

✔ **Watching:** Watching enables you to see when your program stores data in memory and what that data may be. If your program stores incorrect data (such as saving a name instead of a telephone number), you know exactly where in your program the bug is occurring. Figure 4-2 shows a sample debugger at work. This would be like someone telling you to drive 10 miles south down a certain road after turning right. The moment you exceeded 10 miles, a watchpoint would have alerted you so that you would know exactly where you almost made a mistake and got lost.

A debugger essentially shows you exactly how a computer is going to interpret the instructions in your program. This enables you to see where your instructions need to be modified so that the bug doesn't occur anymore. Of course, when you fix one bug, you could introduce several new ones. That's why writing bug-free programs is impossible.

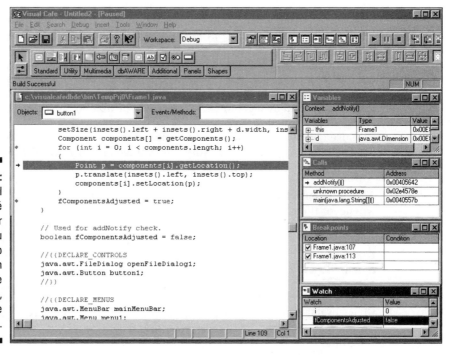

Figure 4-2: The Visual Café debugger enables you to step through your entire program, one line at a time.

Code analyzers

Programming is the art of writing the most efficient programs possible so that they take up less memory and storage space, yet run at blazingly fast speeds. When programmers finish writing a program that actually works, they often examine it line-by-line to optimize the program so that it runs faster or uses less memory.

To make analyzing and optimizing programs easier, people have developed special source code analyzing programs. These programs examine the source code of a program and determine which parts of the program are used most often and which parts are hardly used at all. With this information, you can optimize the most frequently used parts of your program so that it runs faster.

Writing a Help File

Nobody has trouble using a doorknob, a toaster, or a microwave oven, but people still complain that computers and VCRs are too hard to use.

The problem with VCRs lies in the cryptic controls that aren't easy to figure out just by looking at them. Similarly, the problem with computers is that programs are too complicated to use at first glance. If you can make a program that's actually easy to use, people will be able to use it.

Because computers are still being designed for programmers by other programmers, computers still mystify the average user. To help the poor befuddled user, most programs now offer Help files.

A Help file provides instructions and explanations on-screen. Theoretically, whenever the user has trouble with the program, he can browse through the Help file, find an explanation or step-by-step instructions, and continue using the program. Figure 4-3 shows Microsoft PowerPoint 2000, which desperately tries to guide users through its complicated maze of commands by providing a Help file and a cartoon Office Assistant.

Although Help files still can't substitute for designing a program that's easy to use in the first place, most programs offer Help files anyway. To keep your program modern and up to date, you should include a Help file with your program.

To create a Help file, you can use a special Help file authoring program, which simplifies the process of creating and organizing topics for your Help file, as shown in Figure 4-4.

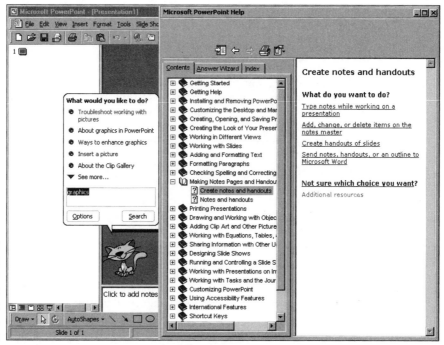

Figure 4-3:
Help files for
Microsoft
PowerPoint
2000.

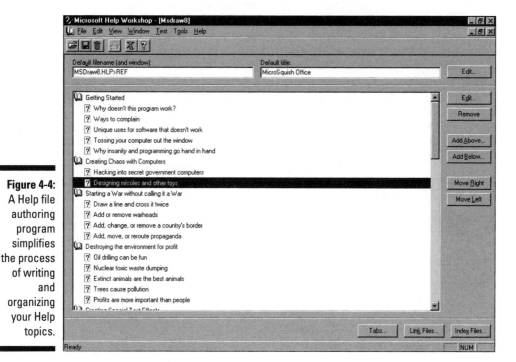

Figure 4-4:
A Help file
authoring
program
simplifies
the process
of writing
and
organizing
your Help
topics.

Creating an Installation Program

After you've written your program, tested it, debugged it, and written a Help file for it, the final step is giving or selling copies of your program to others. Although you can copy your program onto a floppy disk or CD and force buyers to manually copy your program to their hard disk, that can cause problems. Users may not copy all the files correctly, or forcing users to manually copy your program to their hard disk will be such a nuisance that people won't bother even trying to use your program.

To make copying a program to a user's hard disk as easy as possible, most commercial programs include a special installation program. Users run this installation program, which automatically copies a program and all necessary files to the appropriate location on the user's hard disk. By making the installation of a program practically foolproof, software publishers make sure that the user installs the programs correctly.

So the final step to distributing your program to others is to use a special installation program, which can smash all your program files into a single file that can automatically install itself on another computer.

Installation programs offer these features for distributing programs to others:

✔ **File compression:** Most programs are fairly large, which means that they can't fit on a single floppy disk. Rather than force users to insert a stack of floppy disks into their computer to install your program, an installation program smashes your files so that they can fit on as few floppy disks as possible.

✔ **Display graphics and play sounds:** Installing a program usually takes a few minutes while the computer copies files from the floppy or CD to its hard disk. Rather than force the user to stare into space, an installation program can display advertisements or messages to make the installation process mildly interesting.

✔ **Simplify the copying process:** Most important, an installation program simplifies copying your program to the user's hard disk, making the whole process accurate, fast, and fool-proof.

The first impression that people get from your program is through its installation process, so an installation program helps give your program a professional appearance.

Of course, you better make sure that your installation program installs your program correctly or the first impression that users get from your program is likely to be a highly negative one.

Part II

Learning Programming with QBASIC

The 5th Wave — By Rich Tennant

HERE'S THE DEAL — MANAGEMENT IS WILLING TO PAY BIG BUCKS TO ANY PROGRAMMER WHO CAN WORK WITH APPLETS.

AWRIGHT!!

In this part . . .

No matter what programming language you use (C/C++, BASIC, COBOL, Ada, Modula-2, and so on), all computer programs tend to follow the same general principles. When you understand how to write a program using one language (such as BASIC), you'll find that understanding a second or third programming language (such as C/C++ and Java) is much easier.

To give you a chance for hands-on programming, this book sprinkles plenty of QBASIC programs in each chapter. Just type these programs into your computer and run them to see how they work.

Occasionally in this part, you see a QBASIC program along with an equivalent program written in another language (such as C/C++, Pascal, or Java) in order to expose you to other programming languages. You can look at these programs to see how other programming languages accomplish the same tasks while looking entirely different from equivalent QBASIC programs.

Chapter 5

Getting Your Hands on a Real Language: QBASIC

In This Chapter

▶ Understanding why you should learn QBASIC

▶ Installing QBASIC

▶ Writing your first QBASIC program

▶ Using keystroke commands in QBASIC

▶ Getting help using QBASIC

▶ Exiting QBASIC

*T*he best way to learn anything is to start practicing it. If you want to learn computer programming, you should start writing programs on your computer.

You can learn to program with one of hundreds of programming languages, such as Pascal, LOGO, and SmallTalk, but the most popular beginner's programming language is still BASIC. BASIC is simple enough to help you understand the concepts behind programming, yet powerful enough to enable you to create commercial-quality programs.

If you have a copy of Windows 95/98, Microsoft has given you a free copy of its version of BASIC, called QBASIC. (In case you're still using MS-DOS, check which version you have. If you have MS-DOS 5.0, you also have a free copy of QBASIC buried on your computer.) To get you started on programming, the majority of this book shows you how to program by using QBASIC. You can read the book and type the QBASIC programs in your own computer to see how they work.

If you have a Macintosh, you don't have a free copy of QBASIC. In this case, you can use a free BASIC interpreter called Chipmunk BASIC, which you can download from www.nicholson.com/rhn/basic/. Chipmunk BASIC isn't quite identical to QBASIC. But both QBASIC and Chipmunk BASIC use the BASIC language, so programs written for QBASIC should run under Chipmunk

---

The evolution of BASIC on MS-DOS

In the world of MS-DOS and Windows, BASIC has gone through various changes. In the early days of MS-DOS, Microsoft gave us a free BASIC interpreter called BASICA, which stood for BASIC Advanced. Later, they gave us an improved BASIC interpreter called GW-BASIC, which stood for Gee Whiz BASIC.

After programmers started clamoring for a BASIC compiler so that they could sell and distribute their BASIC programs, Microsoft responded by offering QuickBASIC. A rival company, called Borland International, soon sold a similar BASIC compiler called Turbo BASIC, which was later sold and marketed under the new name of Power BASIC.

With the introduction of MS-DOS 5.0, Microsoft included a new BASIC interpreter called QBASIC, which they've continued to give away with Windows 95 and Windows 98. (After releasing Visual Basic for Windows, Microsoft tried to market a version of Visual Basic for MS-DOS, but they quickly dropped this product after everyone started using Windows.)

BASIC with a little modification. If you're running Linux, you can download a free BASIC interpreter called YABASIC (which stands for Yet Another BASIC) by visiting www.yabasic.de.

Why Learn QBASIC?

QBASIC doesn't enable you to write programs that can run on Windows 95/98/NT. If you try to sell your QBASIC programs, users will need a copy of the QBASIC interpreter before they can run your programs. Given these massive disadvantages, you may be wondering "What's the point of learning QBASIC?"

QBASIC is free

QBASIC comes free with every computer that has MS-DOS 5.0 or later or Windows 95 or later. If you want to learn programming but aren't sure which programming language to use first, don't waste your money buying a separate language compiler (such as Visual C++). Start by learning QBASIC and then graduate to other programming languages later. Consider QBASIC your free trial programming language, courtesy of Microsoft.

QBASIC is easy

QBASIC can teach you the fundamentals of programming so that you can get real-life experience programming your own computer. Other programming languages, such as C++ or Java, can force you to master needlessly complicated topics, such as pointers, object-orientation, and memory allocation. Rather than let these other programming languages bury you under an additional layer of complexity that only gets in your way, learn QBASIC.

After you learn the fundamentals of programming with QBASIC, you're better able to learn another programming language, such as C++ or Java.

You can start using QBASIC today

QBASIC comes free with every copy of MS-DOS and Windows, so everyone reading this book can start using QBASIC right away (unless, of course, you're using a Macintosh or an operating system other than Windows, in which case you can find a different version of BASIC for your computer, as I explain at the beginning of this chapter). That makes QBASIC a natural learning tool to complement this book.

If you get confused trying to understand certain programming concepts, type a sample QBASIC program and see for yourself exactly how certain programming features work. By combining theory with hands-on experience, this book and QBASIC can help you learn computer programming in no time.

If you like programming in QBASIC but want to write and sell programs that run on Windows 95/98/NT, you must buy Visual Basic or another BASIC compiler for developing Windows programs.

Installing QBASIC

Even though QBASIC comes free with every copy of Windows 95/98, you probably can't find it on your computer. That's because Microsoft cleverly hid QBASIC so that it doesn't install on your computer unless you specifically load it.

If you're still using MS-DOS 5.0 or later instead of Windows 95/98, QBASIC should already be installed on your computer. Just type **QBASIC** from your DOS directory (most likely at this path: C:\DOS), and you can skip the following instructions about installing QBASIC for Windows 95/98.

To load QBASIC on a computer that runs Windows 95/98, follow these steps:

1. **Insert the Windows 95/98 CD in your CD-ROM drive.**

   If the Windows 95/98 installation program appears, click the close box of the installation window to make it go away.

2. **Right-click the Start button on the Windows taskbar.**

   A pop-up menu appears.

3. **Click Explore.**

   The Windows Explorer appears, displaying the Windows CD in the left pane, like this: Windows 98 (D:).

4. **Click the plus sign that appears to the left of Windows CD icon.**

   Various folders appear directly underneath the Windows CD icon.

5. **Click the plus sign that appears to the left of the Tools folder.**

   Another list of folders appears directly under the Tools folder.

6. **Click the oldmsdos folder.**

   The Windows Explorer displays a variety of different files, but look for the two QBASIC files: the QBASIC Help file and the QBASIC interpreter program, as shown in Figure 5-1.

7. **Press and hold the Ctrl key and click both QBASIC files.**

   The Windows Explorer highlights both QBASIC files.

8. **Click the plus sign that appears to the left of your Windows folder in the left pane of the Windows Explorer.**

   A list of folders appears, with names such as All Users, Command, and Cookies. You may need to click the plus sign that appears to the left of the My Computer icon to see the Windows folder.

9. **Move the mouse over one of the highlighted QBASIC files and press and hold the left mouse button.**

10. **Drag the mouse so that the QBASIC files appear over the Command folder (which appears underneath the Windows folder).**

11. **Release the left mouse button.**

After you copy the two QBASIC files into the Command folder inside your Windows folder (at this path: C:\WINDOWS\COMMAND), you can run QBASIC from within an MS-DOS window.

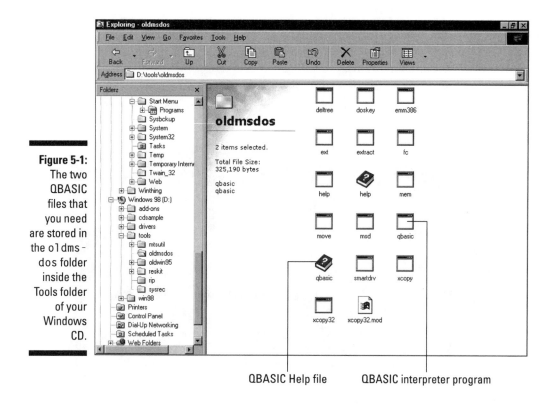

Figure 5-1:
The two
QBASIC
files that
you need
are stored in
the oldms-
dos folder
inside the
Tools folder
of your
Windows
CD.

QBASIC Help file   QBASIC interpreter program

Loading QBASIC

After you install QBASIC on your computer, the next step is to load QBASIC so that you can start using it.

If you are using MS-DOS 5.0 or later, you can load QBASIC just by switching to the C:\DOS directory, typing **QBASIC**, and pressing the Enter key.

To load QBASIC from within Windows 95/98, follow these steps:

1. **Click the Start button on the Windows taskbar.**

2. **Click Run.**

   A Run dialog box appears.

3. **Type** QBASIC **and press Enter.**

   A dialog box named Microsoft QuickBASIC appears. This dialog box enables you to enter any program parameters that you may want to use when running QBASIC. You don't need any at this time.

4. **Click OK or press Enter.**

The QBASIC editor appears with an opening dialog box, as shown in Figure 5-2.

5. **Press Esc to close the opening dialog box.**

At this point, you are ready to type and run a BASIC program.

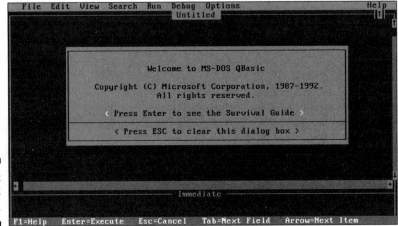

```
 File  Edit  View  Search  Run  Debug  Options                    Help
                            Untitled




                     Welcome to MS-DOS QBasic

           Copyright (C) Microsoft Corporation, 1987-1992.
                        All rights reserved.

              < Press Enter to see the Survival Guide >

              < Press ESC to clear this dialog box >




                            Immediate
 F1=Help    Enter=Execute    Esc=Cancel    Tab=Next Field    Arrow=Next Item
```

Figure 5-2:
The QBASIC
editor.

You can switch out of QBASIC and back to Windows 95/98 by pressing Ctrl+Esc. To switch back to QBASIC, click the Microsoft QuickBASIC button that appears in the Windows 95/98 taskbar.

The mouse pointer in QBASIC looks like a rectangle and works just like the mouse pointer in Windows 95/98; it can just look a bit strange if you've never used an MS-DOS program before.

Your First QBASIC Program

The QBASIC editor is where you write, edit, and run your BASIC program. To see the power of QBASIC, type the following into the QBASIC editor:

```
CLS
PRINT "This BASIC program mimics a really bad boss."
PRINT
PRINT "What is your name?"
INPUT Name$
PRINT "Hello " + Name$ + ". You're fired! Have a nice day."
END
```

You don't need to type the word PRINT in uppercase; the QBASIC editor does so for you automatically. This is QBASIC's way of identifying special BASIC commands. In the preceding program, the four special BASIC commands are CLS, PRINT, INPUT, and END.

Unlike a word processor, the QBASIC editor doesn't wrap words from one line to the other, which means that you can keep typing all the way to the far right until your text scrolls out of view.

This program tells the computer to perform the following tasks:

1. The first line clears the screen.

2. The second line prints on-screen the message "This BASIC program mimics a really bad boss."

3. The third line prints (adds) a blank line directly underneath.

4. The fourth line prints "What is your name?" on-screen.

5. The fifth line waits for the user to type a name. As soon as the user presses the Enter key, the BASIC program stores whatever the user types into a temporary memory location identified as Name$.

6. The sixth line prints the message "Hello (followed by the name that the user typed in the fourth line). You're fired! Have a nice day." The plus sign (+) tells QBASIC to add the word "Hello" with the words stored in Name$.

7. The seventh line tells the computer that this is the end of the program.

Running a QBASIC program

After you finish typing a BASIC program, press Shift+F5 or choose Run⇨Start to run the program. Figure 5-3 shows what the BASIC program from the preceding section looks like when run on QBASIC.

Saving a QBASIC program

Although you could type your QBASIC programs over and over whenever you want to run them, saving your program to a hard or floppy disk is much easier. Then you can load and edit the program later.

```
This program mimics a really bad boss.

What is your name?
? Bill McPherson
Hello Bill McPherson. You're fired! Have a nice day.




Press any key to continue
```

Figure 5-3:
QBASIC
shows what
the BASIC
program
looks like
when actu-
ally run on a
computer.

To save a program, follow these steps:

1. **Choose File⊅Save.**

   The Save dialog box appears.

2. **Type a name for your file.**

   The name should be eight characters or less. (If you don't change the directory or drive, QBASIC saves your file in the C:\WINDOWS\COMMAND directory.)

3. **Click OK or press Enter.**

QBASIC automatically adds a .BAS file extension to QBASIC programs that you save. Unless you have a good reason to change this file extension, you should use the .BAS extension to help you identify your BASIC programs.

Loading an existing or starting a new QBASIC program

Unlike modern Windows programs that can open up multiple windows, QBASIC works with only one window at a time. Any time that you want to view another BASIC program, you must get rid of the BASIC program currently being displayed.

To create a brand new program, follow these steps:

1. **Choose File⊅New.**

   If you haven't saved your currently displayed BASIC program, a dialog box pops up.

2. **Click Yes to save the current file or click No if you don't want to save your changes.**

   QBASIC displays a blank screen, ready for you to type a new BASIC program.

To load a previously saved program, follow these steps:

1. **Choose File➪Open.**

   The Open dialog box appears. You may need to change directories or drives to find where you saved the file.

2. **Click the file that you want to open and then click OK.**

   If you haven't saved your currently displayed BASIC program, a dialog box pops up.

3. **Click Yes to save the current file or click No if you don't want to save your changes.**

   QBASIC displays the BASIC program that you chose in Step 2.

Using Keystroke Commands in QBASIC

The QBASIC editor works like a simple word processor. You can use the mouse or the keyboard to navigate a BASIC program. Table 5-1 shows the different keys that you can press and what they do.

Table 5-1	Keystroke Commands for the QBASIC Editor
Keystroke Command	**What It Does**
Home	Moves the cursor to the front of the line
End	Moves the cursor to the end of the line
Ctrl+Home	Moves the cursor to the beginning of your program
Ctrl+End	Moves the cursor to the end of your program
Ctrl+Left arrow	Moves the cursor one word to the left
Ctrl+Right arrow	Moves the cursor one word to the right
Shift+Arrow key	Highlights text in the direction of the arrow
Delete	Deletes the character directly above the cursor or deletes an entire highlighted block of text

(continued)

Table 5-1 (continued)

Keystroke Command	What It Does
Backspace	Deletes the character to the left of the cursor
Ctrl+T	Deletes the word that the cursor is on
Ctrl+Y	Deletes the entire line that the cursor is on
Ctrl+V	Toggles between Insert mode and Overtype mode

Getting Help Using QBASIC

Because Microsoft has pretty much abandoned QBASIC, you can't find any official Microsoft manuals explaining how to use QBASIC. In fact, you'll be hard pressed to find any third-party books for learning QBASIC.

So if you need help using QBASIC, you must rely on the built-in Help in QBASIC, which comes in three flavors:

✔ **The Help index** explains the purpose of QBASIC language commands (also known as *keywords*) that you can use to write your own QBASIC programs.

✔ **The Help table of contents** provides information for using the QBASIC editor, along with general programming information.

✔ **Context-sensitive Help** provides help for using specific QBASIC keywords in your own programs.

The Help index

The Help index provides explanations for using all the QBASIC programming language commands, such as PRINT, STOP, and INPUT. To view the Help index, follow these steps:

1. **Choose Help⇨Index.**

   The Help Index window appears, listing all QBASIC keywords alphabetically in uppercase.

2. **Move the mouse pointer over a QBASIC keyword and double-click the left mouse button.**

QBASIC displays an explanation for your chosen QBASIC keyword. If you want to continue looking up explanations for using different QBASIC keywords, double-click Index or Back.

3. **Press Esc to close the Help Index window.**

The Help Index window lists all the QBASIC keywords available for your programs. If you want to learn everything possible about QBASIC programming, spend some time browsing through the Help index.

The Help table of contents

The Help table of contents contains all the general information for using QBASIC. To view the Help table of contents, follow these steps:

1. **Choose Help⇨Contents.**

   The Help Table of Contents window appears, listing various Help topics between green triangles.

2. **Move the mouse pointer over any topic surrounded by green triangles and double-click the left mouse button.**

   Depending on the topic you choose, you may need to double-click additional topics. To return to the beginning of the table of contents, double-click Contents or Back.

3. **Press Esc to close the Help Table of Contents window.**

Context-sensitive Help

As you're writing a program, you may have a question about using a specific QBASIC keyword. (QBASIC identifies all keywords by displaying them in uppercase.) To get Help using a QBASIC keyword, follow these steps:

1. **Click the QBASIC keyword that you want to get help on (or move the cursor in the QBASIC keyword).**

2. **Press F1.**

   QBASIC displays a Help window explaining how to use the QBASIC keyword you chose in Step 1.

3. **Press Esc to close the Help window.**

Exiting QBASIC

Eventually you need to exit QBASIC so that you can do something else with your computer. To exit QBASIC, follow these steps:

1. **Choose File➪Exit.**

   If you haven't saved the currently displayed QBASIC program, a dialog box pops up and asks whether you want to save the file.

2. **Click Yes to save the current file or click No if you don't want to save your changes.**

   QBASIC politely disappears from view.

If your QBASIC program displayed anything on-screen, you may see a Finished - Microsoft QuickBASIC window from within Windows 95/98. Just click the close box of this window to make it go away.

Chapter 6

Handling Input and Output

In This Chapter

- Spitting out data
- Using the `PRINT` and `LPRINT` commands
- Getting input

Every program takes in data (input), manipulates that data in some way, and spits the data back out in some form (output).

In the old days, programmers gave input to the computer by using a variety of methods, ranging from physically rearranging switches on the computer to using paper tape, punch cards, teletype machines (which resembled typewriters), and finally keyboards and monitors. When computers spit back some form of output, it usually appears on paper or on the screen of a monitor.

Despite the fact that today's computers include pop-up windows, dialog boxes, command buttons, and scroll bars, most of today's programming languages are still rooted in the past when programs would wait for the user to type a name or a number. Then the program would shove that information up a line and print the resulting output directly underneath, as shown in Figure 6-1.

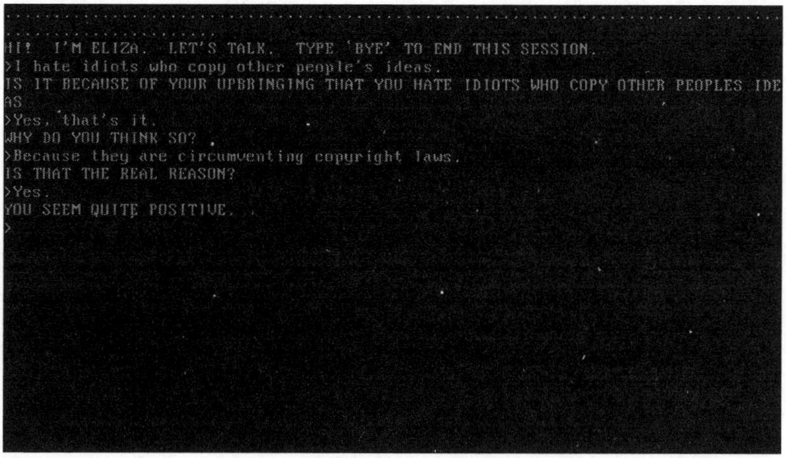

Figure 6-1: An old-style program asks for input and spits back the result, one line at a time.

That's why most programming languages such as QBASIC (and even C/C++) contain built-in commands for reading and displaying data one line at a time on-screen. Naturally, such programs look fairly primitive, especially compared with today's modern programs, but be patient. When you're learning programming for the first time, understanding how programs can accept input and spit data back out is much more important than worrying about how a program actually looks on-screen.

Spitting Out Data

When you write a program, you must organize your instructions one after another, as in a list. At the simplest level, you could have a program that does nothing more than print a message on the screen, such as the following:

```
CLS
PRINT "What are you looking at?"
END
```

Each time that you run this program, it prints the message, "What are you looking at?" on-screen.

Whenever you write a QBASIC program, make sure that you start off with the CLS command and end with the END command. The CLS command clears the screen so that your program can run without bumping into the residue output that another program may have left on-screen. The END command is optional, but it clearly identifies the end of your program.

In QBASIC, you can use two commands (otherwise known as *keywords*) that can make your program display information on-screen:

✔ PRINT

✔ WRITE

Both the PRINT and WRITE commands can print numbers (such as 34, 1.209, or -9038) or strings (such as "Hello, moron" or "Greetings!") on-screen. However, each command prints data slightly differently, as the following BASIC program demonstrates:

```
CLS
PRINT "PRINT => What are you looking at?"
WRITE "WRITE => You looking at me?"
PRINT 98.5
WRITE 98.5
END
```

When you run this program, you see how the PRINT and WRITE commands differ (as shown in Figure 6-2). Table 6-1 points out all the areas in which the commands differ.

Figure 6-2:
Seeing how
the PRINT
and WRITE
commands
differ.

Table 6-1 Comparing the PRINT and WRITE Commands in QBASIC

Data	PRINT *Command*	WRITE *Command*
Strings	Does not print quotation marks	Prints quotation marks
Numbers	Leaves a blank space in front of the number (for a negative sign)	Does not leave a blank space in front of the number

You can use either the PRINT command or the WRITE command to display data on-screen. Just remember that each command displays strings and numbers slightly differently. To make your program easier to read and understand, you should use only one command consistently. When most people use BASIC, they usually use the PRINT command to display data on the screen and the WRITE command to store data to a disk.

Printing multiple chunks of data on one line

The previous examples show how the PRINT command prints one chunk of data per line, such as displaying "What are you looking at?" on-screen. However, if you want to print two or more chunks of data on-screen, you can use the magic of a semicolon (;), as shown in the following example:

```
CLS
PRINT "Please pay this amount ="; 100
END
```

This program displays "Please pay this amount = 100" on-screen.

If you forget to type the semicolon in the preceding program, the QBASIC editor adds the semicolon automatically.

The whole purpose of the semicolon is to allow the PRINT command to print two or more chunks of data, whether that data is a string or a number:

```
CLS
PRINT "Here are the dimensions of my dog"
PRINT 34; 28; 32
PRINT -34; -28; -32
END
```

Figure 6-3 shows how the semicolon separates numbers by one space (plus an additional space for the negative sign, even if the negative sign isn't used, as shown in the first PRINT command).

Figure 6-3:
Semicolons enable the PRINT command to display multiple chunks of data on a single line.

When the semicolon separates two numbers, or a string and a number, it puts a blank space after each item. But look at what happens if you squeeze a semicolon between two strings, as in the following example:

```
CLS
PRINT "Stay healthy!"; "Eat more"; "food coloring!"
END
```

In this case, the semicolon does not put a blank space between the two items and smashes each string together, printing the output "Stay healthy!Eat more food coloring!"

If you use the semicolon to separate two strings, put an extra space at the end or the beginning of one of the strings, like this:

```
CLS
PRINT "Stay healthy!"; " Eat more "; "food coloring!"
END
```

If you want to print multiple chunks of data on one line, you have two choices. You can type one PRINT command followed by all the chunks of data that you want to print. Or you can use multiple PRINT commands with a semicolon at the end of each PRINT command, except for the last one.

When a semicolon appears at the end of a PRINT command, it tells QBASIC, "Print the next chunk of data on the same line as this line." For example, the following QBASIC program prints all data on a single line:

```
CLS
PRINT "Stay healthy!";
PRINT " Eat more";
PRINT " food coloring!"
END
```

This program simply prints "Stay healthy! Eat more food coloring!" on a single line. Notice that the semicolon appears at the end of the first two PRINT commands but not the last one.

Spacing data on a single line

For another way to print data on a single line, use a comma (,) between chunks of data, as in this example:

```
CLS
PRINT "This is the IQ", 32, "of my teacher."
PRINT "This is the IQ", " of my government =", -45
END
```

When used with the PRINT command, commas print each chunk of data exactly 14 spaces apart in its own print zone, as shown in Figure 6-4.

Figure 6-4:
How
commas
divide the
screen into
separate
print zones.

Commas always align each chunk of data in its own print zone. Print zones begin in columns 1, 15, 29, 43, and 57. If you want to define the specific column in which your data should appear, you can use the TAB command with semicolons, as shown in the following code:

```
CLS
PRINT "This is the IQ"; TAB(21); 32; TAB(47); " of my
          teacher."
PRINT "This is the IQ"; TAB(26); " of my government
          =";TAB(53); -45
END
```

Using the TAB command, you can specify the column where you want your data to appear, whether that data consists of numbers or strings. The TAB(21) command tells QBASIC to print the next chunk of data in column 21, the TAB(26) command prints the next chunk of data in column 26, the TAB(47) command prints the next chunk of data in column 47, and the TAB(53) command prints the next chunk of data in column 53.

What happens if you use the TAB command to specify a column that already contains data? Rather than overwriting the existing data, QBASIC simply prints the next chunk of data on a separate line (as shown in Figure 6-5). The following program demonstrates:

```
CLS
PRINT "Morons are that way by choice."; TAB(6); "That's why
          they're morons."
END
```

If you want to define exactly how many spaces should separate each chunk of data, you can use the SPC command, which specifies exactly how many spaces QBASIC prints between chunks of data. For example, the following QBASIC program prints exactly seven spaces between two strings:

```
CLS
PRINT "If the theory of evolution is true,"; SPC(7); "then
          where do creationists come from?"
END
```

Formatting your numbers with the PRINT USING command

Normally the PRINT command just displays data exactly as it appears. However, you may want to format your data so that it appears slightly differently. For example, rather than display the number 35.9873, you could have the computer automatically format that number so that it appears as 3.59873E+01 or 35.99.

The magic command that can format the appearance of data is the PRINT USING command, which enables you to define the data that you want to display, along with the way you want it to look, as in the following example:

```
CLS
INPUT "Type a decimal number such as 38.1625"; Number
PRINT USING "##.###"; Number
END
```

In the preceding program, each # symbol tells QBASIC where to display a single digit. So the two ## symbols before the period and the three ### symbols after the period tell QBASIC, "Display only two digits before the decimal point and three digits after the decimal point." If you type in a number with more than two digits before the decimal point (such as 103.95), the PRINT USING command displays %103.95 where the % means, "Hey stupid! You didn't allocate enough digits in front of the decimal point!"

Always allocate enough digits before the decimal point when using the PRINT USING command, or QBASIC prints the percent sign as a reminder that you made a mistake. You're better off to allocate too many digits before the decimal point than too few.

If you type a number with more than three digits after the decimal point, the preceding PRINT USING command rounds the digits, so that a number such as 4.9836 appears as 4.984.

In the preceding program, the PRINT USING command prints three digits after the decimal point. If you type a number such as 4.1, the PRINT USING command prints 4.100, adding zeros to fill in the extra digits.

In addition to giving you the chance to define exactly how many digits should appear before and after the decimal point, the PRINT USING command also gives you the chance to format numbers using scientific notation.

To specify scientific notation, define the number of digits before and after the decimal point using the # symbol, followed by four caret (^) symbols, like this:

```
CLS
INPUT "Type a decimal number such as 38.1625"; Number
PRINT USING "##.##^^^^"; Number
END
```

If you run this program and type the number 34.7612, QBASIC displays the number as 3.48E+01.

When you display numbers in scientific notation, always allocate at least two digits before the decimal point. If you allocate only one digit before the decimal point (as in PRINT USING "#.##^^^^"), QBASIC displays the number slightly differently: 0.35E+02.

Sending output to the printer

The PRINT and WRITE commands send data to the monitor. But you may want to send data to the printer instead. In that case, you use the LPRINT command, as follows:

```
CLS
LPRINT "Save the dolphins! Kill the tuna!"
END
```

The LPRINT command works exactly like the PRINT command except that it sends data to your printer instead of to the monitor. You can use the TAB, SPC, comma, and semicolon with the LPRINT command just as you can use them with the PRINT command.

If you want to send identical output to both the screen and the printer, you must use both the PRINT and LPRINT commands.

Getting Input

A program that does nothing but spit out data is pretty useless because it can't respond and adapt to outside data. In addition to spitting out data, a program needs to accept data.

When a program accepts data, it stores that data temporarily in a chunk of memory identified by a name, called a *variable*. The following QBASIC program asks for input from the user, stores the data in a variable called Myboss$, and spits back output:

```
CLS
PRINT "What is the name of your boss?"
INPUT Myboss$
PRINT Myboss$ + "? That sounds like the name of a moron!"
END
```

See Figure 6-6 for an example of what this program looks like on-screen. This QBASIC program tells the computer to do the following:

1. The first line clears the screen.

2. The second line tells the computer to print on-screen, "What is the name of your boss?"

3. The third line tells the computer, "Wait for the user to type something; then store that information in memory in an arbitrarily named variable called Myboss$."

4. The fourth line tells the computer, "Print the information stored in the variable named Myboss$ and then print the following after it: '? That sounds like the name of a moron.'"

5. The fifth line tells the computer that this is the end of the program.

In QBASIC, the program starts with the first instruction at the top and keeps going until it either runs out of instructions to follow or until it finds the END command that defines (what else?) the end of the program.

As soon as QBASIC sees the END command, it assumes that it has found the end of the program, even if more BASIC instructions follow the END command.

Figure 6-6:
What the
BASIC pro-
gram looks
like when
run in
QBASIC.

Combining the PRINT and INPUT commands

You can combine the PRINT command with the INPUT command as follows:

```
CLS
INPUT "How old is your boss"; Bossage
PRINT "Your boss is "; Bossage; "? Shouldn't he be dead by
        now?"
END
```

When the INPUT command contains a string such as "How old is your boss", you don't need to type a question mark at the end because QBASIC automatically types a question mark when the program runs.

When your program expects the user to type a string of letters, variable names must end with a dollar sign ($). If a variable does not end with a dollar sign, your program refuses to store anything other than numbers in that variable. When your program expects a number, your variables don't need a dollar sign at the end.

Using variables repeatedly

Because a variable temporarily stores data, you can use the same variable repeatedly. Just remember that a variable can hold only one piece of information at a time. The moment that you stuff a new piece of information into a variable, it automatically forgets what it previously stored.

An equivalent C program

Unlike BASIC, other programming languages force you to enclose instructions inside special words or symbols that act as parentheses (so to speak) that wrap around the beginning and ending of your program. In the C/C++ language, a program consists of nothing more than the word main followed by parentheses and curly brackets, as in the following example:

```
main ()
{
}
```

When you write instructions using C/C++, you must enclose them inside these strange curly brackets, as shown here:

```
main ()
{
   char myboss[15];
   printf ("What is the name of
      your boss.\n");
   scanf ("%s", &myboss);
   printf ("%s", myboss);
   printf ("? That sounds like
      the name of a moron!");
}
```

Examine the following QBASIC program to see how the computer uses the Myboss variable twice:

```
CLS
PRINT "What is the name of your boss?"
INPUT Myboss$
PRINT Myboss$ + "? That sounds like the name of a moron!"
PRINT
PRINT "What is your name?"
INPUT Myboss$
PRINT "Congratulations, " + Myboss$ + "! You are now the
            boss."
END
```

This BASIC program tells the computer to do the following:

1. The first line clears the screen.

2. The second line tells the computer to print on-screen, "What is the name of your boss?"

3. The third line tells the computer, "Wait for the user to type something and then store that information in a variable named Myboss$." (If you type **Joe** in line two, the variable Myboss$ holds the name Joe.)

4. The fourth line tells the computer, "Print the information stored in the variable named Myboss$ and then print the following after it, '? That sounds like the name of a moron.'"

5. The fifth line prints a blank line.

6. The sixth line prints on-screen "What is your name?"

7. The seventh line tells the computer, "Wait for the user to type something and then store that information in the variable named Myboss$." (If you type **David** in line six, the variable Myboss$ now holds the name David, completely forgetting the fact that it used to hold the name Joe.)

8. The eighth line tells the computer, "Print the information stored in the variable Myboss$ and then print the following after it: '! You are now the boss.'"

9. The ninth line tells the computer that this is the end of the program.

With most programming languages such as BASIC (and QBASIC), you just need to create variables and the computer takes care of storing your data in a specific location in its memory. But when you write programs in machine language, assembly language, and C/C++, you can specify the exact location in memory to store your data, even if that portion of the computer's memory is currently being used by another program. If this happens, your program or computer probably crashes.

When you use modern programs that use a graphical user interface such as the Macintosh or Windows, you often give input to a program by typing in a box or clicking a button. Then the program spits back output in the form of graphs, text, or numbers displayed on-screen. The crude QBASIC commands for getting input and spitting back output simply show you how primitive programming used to be.

Chapter 7

Variables, Constants, and Comments

In This Chapter

▶ Using variables

▶ Using constants

▶ Commenting your code

*V*ariables are the most powerful part of programming because they allow programs to store and manipulate data so that the computer can react to different types of conditions.

Besides storing different data using variables, programs also use things called *constants* and *comments*. Constants represent a fixed value that a program might need, and comments are explanations that programmers use to explain how a program works.

Although the idea of using variables, constants, and comments may seem mysterious to you, relax. You'll see their purpose as soon as you start writing your own programs.

Why Use Variables?

If you typed your name into a computer and the computer couldn't remember what you typed, you might think that the computer was pretty useless. To keep computers from being useless, programs have to tell the computer to store any data that it receives so that it can use it later on.

When you feed information into a program, the program temporarily stores this information in its memory. Because programs may get bombarded with several pieces of information at once, programs give each piece of information a specific name to help keep the data organized in the computer's memory. Each name is called a *variable*, because the specific information that the name can represent may vary. Variables have two uses:

✔ For storing inputted data

✔ For storing calculations that use inputted data or previous calculations

A variable temporarily stores any information that it receives so that the program can use this information later. Although you can name variables anything you want, you should use variable names that describe the type of information that it will hold. For example, if you want a variable to hold phone numbers, a good variable name would be PhoneNumbers or something equally descriptive.

Although you should always give your variables descriptive names, keep in mind that every programming language has slightly different rules for what is an acceptable name for a variable. In QBASIC, the rules for naming variables are as follows:

✔ Variable names must be 40 characters or less.

✔ The first character of a variable name must be a letter, such as A or S. You can't create a variable in which the first character is a number, as in 8me.

✔ Variables cannot consist of more than one word. Myboss is an acceptable variable name but My boss is not (because of the space between the two words).

✔ The name of a variable can't be identical to a QBASIC keyword, such as END, STOP, or TAB.

The following example uses two variables. One variable (called Salary) stores the data that the user types and the second variable (called TaxOwed) stores a calculation.

```
CLS
INPUT "How much money did you make last year"; Salary
TaxOwed = Salary * .95
PRINT "This is how much tax you owe ="; TaxOwed
END
```

This BASIC program tells the computer to do the following:

1. The first line clears the screen.

2. The second line tells the computer to print on the screen, "How much money did you make last year?" When the user types a number, the program stores that number in a variable called Salary.

3. The third line tells the computer, "Multiply the number stored in a variable called Salary by the number .95. Then store the value of this calculation in another variable called TaxOwed."

4. The fourth line tells the computer, "Print 'This is how much tax you owe =" followed by the number represented by the variable called TaxOwed.

5. The fifth line tells the computer that this is the end of the program.

An equivalent C program

Just so you don't start thinking that all programs look like BASIC, here's what a C program looks like that is equivalent to the one in the "Why Use Variables?" section:

```
main ()
{
   float salary, taxowed;
   printf ("How much money did you make last
             year? ");
   scanf ("%f", &salary);
   taxowed = salary * .95;
   printf ("This is how much tax you owe =
             %8.2f", taxowed);
}
```

Assigning a value to a variable

In BASIC, variables contain nothing until you assign a value to them. Because the whole purpose of a variable is to store data, you can assign a value to a variable in three ways:

- Use the INPUT command.
- Assign a fixed value to a variable.
- Assign the result of a calculation to a variable.

Later in this chapter, I explain in more detail that variables can hold either numbers or characters (anything you can type from the keyboard, such as a letter, number, or punctuation mark). A variable created to hold a number initially holds 0. A variable created to hold characters initially holds "".

Stuffing a value into a variable with the INPUT command

The INPUT command waits for the user to type a number or a character. (If the user types two or more characters, that's called a *string*, as in "a string of characters.") Then the INPUT command stuffs the string into a variable, like this:

```
INPUT YourName$
```

When the program runs this command, the computer stores whatever the user types into a variable called YourName$.

If you want to store a string (such as a company name), make sure that you use the dollar sign ($) at the end of the variable name. If you need to store only numbers, you don't need the dollar sign at the end of the variable name.

If you want to get fancy and prompt the user to type some data, you can include some text, such as the following:

```
INPUT "Type your age now, stupid!", YourAge
```

When you use the INPUT command with text, you can use a semicolon or a comma to separate the text from the variable. If you use a semicolon, QBASIC automatically types a question mark after your text. If you use a comma (as shown in the preceding INPUT command), QBASIC doesn't display a question mark after the text.

The INPUT command depends on the user to type a number or string to stuff into a variable.

Putting a fixed value in a variable

The simplest way to assign a value to a variable is to use the equal sign. This allows you to assign a number or a string to a variable, like this:

```
CEOSalary = 9000000
Message2Workers$ = "So I make more than I'm worth. So what?"
```

In the first line, the number 90000000 gets assigned to a variable named CEOSalary. In the second line, the string "So I make more than I'm worth. So what?" gets assigned to the variable Message2Workers$.

When you assign a string to a variable, the variable name must include the dollar sign ($) at the end. If you assign a number to a variable, do not include a dollar sign.

Until you assign a value to a variable, its value will either be zero (0) or a blank string ("").

Assigning a calculated value to a variable

Because variables can represent numbers or strings that may change, it's only natural that you can assign calculations to a variable. If you want to store a numerical value into a variable, just assign a mathematical calculation as follows:

```
DumbestPersonIQ = 4
BossIQ = DumbestPersonIQ / 2
```

In this example, QBASIC creates a variable called BossIQ. Then it takes the value stored in the variable DumbestPersonIQ and divides it by two. The result is then assigned to the BossIQ variable. In this case, the value assigned to BossIQ is 2.

You can also assign a string calculation to a variable, like this:

```
Cry$ = "I want to eat"
NewCry$ = Cry$ + " food that is really bad for me!"
```

In this example, the first line stores the string "I want to eat" in a variable called Cry$. The second line creates a new variable called NewCry$. Then it combines the value of the Cry$ variable ("I want to eat") with the string " food that is really bad for me!"

Thus, the NewCry$ variable now represents the string, "I want to eat food that is really bad for me!"

To see how QBASIC can assign numbers and strings to variables, type the following program:

```
CLS
Parents = 2
Whacks = 20
MotherAxWhacks = Parents * Whacks
FatherAxWhacks = MotherAxWhacks + 1
FirstName$ = "Lizzie"
LastName$ = " Borden"
FullName$ = FirstName$ + LastName$
PRINT FullName$ + " had an ax, gave her mother ";
            MotherAxWhacks;
PRINT " whacks. When she saw what she had done, gave her";
PRINT " father "; FatherAxWhacks
END
```

This BASIC program tells the computer to do the following:

1. The first line clears the screen.

2. The second line creates a variable called Parents and assigns it a value of 2.

3. The third line creates a variable called Whacks and assigns it a value of 20.

4. The fourth line creates a variable called MotherAxWhacks. Then it multiplies the value of the Parents variable (which is 2) by the value of the Whacks variable (which is 20). Thus, the value of the MotherAxWhacks variable is assigned the value of 2 * 20, or 40.

5. The fifth line creates a variable called `FatherAxWhacks`. Then it adds 1 to the value of the `MotherAxWhacks` variable (which is 40). Thus, the value of the `FatherAxWhacks` variable is assigned the value 40 + 1, or 41.

6. The sixth line creates a variable called `FirstName$` and assigns it the value of `"Lizzie"`. (Notice that the `FirstName$` variable includes a dollar sign, to tell the computer that you want this variable to hold only strings.)

7. The seventh line creates a variable called `LastName$` and assigns it the value of `"Borden"`.

8. The eighth line creates a variable called `FullName$` and assigns it the combination of the `FirstName$` variable and the `LastName$` variable. Thus, the value of the `FullName$` variable is `"Lizzie"` plus `" Borden"`, or `"Lizzie Borden"`. (Notice that you need to insert a space, or QBASIC rams two strings together like this: `"LizzieBorden"`.)

9. The ninth line prints the value assigned to the variable `FullName$` (which is `"Lizzie Borden"`) along with the string `" had an ax, gave her mother "` and the value assigned to the `MotherAxWhacks` variable (which is 40).

10. The tenth line prints the string `" whacks. When she saw what she had done, gave her"`.

11. The eleventh line prints the string `" father "` and the value assigned to the `FatherAxWhacks` variable (which is 41). The output of the program appears in Figure 7-1.

If you mistype a variable name, such as typing `FatherWhacks` instead of `FatherAxWhacks`, QBASIC assumes that you want to create a new variable and gives it a value of zero (0) or a blank (`" "`). If your program doesn't work right, make sure that you have typed all variable names correctly.

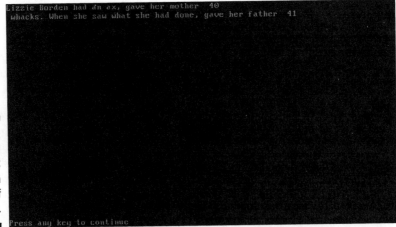

Figure 7-1:
What the QBASIC program looks like if you run it.

Declaring your variables

Variables allow a program to store and manipulate data. As a result, identifying all the variables that a program uses and what type of data it stores in them can help you understand how a specific program works.

Unfortunately, BASIC allows you to create and use variables anywhere in a program. Although this can be convenient when writing a program, it can be difficult to understand later when trying to modify that same program.

For example, study the preceding Lizzie Borden program. Quick! How many variables does this program use? If you can't tell right away, then you'll have to waste time going through the entire program, line by line, to find the answer.

To make it easier for you (or anyone else) to identify all the variables used in a program, QBASIC gives you the option of declaring your variables at the beginning of your program. Choosing to declare your variables at the beginning has two uses:

- ✔ To identify the names of all variables used by a program
- ✔ To identify all the variables used in a program

Knowing all the variables that a program uses can help you better understand how the program works, because you can determine all the places where the program might store data.

To declare a variable ahead of time in QBASIC, you use the DIM command, like this:

```
DIM Eyeballs
```

The preceding command tells your computer, "Create a variable named Eyeballs." You can define multiple variables at once, just by separating them with a comma:

```
DIM Eyeballs, Bullets, Logs
```

The preceding command tells your computer, "Create three variables named Eyeballs, Bullets, and Logs."

Now if you rewrite the preceding Lizzie Borden program and declare all variables at the start of the program, you can easily identify and count all variables used by the program. As you can see in the following revised version that declares variables ahead of time, you can easily determine the total number of variables used (which is 7):

```
CLS
DIM Parents, Whacks, MotherAxWhacks, FatherAxWhacks
DIM FirstName$, LastName$, FullName$
Parents = 2
Whacks = 20
MotherAxWhacks = Parents * Whacks
FatherAxWhacks = MotherAxWhacks + 1
FirstName$ = "Lizzie"
LastName$ = " Borden"
FullName$ = FirstName$ + LastName$
PRINT FullName$ + " had an ax, gave her mother ";
        MotherAxWhacks;
PRINT " whacks. When she saw what she had done, gave her";
PRINT " father "; FatherAxWhacks
END
```

TECHNICAL STUFF

An equivalent Java program

Java closely resembles C/C++, so if you learn C/C++, you should have little trouble learning Java. Just to give you some exposure to what a Java program looks like, study the following program to get a better idea how another programming language accomplishes the same task as the preceding QBASIC program:

```
public class TrivialApplication {
  public static void main(String args[]) {
      int parents, whacks, motheraxwhacks, fatheraxwhacks;
      String firstname, lastname, fullname;
      parents = 2;
      whacks = 20;
      motheraxwhacks = parents * whacks;
      fatheraxwhacks = motheraxwhacks + 1;
      firstname = "Lizzie";
      lastname = " Borden";
      fullname = firstname + lastname;
      System.out.println(fullname + " had an ax, gave her mother "
+ motheraxwhacks);
      System.out.println("whacks. When she saw what she had done,
gave her");
      System.out.println(" father " + fatheraxwhacks);
      }
}
```

When you run this program, it behaves just like the preceding version. However, identifying the program variables at a glance is much easier.

Declaring variables isn't just for the convenience of the computer; it's for the convenience of the programmer who has to read, understand, and modify a program later.

Defining the type of data that variables can hold

In addition to creating and naming your variables at the beginning of a program, you should also define the type of data that each variable can hold. Defining your data types serves two purposes:

- ✔ It identifies the type of data that each variable can hold. When you clearly identify what type of data a variable can hold, you (or another programmer) can better understand where a program may store data and what type of data it can store in each specific variable.

- ✔ It prevents bugs by keeping variables from storing the wrong type of data by mistake.

In QBASIC, variables can hold five different types of data:

- ✔ Strings

- ✔ Integers

- ✔ Long integers

- ✔ Single-precision decimal numbers

- ✔ Double-precision decimal numbers

An integer is a whole number, such as 3, 149, or 9043. A decimal number represents partial numbers, such as 3.14, 98.048, or 1.03846.

Table 7-1 shows the maximum and minimum values of each data type, along with examples of how you declare a variable to be a specific data type.

Table 7-1	Types of Data That QBASIC Variables Can Store		
Data Type	**Minimum Value**	**Maximum Value**	**Sample Declaration**
String	0 characters	32,767 characters	DIM Myboss$ or DIM Myboss AS STRING

(continued)

Table 7-1 (continued)

Data Type	Minimum Value	Maximum Value	Sample Declaration
Integer	-32,768	32,767	`DIM Age%` or `DIM Age AS INTEGER`
Long integer	-2,147,483,648	2,147,483,647	`DIM BigPay&` or `DIM BigPay AS LONG`
Single-precision	-3.402823E+38	3.402823E38	`DIM Salary!` or `DIM Salary AS SINGLE`
Double-precision	-1.79769313486231D+308	1.79769313486231D+308	`DIM PreciseAngle#` or `DIM PreciseAngle AS DOUBLE`

QBASIC gives you the choice of declaring variables using cryptic symbols ($, %, !, or #) or using more descriptive names (STRING, INTEGER, LONG, SINGLE, or DOUBLE). QBASIC doesn't care which method you use, and you can use both methods in the same program if you choose.

However, for consistency's sake, stick to one method or the other. For brevity's sake, some programmers prefer using symbols, such as the following:

```
DIM Parents%, Whacks%, MotherAxWhacks%, FatherAxWhacks%
DIM FirstName$, LastName$, FullName$
```

Other programmers prefer the descriptive method for readability, which looks like this:

```
DIM Parents AS INTEGER, Whacks AS INTEGER, MotherAxWhacks AS
      INTEGER, FatherAxWhacks AS INTEGER
DIM FirstName AS STRING, LastName AS STRING, FullName AS
      STRING
```

You can declare all variable types using either symbols or more descriptive declarations. For example, if you declare a string variable using the AS STRING declaration, you don't need to tack on the dollar sign ($) at the end of your string variable names.

As a further aid, you may also want to use a descriptive prefix in front of each variable name to identify what type of data it holds. For example, because the variable `FirstName` represents a string, you could rename the variable as `strFirstName`. By using prefixes on your variables, you can quickly see which variables represent strings and which ones represent integers. Table 7-2 shows the three-letter prefixes that you can use to identify different variable data types.

Table 7-2	Three-Letter Prefixes for Identifying Data Types	
Data Type	*Suggested Prefix*	*Sample Declaration*
String	str	`DIM strMyboss$` or `DIM strMyboss AS STRING`
Integer	int	`DIM intAge%` or `DIM intAge AS INTEGER`
Long integer	lng	`DIM lngBigPay&` or `DIM lngBigPay AS LONG`
Single-precision	sng	`DIM sngSalary!` or `DIM sngSalary AS SINGLE`
Double-precision	dbl	`DIM dblPreciseAngle#` or `DIM dblPreciseAngle AS DOUBLE`

Using prefixes for your variables makes the Lizzie Borden QBASIC program look like this:

```
DIM intParents AS INTEGER, intWhacks AS INTEGER,
        intMotherAxWhacks AS INTEGER, intFatherAxWhacks AS
        INTEGER
DIM strFirstName AS STRING, strLastName AS STRING,
        strFullName AS STRING
```

Because a long integer variable can hold the same range of numbers as an integer variable, and a double-precision variable can hold the same range of numbers as a single-precision variable, why not declare all variables as either long integer or double-precision? Good question, and here's the answer.

Long integer and double-precision variables require more memory than either integer or single-precision variables to hold the same value. To conserve memory, you should declare a variable as a long integer or double-precision only when that variable absolutely must hold a large or extremely small number. Otherwise, use the smallest data type that you can, such as integer or single-precision, so that your program requires less memory.

What happens if you create a variable to hold an integer, but somewhere in your program you try to store a single-precision number in the variable instead? The following example illustrates my point:

```
CLS
DIM NumberofLegs AS INTEGER
NumberofLegs = 4.8
PRINT NumberofLegs ' Prints 5 on the screen
END
```

In this specific case, the NumberofLegs variable can hold only integer values, so it rounds the number 4.8 to 5, and because the NumberofLegs variable represents the number 5, the number 5 gets printed on the screen.

If you try to stuff a number into a string variable, or a string into a number variable, QBASIC will scream and refuse to run your program.

Using Constants

Variables can change values while the program is running; that's why they're called variables (because their values can vary). However, sometimes you may want to use a fixed value throughout your program. For example, look at the following program. Can you figure out what the number .1975 stands for?

```
CLS
Balance = 43090
OurProfit = Balance * .1975
Balance = Balance + OurProfit
PRINT "Pay this amount, or we'll kill you = "; Balance
PRINT "(Have a nice day!)"
END
```

If you have no idea what the number .1975 represents, you know why programmers use constants. Essentially, a constant represents a fixed value. The main advantage is that a constant can be a descriptive name, which you can define by using the CONST command, like this:

```
CONST InterestRate = .1975
```

Then you can use your constant value in a program such as the following:

```
CLS
CONST InterestRate = .1975
Balance = 43090
OurProfit = Balance * InterestRate
Balance = Balance + OurProfit
PRINT "Pay this amount, or we'll kill you = "; Balance
PRINT "(Have a nice day!)"
END
```

Naturally, you can use a constant as many times as you want throughout your program. If you didn't use constants, you would have to type the same number repeatedly throughout your program, as in the following program:

```
CLS
HusbandBalance = 4390
WifeBalance = 8930
ProfitOffHusband = HusbandBalance * .1975
ProfitOffWife = WifeBalance * .1975
Balance = HusbandBalance + WifeBalance + ProfitOffHusband +
          ProfitOffWife
PRINT "Pay this amount, or we'll kill you = "; Balance
PRINT "(Have a nice day!)"
END
```

Looking at this program, you may have difficulty knowing what the number .1975 represents. Even if you know that it represents an interest rate, you have a second problem. What happens if the interest rate changes from .1975 to .1455? In the preceding program, you would have to change .1975 to .1455 in two locations. For a small program, this isn't inconvenient, but for a large program, this would be time-consuming and possibly error-prone as well.

By using constants, you need to change a value only once, and the rest of the program automatically uses the new constant value. Here's how to do this:

```
CLS
CONST InterestRate = .1975
HusbandBalance = 4390
WifeBalance = 8930
ProfitOffHusband = HusbandBalance * InterestRate
ProfitOffWife = WifeBalance * InterestRate
Balance = HusbandBalance + WifeBalance + ProfitOffHusband +
          ProfitOffWife
PRINT "Pay this amount, or we'll kill you = "; Balance
PRINT "(Have a nice day!)"
END
```

Now you need to change the value of the *InterestRate* constant only in the second line from .1975 to .1455.

Constants have two key advantages:

✔ They identify numeric or string values with a descriptive name.

✔ Changing the value of a constant can automatically modify your entire program quickly and accurately.

An equivalent C++ program

Because C++ is so popular, you may want to start studying how C++ programs look compared to QBASIC programs:

```
#include <iostream>
using namespace std;       //introduces namespace
                std
int main( void )
{
    const float interestrate = .1975;
    float husbandbalance, wifebalance, prof-
            itoffhusband, profitoffwife, balance;
    husbandbalance = 4390;
    wifebalance = 8930;
    profitoffhusband = husbandbalance * intere-
            strate;
    profitoffwife = wifebalance * interestrate;
    balance = husbandbalance + wifebalance + prof-
            itoffhusband + profitoffwife;
    cout << "Pay this amount, or we'll kill you =
            " << balance << "\n";
    cout << "(Have a nice day!)";
    return 0;
}
```

Commenting Your Code

When you write a small program, anyone can readily understand how it works by following it line-by-line, but when you write a large program, it can be difficult for others (and even you) to understand what the program does without spending a long time studying each line.

To make understanding (and ultimately maintaining) a program easier (because programmers are a notoriously lazy bunch), every programming language lets you insert comments into your source code. Comments let you store directly in your source code explanations that can identify the following information:

✔ Who wrote the program

✔ The date the program was created and last modified

✔ What the program is supposed to do

✔ How the program works

✔ Where the program gets, saves, and outputs data

✔ Any known problems with the program

In QBASIC, you can add comments in one of two ways:

✔ With the REM (short for REMark) statement

✔ With the apostrophe (')

The following program shows how to use both the REM statement and the apostrophe to insert comments into a program. Although you can use both types of comments in a single program, use one or the other for consistency's sake.

```
' Created on March 29, 1999
' Written by John Doe
' This program displays a not so subtle
' message to potential copycats to
' come up with their own ideas rather
' than steal mine.
CLS ' This first line clears the screen
REM This program does nothing more than
REM print a message on the screen to
REM insult any potential authors browsing
REM through this book in hopes of stealing
REM ideas to use in a competing book.
PRINT "Don't steal ideas from this book!"
END ' This last line ends the program
```

Because comments are for the benefit of humans only, the computer looks at the preceding QBASIC program like this:

```
CLS
PRINT "Don't steal ideas from this book!"
END
```

The apostrophe is more versatile than the REM statement for making a comment because the apostrophe can create a comment that appears as a separate line or as part of an existing line. The REM statement can create only a comment that appears on a separate line.

Comments exist solely for your benefit. The computer completely ignores any comments that you insert in a program. So make your comments useful but not too wordy, or they'll be more of a nuisance than an aid.

Comments can be valuable for telling QBASIC to temporarily ignore one or more lines of code. For example, rather than delete an entire line, test to see whether the program works, and then retype the previously deleted line, you can just comment out the line, like this:

```
CLS
' A = SQR((B * B) + (C + C))
END
```

If you run this program, QBASIC sees only this:

```
CLS
END
```

To restore the commented line, just remove the apostrophe so that QBASIC sees the program as this:

```
CLS
A = SQR((B * B) + (C + C))
END
```

Chapter 8

Crunching Numbers and Playing with Strings

• •

In This Chapter

▶ Performing mathematical operations

▶ Using QBASIC's built-in math functions

▶ Pulling strings with your data

▶ Converting strings into numbers

• •

*O*ne of the most important parts of a computer program is its capability to manipulate any data that it receives and spit out a useful answer that people are willing to pay for (so that you can make money). The two types of data your program must manipulate are numbers and words (called *strings* by the programming community).

Some common number-manipulating programs include spreadsheets, accounting programs, and even video games (because they need to calculate the correct way to display jet fighters or dragons popping on-screen to enable you to mow them down with a machine gun). Common string-manipulating programs include databases (that store, sort, and rearrange data such as names), word processors, and foreign-language translation programs.

Adding, Subtracting, Dividing, and Multiplying

The four basic ways to manipulate numbers are adding, subtracting, dividing, and multiplying. By using these four mathematical operations, you can create any type of complicated mathematical formula.

To add, subtract, divide, or multiply two numbers (or two variables that represent numbers), you use the symbols shown in Table 8-1.

Table 8-1	Mathematical Operators		
Mathematical Operation	*Symbol to Use*	*Example*	*Result*
Addition	+	2 + 5	7
Subtraction	-	77 - 43	34
Division	/ (forward slash)	20 / 4	5
Multiplication	*	4 * 7	28
Integer division	\ (backward slash)	7 \ 4	1
Exponentiation	^	2 ^ 3	8

The division symbol (/) usually appears in two places on your keyboard: once on the same key as the question mark (?) and once on the numeric keypad. The integer division symbol (\) appears on the same key as the line symbol (|). The exponentiation symbol (^) appears on the 6 key. The subtraction symbol (-) can also be used to create negative numbers, such as -34.5 or -90.

Although you should already understand how addition, subtraction, division, and multiplication work, you may be less familiar with integer division and exponentiation.

Integer division always returns a whole number (an integer) that represents the number of times one number can be divided by another number. Table 8-2 shows the differences between ordinary division and integer division. To verify these results for yourself, type and run the following QBASIC program:

```
CLS
PRINT "Normal division"; TAB(20); "Integer division"
PRINT "5 / 2 = "; 5/2; TAB(20); 5 \ 2 = "; 5 \ 2
PRINT "13 / 4 = "; 13 / 4; TAB(20); 13 \ 4 = "; 13 \ 4
PRINT "39 / 5 = "; 39 / 5; TAB(20); 39 \ 5 = "; 39 \ 5
END
```

Table 8-2	Normal Division and Integer Division
Normal Division	*Integer Division*
5 / 2 = 2.5	5 \ 2 = 2
13 / 4 = 3.25	13 \ 4 = 3
39 / 5 = 7.8	39 \ 5 = 7

Integer division essentially divides two numbers and drops anything that appears to the right of the decimal point.

Exponentiation simply multiplies one number by itself several times. For example, 4 ^ 3 tells QBASIC, "Take the number 4 and multiply it by itself three times. So 4 ^ 3 really means 4 * 4 * 4, or 64."

Using variables

Any mathematical calculation (addition, subtraction, division, or multiplication) creates a single value, which you can store in a variable like this:

```
TaxYouOwe = 125000 * 1.01
```

But rather than use specific numbers to create mathematical formulas (12500 * 1.01), you can substitute variables in this way:

```
CLS
INPUT "How much money did you make last year"; NetIncome
TaxYouOwe = NetIncome * 1.01
PRINT "You owe this much in taxes = "; TaxYouOwe
END
```

To make your mathematical calculations easier to understand, always use variables or constants rather than actual numbers. In the preceding example, you can't tell what the number 1.01 represents. Rather than use an actual number, substitute a descriptive constant in the formula as follows:

```
CLS
TaxRate = 1.01
INPUT "How much money did you make last year"; NetIncome
TaxYouOwe = NetIncome * TaxRate
PRINT "You owe this much in taxes = "; TaxYouOwe
END
```

If you use a constant (in this case, having `TaxRate` represent the number 1.01), you can quickly understand what the number 1.01 means and why it's used in the mathematical formula.

You can use variables in two ways in mathematical formulas:

- ✔ To represent numbers used by the mathematical formula
- ✔ To store the value calculated by the mathematical formula

Be careful when naming variables. If you mistype a variable name, QBASIC assumes that you're creating a new variable, so it assigns a value of zero or a blank to the "new" variable. If your program isn't working right, check to make sure that you spelled the variables correctly.

Working with precedence

Simple formulas such as `NetIncome * TaxRate` are easy to understand; you just multiply the values represented by both variables. However, you can create more powerful mathematical formulas by combining addition, subtraction, division, or multiplication, as in this example:

```
TaxYouOwe = PastTaxes + NetIncome * TaxRate
```

If the value of `NetIncome` is 50,000, `TaxRate` is 1.01, and `PastTaxes` is 2,500, the formula looks like this:

```
TaxYouOwe = 2500 + 50000 * 1.01
```

So now the question is this: Does QBASIC add 2,500 to 50,000 and then multiply the whole thing by 1.01 (in which case the answer would be 53,025), or does QBASIC multiply 50,000 by 1.01 first and then add 2,500 (in which case the answer would be 53,000)?

Because the result of combining addition, subtraction, division, and multiplication in a single formula can confuse the living daylights out of people, programming languages have created something mysterious called *precedence* that tells the computer which mathematical operations to calculate first. QBASIC calculates mathematical operators in this order from top (first) to bottom (last):

- Exponential (^)
- Multiplication (*) and division (/)
- Integer division (\)
- Addition (+) and subtraction (-)

Before running the following QBASIC program, try to figure out how the computer calculates a result:

```
CLS
MyMoney = 3 + 4 ^ 5 \ 3 - 8 / 5 * -7
PRINT MyMoney
END
```

This QBASIC program tells the computer to do the following:

1. The first line clears the screen.
2. The second line tells the computer to create a variable called `MyMoney`.

   Because the computer calculates exponential values first, QBASIC calculates the value of 4 ^ 5, which is 1,024. The formula now looks like this:

   ```
   MyMoney = 3 + 1024 \ 3 - 8 / 5 * -7
   ```

   Next, the computer calculates all multiplication and division (/). Because multiplication and division have equal precedence, the computer starts calculating with the first multiplication or division (/) operator that it finds, moving from left to right. The computer calculates the value of 8 / 5 first (1.6) and then multiplies it by -7. So the formula now looks like this:

   ```
   MyMoney = 3 + 1024 \ 3 - -11.2
   ```

   Now the computer calculates any integer division. It calculates 1024 \ 3, which is 341. The formula now looks like this:

   ```
   MyMoney = 3 + 341 - -11.2
   ```

   Finally, the computer calculates all addition and subtraction, moving from left to right. First it calculates the value of 3 + 341 (which is 344); then it subtracts –11.2 from it. (Subtracting a negative number is the same as adding that number — you know, the old "two negatives make a positive" trick that you learned in junior-high math. Bet you never thought you'd use that stuff again!) Thus the final answer looks like this:

   ```
   MyMoney = 355.2
   ```

3. The third line tells the computer to print the value stored in the `MyMoney` variable, which is `355.2`.
4. The fourth line tells the computer that this is the end of the program.

The computer always calculates operators from left to right if operators have equal precedence, such as multiplication and division or addition and subtraction.

Using parentheses

Trying to remember the precedence of different mathematical operators can be confusing. Even worse is that the ordinary precedence of mathematical operators can mess up the way that you want the computer to calculate a result. For example, suppose that you type the following:

```
CLS
BigValue = 3 + 4 ^ 5
PRINT BigValue
END
```

With this program, the computer first calculates the exponential of 4 ^ 5 (which is 1,024), and then it adds 3 to it, for a total of 1,027.

But what if you really want the computer to add 3 to 4 and then perform the exponential? In this case, you must use parentheses to tell the computer, "Hey, add 3 to 4 first and then calculate the exponential," as in this example:

```
CLS
BigValue = (3 + 4) ^ 5
PRINT BigValue
END
```

This program adds 3 and 4 to get 7, so the formula becomes `BigValue = 7 ^ 5`, or 16,807.

Anytime the computer sees something trapped within parentheses, it calculates those values first. Then it uses its normal rules of precedence to figure out how to calculate the rest of the formula.

Use parentheses to enclose only one mathematical operator at a time, such as `(3 + 4)`. Although you could use parentheses to enclose multiple mathematical operators, such as `(3 + 4 ^ 5)`, this essentially defeats the purpose of using parentheses to make clear what the computer should calculate first. You can use multiple parentheses to create fairly complex formulas, such as the following formula:

```
EasyTaxCode = ((3 + 4) ^ 5 \ 3 - 8) / 5 * -7.
```

(Without the parentheses in the preceding formula, QBASIC would calculate an entirely different result.)

Using QBASIC's Built-In Math Functions

By combining mathematical operators, you can create practically any type of mathematical formula. But creating some mathematical formulas may be too cumbersome, so as a shortcut, QBASIC (and many other programming languages) provides built-in mathematical functions that you can use, as shown in Table 8-3.

Table 8-3	QBASIC's Built-in Mathematical Functions
Function	**What It Does**
ABS (x)	Returns the absolute value of x.
ATN (x)	Returns the arctangent of x.
CINT (x)	Rounds a number (x) to an integer.
COS (x)	Returns the cosine of x.
EXP (x)	Returns a number raised to a specified power (x).
FIX (x)	Returns an integer after dropping any numbers to the right of the decimal point.
INT (x)	Returns the largest integer less than or equal to a specific number or expression.
LOG (x)	Returns the natural logarithm of x. (***Note***: The value of x must be a positive, nonzero number.)
SIN (x)	Returns the sine of x.
SGN (x)	Returns a value indicating the sign of x. If x is a negative number, SGN returns a value of -1. If x is a positive number, SGN returns a value of 1. If x is zero, SGN returns zero.
SQR (x)	Returns the square root of x. (***Note***: The value of x must be a positive, nonzero number.)
TAN (x)	Returns the tangent of x.

To see how QBASIC's mathematical functions work, run the following program and type different numbers (negative, positive, decimal, and so on) to see how the program works:

```
DO
  CLS
  INPUT "Type in a number"; AnyNumber
  PRINT "The ABS value = "; ABS(AnyNumber)
  PRINT "The ATN value = "; ATN(AnyNumber)
  PRINT "The CINT value = "; CINT(AnyNumber)
  PRINT "The COS value = "; COS(AnyNumber)
  PRINT "The EXP value = "; EXP(AnyNumber)
  PRINT "The FIX value = "; FIX(AnyNumber)
  PRINT "The INT value = "; INT(AnyNumber)
  PRINT "The LOG value = "; LOG(ABS(AnyNumber))
  PRINT "The SIN value = "; SIN(AnyNumber)
  PRINT "The SGN value = "; SGN(AnyNumber)
  PRINT "The SQR value = "; SQR(ABS(AnyNumber))
```

```
    PRINT "The TAN value = "; TAN(AnyNumber)
    PRINT
    INPUT "Do you want to run the program again (Y or N)";
          Answer$
LOOP UNTIL UCASE$(Answer$) = "N"
END
```

The UCASE$ function in the second to last line of the preceding code is explained in the "Playing with UPPERCASE and lowercase" section, later in this chapter.

You can use only positive numbers with the LOG or SQR functions.

Manipulating Strings

Besides manipulating numbers, computers can also manipulate strings. A string is anything that you can type from the keyboard, including letters, symbols (such as #, &, and +), and numbers.

In QBASIC, a string is anything that appears inside quotation marks, as in this example:

```
CLS
PRINT "Everything enclosed in quotation marks"
PRINT "is a string, including the numbers below:"
PRINT "72 = 9 * 8"
PRINT "You can even mix letters and numbers like this:"
PRINT "I made $4,500 last month and still feel broke."
END
```

In the preceding program, the formula 72 = 9 * 8 is actually a string, even though it consists of numbers. That's because the numbers are enclosed in quotation marks.

Declaring variables as strings

As with numbers, you can use strings directly in your program like this:

```
CLS
PRINT "Print me."
PRINT 54
END
```

How C/C++ handles strings

Unlike BASIC (and many other languages, including Java), the C/C++ language does not have a string data type. Instead, C/C++ programs use a more primitive data type called a character (abbreviated `char`).

A character data type can hold only one character (such as a letter, symbol, or number), so to manipulate strings, C/C++ programs must use an array of characters. (Don't worry. Chapter 15 explains more about arrays. The important thing right now is to realize that C/C++ programs must handle strings differently from QBASIC.)

Just to give you an idea of how C/C++ programs handle strings, look at the following program. In this example, this C program defines a variable

called `myrelative` and defines it as an array that can hold 10 characters:

```
main ()
{
    char myrelative[10];
    printf ("Type the name of a
      male relative you
      hate.\n");
    scanf ("%s", &myrelative);
    printf ("%s", myrelative);
    printf (" says he doesn't
      like you either!");
}
```

However, you're more likely to store strings in variables and then manipulate the variables. That way, your program can receive a string, store the string in a variable, and then manipulate the string to create a useful result, such as displaying a message to the user on-screen.

When you create a variable, you must tell QBASIC, "Hey, I want this variable to hold only strings!" In technical terms, you're declaring a string to be a *string data type*. To create a variable to hold a string, QBASIC provides two different but equally effective methods:

✔ Create a variable and add the dollar sign ($) on the end of the variable name like this:

```
StringVariable$ = "This variable can hold only strings."
```

✔ Declare a variable as a string data type, like this:

```
DIM StringVariable AS STRING
```

or

```
DIM StringVariable$
```

If you fail to declare a variable as a string data type, but you still try to stuff a string into the variable, your program doesn't work correctly.

Smashing strings together

Unlike with numbers, you can't subtract, divide, or multiply strings. But you can add strings (which is technically called *concatenating strings*). To concatenate two strings, use the plus sign (+) to essentially smash two strings into a single string.

```
CLS
INPUT "What is your name?"; MyName$
PRINT "Hello, " + MyName$ + ". Isn't it time to take"
PRINT "an early lunch from your job now?"
END
```

This QBASIC program tells the computer to do the following:

1. The first line clears the screen.

2. The second line tells the computer to print the message, "What is your name?" on-screen and then wait for the user to type something. Whatever the user types gets stuffed into a string variable called MyName$.

3. The third line tells the computer to create one big string using the string stored in the MyName$ variable. If the name "Tasha" is stored in the MyName$ variable, the third line prints, "Hello, Tasha. Isn't it time to take".

4. The fourth line prints, "an early lunch from your job now?".

5. The fifth line tells the computer that this is the end of the program.

When you concatenate strings, make sure that you leave a space between the two strings so that they don't appear smashed together (likethis).

Playing with QBASIC's String Functions

If just storing and concatenating strings were all you could do, QBASIC would be pretty boring. That's why QBASIC includes a bunch of built-in functions to give you all sorts of fun ways to manipulate strings.

Playing with UPPERCASE and lowercase

If strings consist of letters, they can appear in three ways:

- ✔ in all lowercase, like this sentence.

✔ IN ALL UPPERCASE, LIKE THIS (WHICH CAN LOOK ANNOYING AFTER A WHILE).

✔ A mix of Uppercase and lowercase letters, like this.

To convert every character in a string to lowercase, you can use a special function called LCASE$. Likewise, to convert every character in a string to uppercase, you can use another function called UCASE$.

Both of these functions take a string and convert it to either uppercase or lowercase, like this:

```
UCASE$("hello")      ' HELLO
LCASE$("GOOD-BYE")   ' good-bye
```

Run the following program to see how these two functions work:

```
CLS
INPUT "What would you like to convert"; ThisString$
PRINT "This is what happens when you use LCASE$:"
PRINT LCASE$(ThisString$)
PRINT
PRINT "This is what happens when you use UCASE$:"
PRINT UCASE$(ThisString$)
END
```

Both the LCASE$ and UCASE$ functions work only with letters. They don't do anything with symbols (such as $, %, or @) or numbers.

Counting the length of a string

When you need to manipulate strings, you may want to know the actual length of a string. To count the number of characters in a string, use the LEN function, which looks like this:

```
LEN("Greetings from Mars!")
```

In this example, the length of the string is 20 characters, including spaces and the exclamation point. Run the following program to see how the LEN function works:

```
CLS
DIM CountMe AS STRING
DIM TotalLength AS INTEGER
PRINT "Give me a string:"
INPUT CountMe
TotalLength = LEN(CountMe)
PRINT "The total number of characters in your string is:"
PRINT TotalLength
END
```

The actual length of a string can be deceiving because a string can consist of several spaces before or after any visible characters. When calculating the total length of a string, the LEN function counts any spaces before or after any visible characters, as shown in Table 8-4.

Table 8-4   How the LEN Function Counts Spaces in a String

String	String Length
" Hello!"	11 (6 characters plus 5 spaces in front of the string)
"What are you looking at? "	29 (24 characters plus 5 spaces at the end of the string)
" Boo! Go away! "	28 (16 characters plus 12 spaces before and after the string)

If you use the INPUT statement to accept a string and the user types in a bunch of spaces before or after the string, QBASIC automatically removes any spaces before or after the string. For example, suppose that a user types the following:

"   Hello!   "

QBASIC's INPUT statement would store this string as simply "Hello!"

Trimming the front and back of a string

Because strings can have spaces before (called *leading spaces*) or after (called *trailing spaces*) any visible character, you may want to eliminate these leading or trailing spaces before counting the length of a string.

Fortunately, QBASIC includes two special functions to do just that:

```
LTRIM$("    Hello, there!")    ' "Hello, there!"
RTRIM$("Good-bye!    ")        ' "Good-bye"
```

To see how the LTRIM$ function can strip away leading spaces, try the following program:

```
CLS
AString$ = "    Hello, there!"
PRINT "The original length of the string = "; LEN(AString$)
TempString$ = LTRIM$(Astring$)
PRINT TempString$
PRINT "The new length is now = "; LEN (TempString$)
END
```

You can combine the LTRIM$ and RTRIM$ functions to remove both leading and trailing spaces at the same time, as in this example:

```
LTRIM$(RTRIM$("    Wow!  "))  '  "Wow!"
```

Inserting spaces

Sometimes you may want to create spaces without pressing the space bar multiple times to do so. For an easy way to create spaces, QBASIC provides the SPACE$ function, which looks like this:

```
SPACE$(X)
```

In this example, X represents the number of spaces that you want to insert. The SPACE$ function in the following program simply inserts five spaces between the string "Hello" and the string "Bo the Cat.":

```
CLS
AString$ = "Bo the Cat."
PRINT "Hello" + SPACE$(5) + AString$
END
```

Yanking characters out of a string

If you have a long string, you may want only part of that string. For example, you may have a string consisting of somebody's first and last name, but you want only the last name. You can use one of the following QBASIC functions to rip away one or more characters from a string:

- ✔ LEFT$ (string, X) rips away X number of characters starting from the left of the string.

- ✔ RIGHT$ (string, X) rips away X number of characters starting from the right of the string.

- ✔ MID$ (string, X, Y) rips away Y number of characters, starting at the *Xth* character from the left.

To see how these three functions work, run the following program and see what happens:

```
CLS
FakeName$ = "John Barkley Doe"
FirstName$ = LEFT$(FakeName$, 4)
PRINT "This is the first name = "; FirstName$
LastName$ = RIGHT$(FakeName$, 3)
```

```
PRINT "This is the last name = "; LastName$
MiddleName$ = MID$(FakeName$, 6, 7)
PRINT "This is the middle name = "; MiddleName$
END
```

This program does nothing more than strip out the first, last, and middle names from the longer string `"John Barkley Doe"`.

Looking for a string inside another string

If you have a long string, you may want to know where another word or phrase is located inside the longer string. For example, suppose that you had a string containing a list of names like this:

```
"John, Julia, Matt, Mike, Sam, Chris, Karen"
```

If you wanted to know in what position the name "Matt" appeared in the preceding string, you could use the magical `INSTR` command as follows:

```
CLS
DIM Position AS INTEGER
Names$ = "John, Julia, Matt, Mike, Sam, Chris, Karen"
Position = INSTR (1, Names$, "Matt")
PRINT "The name Matt is located in position = "; Position
END
```

This QBASIC program tells the computer to do the following:

1. The first line clears the screen.

2. The second line creates a variable called `Position` and defines it as an integer data type.

3. The third line creates a string variable called `Names$` that stores the string `"John, Julia, Matt, Mike, Sam, Chris, Karen."`

4. The fourth line tells the computer, "Set the value of the `Position` variable to the value returned by the `INSTR` function."

   The `INSTR` function tells the computer, "Starting at position 1, look at the string represented by the variable `Names$` and look for the string "Matt"." In this case, the string `"Matt"` appears in position 14 in the `Names$` string.

5. The fifth line prints, `"The name Matt is located in position = 14."`

6. The sixth line tells the computer that this is the end of the program.

To use the INSTR function, you need to specify three items:

- ✔ The position where you want to start searching. In the preceding QBASIC example, the position was 1, which represents the start of the string. However, you could tell the computer to start looking from any position. If you told the computer to start looking from position 20, it would never find the name "Matt" in the Names$ variable.

- ✔ The string that you want to search.

- ✔ The string that you want to locate.

Strings are case-sensitive, which means that, to the computer, the strings "MATT" and "Matt" are two completely different strings. In the following program, INSTR can't find the string "MATT" because it thinks the strings "MATT" and "Matt" are not the same:

```
CLS
DIM Position AS INTEGER
Names$ = "John, Julia, Matt, Mike, Sam, Chris, Karen"
Position = INSTR (1, Names$, "MATT")
PRINT "The name Matt is located in position = "; Position
END
```

If the INSTR function can't find the string that you're looking for, the value of the INSTR function is zero.

Converting strings into numbers (and vice versa)

A string can consist of letters, symbols, and numbers. The most common use for storing numbers as a string is when the numbers represent something special such as a telephone number or address. If you wanted the computer to print a telephone number, you must store that number as a string, like this:

```
PRINT "555-1212"
```

This command prints the string 555-1212 on-screen. The quotation marks tell the computer, "Anything inside the quotation marks is a string." What happens if you try the following command?

```
PRINT 555-1212
```

QBASIC interprets this to mean, "Subtract the number 1212 from the number 555 and print the result (which is -657) on-screen."

If you have a number, but you want to treat it like a string, you can use QBASIC's STR$ function, which works like this:

```
STR$(Number)
```

The STR$ function tells QBASIC, "Take a number (such as 45) and turn it into a string." If you had a number 34 and used the STR$ function, QBASIC would convert that number 34 into a string "34".

For example, to print both a string and a number, you would normally need to use the PRINT command with a semicolon, as in this example:

```
CLS
BossIQ = 12
PRINT "This is the IQ of your boss ="; BossIQ
END
```

However, you can use the STR$ function to convert the BossIQ variable into a string:

```
CLS
BossIQ = 12
NewString$ = "This is the IQ of your boss =" + STR$(BossIQ)
PRINT NewString$
END
```

The main difference between the first example and the second example is that now the number, BossIQ, is part of a string called NewString$.

Naturally, QBASIC enables you to convert strings into numbers as well. If you have a string (such as "46"), you can't perform any mathematical operations on it. However, you can convert that string into a number by using QBASIC's VAL function, which works like this:

```
VAL("String")
```

The VAL function tells QBASIC, "Take a string (such as "45") and turn it into a number." If you had a string "45" and used the VAL function, QBASIC would convert that string "45" into the number 45.

If you use the VAL function on a string that doesn't represent a number, such as the string "Hello!", the VAL function returns a zero value.

To see how the VAL function works, run the following program:

```
CLS
YearBorn$ = "1964"
PRINT "You were born in " + YearBorn$
Year = 1999 - VAL(YearBorn$)
PRINT "In 1999, you were this old = "; Year
END
```

Chapter 9

Making Decisions with Control Statements

*T*he whole purpose of a program is to make the computer behave in a certain way. The most primitive programs act exactly the same way each
time you run them, such as displaying, "Hello, world!" or the name of your cat
on the screen.

Such primitive programs may be fine for learning to program, but they're relatively useless, because most programs need to accept data and modify their
behavior based on any data that they receive.

For example, many banks use a computer to analyze risks before they loan
money. If you have an income over a certain amount and don't have a history
of declaring bankruptcy every two years, then the bank's computer may
approve your loan before it approves a loan for someone who has no income
or assets. In this case, the bank's computer program has to accept data and
decide what to do based on that data.

Each time you feed the program different data, the program may spit out a
different answer. To learn how to give your program the ability to make decisions, you have to use something mysterious called *control statements*.

Understanding Boolean Expressions

When you make a decision, such as what to eat for dinner, you ask yourself a
question like, "Do I feel like eating a hamburger?" If the answer is yes, you go
to a restaurant that serves hamburgers.

Computers work in a similar way. Although people can ask questions, computers check a *Boolean expression*. A Boolean expression is anything that represents one of two values, such as true/false or zero/non-zero.

Boolean expressions are part of Boolean algebra, which was named after a man named George Boole. If you study hard and create your own branch of mathematics, you can have something named after you, too. The simplest Boolean expression is one that compares two values as shown in Table 9-1.

Table 9-1	Evaluating Boolean Expressions	
Boolean Expression	*What It Means*	*Boolean Value*
4 < 54	4 is less than 54	True
4 > 54	4 is greater than 54	False
4 = 54	4 is equal to 54	False
4 <= 54	4 is less than or equal to 54	True
4 >= 54	4 is greater than or equal to 54	False
4 <> 54	4 is not equal to 54	True

Symbols like <, >, =, <=, >=, and <> are known as *relational operators*.

Try running the following program to see what it prints:

```
CLS
IF (4 < 54) THEN
  PRINT "This prints out on the screen."
ELSE
  PRINT "Why did you pick this sentence?"
END IF
END
```

This BASIC program tells the computer to do the following:

1. The first line clears the screen.

2. The second line tells the computer to evaluate the Boolean expression *(4 < 54)*. Because this is true, the computer can proceed to the third line.

3. The third line tells the computer to print the message, "This prints out on the screen." Then the computer skips over the fourth and fifth lines to the sixth line of the program.

4. The fourth line tells the computer, "In case the Boolean expression *(4 < 54)* happens to be false, proceed to the fifth line of the program.

5. The fifth line tells the computer to print the message, "Why did you pick this sentence?" Because the Boolean expression *(4 < 54)* is never false, the fourth and fifth lines are never run.

6. The sixth line simply identifies the end of the IF THEN ELSE statement (which you'll find out more about later in this chapter).

7. The seventh line tells the computer that this is the end of the program.

You can assign a variable to a Boolean expression in this way:

```
Guilty = (4 < 54)
```

This assigns the value of true to the variable called Guilty. The preceding statement tells the computer, "The Boolean expression of (4 < 54) is true. Thus the value of the Guilty variable is true."

QBASIC doesn't really know the difference between True and False. Because QBASIC can't assign a True value to a Boolean expression, QBASIC just assigns the number -1 to the Boolean expression, which represents the value True. When QBASIC wants to assign a False value to a Boolean expression, it assigns the number 0 to the Boolean expression.

Try running the following program:

```
CLS
Guilty = (4 < 54)
IF Guilty THEN
   PRINT "Slap him on the wrist and let him go."
ELSE
   PRINT "This sentence never prints out."
END IF
END
```

Each time you run the preceding program, it only prints the message, "Slap him on the wrist and let him go."

Using variables in Boolean expressions

The sample program, in the preceding section, has a Boolean expression (4 < 54) that is fairly useless because it will always be true. Every time you run the program, it just prints out the message, "This prints out on the screen."

For greater flexibility, Boolean expressions usually compare two variables or one variable to a fixed value, as in this example:

```
(MyIQ < AnotherIQ)
(Taxes < 100000)
```

The value of the first Boolean expression (MyIQ < AnotherIQ) depends on the value of the two variables MyIQ and AnotherIQ. Run the following program to see how it follows a different set of instructions, depending on the value of the MyIQ and AnotherIQ variables:

```
CLS
INPUT "What is your IQ"; MyIQ
INPUT "What is the IQ of another person"; AnotherIQ
IF (MyIQ > AnotherIQ) THEN
  PRINT "I'm smarter than you are."
ELSE
  PRINT "You have a higher IQ to make up for your lack of
           common sense."
END IF
END
```

When you run this program and type different values for MyIQ and AnotherIQ, the program behaves in two possible ways, printing on the screen "I'm smarter than you are" or "You have a higher IQ to make up for your lack of common sense."

When you use variables in Boolean expressions, you give the computer more flexibility in making decisions on its own.

Using Boolean operators

Examining a single Boolean expression at a time can be a bit cumbersome, as the following example shows:

```
CLS
INPUT "How much money did you make"; Salary
INPUT "How much money did you donate to political candi-
           dates": Bribes
IF (Salary > 500) THEN
  IF (Bribes > 700) THEN
    PRINT "You don't have to pay any taxes."
  END IF
END IF
END
```

The only time this program prints the message, "You don't have to pay any taxes" on the screen is when both Boolean expressions (Salary > 500) and (Bribes > 700) are true.

Rather than force the computer to evaluate Boolean expressions one at a time, you can have the computer evaluate multiple Boolean expressions by using something called *Boolean operators*. A Boolean operator does nothing more than connect two or more Boolean expressions to represent a true or a false value.

Every programming language uses these four Boolean operators:

✔ AND

✔ OR

✔ XOR

✔ NOT

The AND operator

The AND operator links two Boolean expressions. For example, you can rewrite the program in the preceding section as follows by using the Boolean operator AND:

```
CLS
INPUT "How much money did you make"; Salary
INPUT "How much money did you donate to political candi-
        dates": Bribes
IF (Salary > 500) AND (Bribes > 700) THEN
  PRINT "You don't have to pay any taxes."
END IF
END
```

In this case, the program will print out the message, "You don't have to pay any taxes" only if both (Salary > 500) is true and (Bribes > 700) is true. If either Boolean expression is false, this program won't print anything.

Run the preceding program and type the values listed in Table 9-2 to see what happens.

Table 9-2 Different Values Determine How the AND Operator Works

Value of Salary	Value of Bribes	What the Program Does
100	100	Nothing
900	100	Nothing
100	900	Nothing
900	900	Prints the message

The AND operator can represent a true value only if both Boolean expressions that it connects are also true.

To show how the AND operator works, programmers like to draw something called a *truth table*, which tells you when two Boolean expressions, connected by the AND operator, represent a true or a false value. Table 9-3 is a truth table listing the values for the following two Boolean expressions:

```
(Boolean expression 1) AND (Boolean expression 2)
```

Table 9-3	The Truth Table for the AND Operator	
Value of (Boolean Expression 1)	*Value of (Boolean Expression 2)*	*Value of the Entire (Boolean Expression 1) AND (Boolean Expression 2)*
False	False	False
True	False	False
False	True	False
True	True	True

The OR operator

The OR operator links two Boolean expressions, but produces a true value if either Boolean expression represents a true value. For an example of how this operator works, run the following program:

```
CLS
INPUT "How far can you throw a football"; Football
INPUT "What is your IQ"; IQ
IF (Football > 50) OR (IQ <= 45) THEN
   PRINT "You have what it takes to become a professional
          athlete!"
END IF
END
```

In this case, the program will print the message, "You have what it takes to become a professional athlete!" if either (Football > 50) is true or (IQ <= 45) is true. Only if both Boolean expressions are false will the program refuse to print anything.

Run the preceding program, and type the values listed in Table 9-4 to see what happens.

Table 9-4 Different Values Determine How the OR Operator Works		
Value of Football	*Value of IQ*	*What the Program Does*
5	70	Nothing
70	70	Prints the message
5	5	Prints the message
70	5	Prints the message

The OR operator can represent a false value only if both Boolean expressions that it connects are also false.

Table 9-5 is a truth table to show how the OR operator works for Boolean expressions like this:

```
(Boolean expression 1) OR (Boolean expression 2)
```

Table 9-5	The Truth Table for the OR Operator	
Value of (Boolean Expression 1)	*Value of (Boolean Expression 2)*	*Value of the Entire (Boolean Expression 1) OR (Boolean Expression 2)*
False	False	False
True	False	True
False	True	True
True	True	True

The XOR operator

The XOR operator links two Boolean expressions but produces a true value only if one Boolean expression represents a true value and the other Boolean expression represents a false value. For an example of how this operator works, run the following program:

```
CLS
INPUT "Is your spouse around (Type 1 for Yes or 0 for No)";
          SpouseHere
INPUT "Is your best friend around (Type 1 for Yes or 0 for
          No)"; BestfriendHere
IF (SpouseHere = 0) XOR (BestfriendHere = 0) THEN
   PRINT "You won't be lonely tonight!"
END IF
END
```

The only two times that this program will print the message, "You won't be lonely tonight!" is if your spouse is around (SpouseHere = 1) but your best friend is not (BestfriendHere = 0), or if your best friend is around (Bestfriendhere = 1) but your spouse is not (SpouseHere = 0).

If your spouse is around (SpouseHere = 1) and your best friend is around (BestfriendHere = 1), nothing will happen. Likewise, if your spouse is gone (SpouseHere = 0) and your best friend is gone (BestfriendHere = 0), nothing will happen.

Run the preceding program, and type the values listed in Table 9-6 to see what happens:

Table 9-6 Different Values Determine How the XOR Operator Works

Value of SpouseHere	Value of BestfriendHere	What the Program Does
0	0	Nothing
1	0	Prints the message
0	1	Prints the message
1	1	Nothing

The XOR operator can represent a false value only if both Boolean expressions that it connects are false or if both Boolean expressions are true.

Table 9-7 is the truth table to show how the XOR operator works for the following Boolean expressions:

```
(Boolean expression 1) XOR (Boolean expression 2)
```

Table 9-7	The Truth Table for the XOR Operator	
Value of (Boolean Expression 1)	Value of (Boolean Expression 2)	Value of the Entire (Boolean Expression 1) XOR (Boolean Expression 2)
False	False	False
True	False	True
False	True	True
True	True	False

The NOT operator

The NOT operator affects a single Boolean expression. If the Boolean expression is true, the NOT operator makes it false. If the Boolean expression is false, the NOT operator makes it true. Essentially, the NOT operator converts a Boolean expression to its opposite value.

For example, this Boolean expression is true:

```
(4 < 54)
```

But this Boolean expression is false:

```
NOT(4 < 54)
```

If you want to assign a value of false to the Guilty variable, use the NOT operator like this:

```
Guilty = NOT(4 < 54)
```

This statement tells the computer, "The Boolean expression of (4 < 54) is true. But the NOT operator turns a true value to false, so the value of the Guilty variable is false." To get a better idea how this works, run the following program:

```
CLS
Guilty = NOT(4 < 54)   ' The value of Guilty is false
IF Guilty THEN
  PRINT "This sentence never prints out."
ELSE
  PRINT "The defendant is not guilty because he's rich."
END IF
END
```

Each time you run the preceding program, it prints the message, "The defendant is not guilty because he's rich."

Exploring IF THEN Statements

The most common way to control which instruction the computer follows next is to use the IF THEN statement. This statement checks whether a certain condition is true. If so, it tells the computer to follow one or more instructions.

The IF THEN statement looks like this:

```
IF (Boolean expression) THEN
  ' Follow one or more instructions listed here
END IF
```

For an example of how this statement works, type and run the following program:

```
CLS
INPUT "Do you eat cow lips (Type Y for Yes or N for No)";
          Answer$
IF (Answer$ = "Y") THEN
  PRINT "I have a nice hot dog you might like then."
END IF
END
```

Only if you type **Y** will the program print the message, "I have a nice hot dog you might like then."

If you want the computer to follow exactly one instruction following an IF THEN statement (such as the PRINT instruction in the preceding example), you can shorten the IF THEN statement to the following:

```
CLS
INPUT "Do you eat cow lips (Type Y for Yes or N for No)";
        Answer$
IF (Answer$ = "Y") THEN PRINT "I have a nice hot dog you
        might like then."
END
```

If you want the computer to follow two or more instructions following an IF THEN statement, you must enclose them with the END IF line, like this:

```
CLS
INPUT "How many cats do you own"; Answer
IF (Answer >= 1) THEN
  PRINT "You have my sympathies."
  PRINT "Have you ever thought of getting"
  PRINT "your head examined real soon?"
END IF
END
```

IF THEN ELSE statements

The IF THEN statement tells the computer to follow one or more instructions only if a certain condition is true. If that condition is not true, the computer ignores all the instructions trapped inside the IF THEN statement.

The IF THEN ELSE statement is slightly different because it tells the computer to follow one set of instructions in case a condition is true and a different set of instructions if the condition is false. The IF THEN ELSE statement looks like this:

```
IF (Boolean expression) THEN
  ' Follow one or more instructions listed here
ELSE
  ' If the condition is false, then follow these
  ' instructions instead
END IF
```

For an example of how this statement works, run the following program and see what happens:

```
CLS
INPUT "How long were you in medical school"; Answer
IF (Answer > 4) THEN
    PRINT "Congratulations! You should be able to"
    PRINT "play a good game of golf in no time."
ELSE
    PRINT "You may not have been in medical school for"
    PRINT "very long, but at least you should know"
    PRINT "how to put on a white lab coat."
END IF
END
```

Unlike the IF THEN statement, the IF THEN ELSE statement always forces the computer to follow one set of instructions no matter what. In this program, if the answer is greater than four, the computer prints out, "Congratulations! You should be able to play a good game of golf in no time."

If the answer is not greater than four, the computer prints out, "You may not have been in medical school for very long, but at least you should know how to put on a white lab coat."

The IF THEN ELSE statement always makes the computer follow one set of instructions. With the ordinary IF THEN statement, the computer may or may not follow one set of instructions.

IF THEN ELSEIF statements

The IF THEN ELSEIF statement provides the computer with two different sets of instructions. No matter what happens, the computer must follow one set of instructions.

The IF THEN ELSEIF statement can list two or more different sets of instructions, and the computer still may not follow any of them. The IF THEN ELSEIF statement looks like this:

```
IF (Boolean expression 1) THEN
    ' Follow one or more instructions listed here
ELSEIF (Boolean expression 2) THEN
    ' Follow one or more instructions listed here
END IF
```

For an example of how this statement works, run the following program and see what happens:

```
CLS
INPUT "How long did you go to law school"; Answer
IF (Answer > 4) THEN
```

```
      PRINT "Congratulations! You now know enough to"
      PRINT "sue your law school for wasting your time."
   ELSEIF (Answer > 2) THEN
      PRINT "You may not have finished law school yet,"
      PRINT "but that doesn't mean you can't lie about it."
   END IF
   END
```

If the user types any number greater than 4, this program displays the message, "Congratulations! You now know enough to sue your law school for wasting your time."

Notice that after the computer follows one set of instructions, it stops checking to see whether any additional ELSEIF conditions may also be true.

If the user types the number 3 or 4, the program displays, "You may not have finished law school yet, but that doesn't mean you can't lie about it." What happens if the user types the number 2, 1, or 0? In this case, absolutely nothing happens.

The IF THEN ELSEIF statement can offer multiple conditions, as in the following example:

```
IF (Boolean expression 1) THEN
   ' Follow one or more instructions listed here
ELSEIF (Boolean expression 2) THEN
   ' Follow one or more instructions listed here
ELSEIF (Boolean expression 3) THEN
   ' Follow one or more instructions listed here
END IF
```

The IF THEN ELSEIF statement checks multiple conditions, but the computer still may not follow any instructions. If you want to make sure that at least one set of instructions gets followed, tag an ELSE command at the end, like this:

```
IF (Boolean expression 1) THEN
   ' Follow one or more instructions listed here
ELSEIF (Boolean expression 2) THEN
   ' Follow one or more instructions listed here
ELSEIF (Boolean expression 3) THEN
   ' Follow one or more instructions listed here
ELSE
   ' Follow these instructions if none of the other
   ' instructions are followed
END IF
```

For an honest-to-goodness program to examine, run the following and type **10**, **4**, and **1** to see what happens:

```
CLS
INPUT "How many millions did your government waste last
          year"; Answer
IF (Answer > 8) THEN
   PRINT "Congratulations! You must live in a true"
   PRINT "democracy."
ELSEIF (Answer > 2) THEN
   PRINT "Your government isn't spending enough. Tell them"
   PRINT "to start buying weapons they don't need."
ELSE
   PRINT "Your government is obviously concerned with"
   PRINT "staying under budget, which means it's not"
   PRINT "likely to last much longer."
END IF
END
```

If you type 10, which makes the Boolean expression (Answer > 8) true, the program prints, "Congratulations! You must live in a true democracy."

If you type 4, which makes the Boolean expression (Answer > 2) true, the program prints, "Your government isn't spending enough. Tell them to start buying weapons they don't need."

If you type 1, the program follows the instructions under the ELSE command and prints, "Your government is obviously concerned with staying under budget, which means it's not likely to last much longer."

Working with SELECT CASE Statements

Listing multiple conditions in an IF THEN ELSEIF statement can be tedious and messy, as the following example shows:

```
CLS
INPUT "How old are you"; Answer
IF (Answer = 21) THEN
   PRINT "Congratulations! You may be able to rent a"
   PRINT "car in some states."
ELSEIF (Answer = 20) THEN
   PRINT "You can't rent a car, but you're pre-approved"
   PRINT "for 20 different credit cards."
ELSEIF (Answer = 19) THEN
   PRINT "You're still officially a teenager."
ELSEIF (Answer = 18) THEN
   PRINT "You're old enough to join the military and"
```

```
      PRINT "fire an automatic rifle, but you still can't"
      PRINT "buy beer legally. Figure that one out."
   ELSEIF (Answer = 17) THEN
      PRINT "You can see R-rated movies on"
      PRINT "your own (but you've probably done that for years)."
   END IF
END
```

As an alternative to the IF THEN ELSEIF statement, you can use the SELECT CASE statement, which looks like the following:

```
SELECT CASE Variable
CASE Value1
   ' Follow these instructions if the Variable = Value1
CASE Value2
   ' Follow these instructions if the Variable = Value2
END SELECT
```

Like the IF THEN ELSEIF statement, the SELECT CASE statement provides different instructions depending on the value of a particular variable. Rewriting the preceding IF THEN ELSEIF statement looks like this:

```
CLS
INPUT "How old are you"; Answer
SELECT CASE Answer
CASE 21
   PRINT "Congratulations! You may be able to rent a"
   PRINT "car in some states."
CASE 20
   PRINT "You can't rent a car, but you're pre-approved"
   PRINT "for 20 different credit cards."
CASE 19
   PRINT "You're still officially a teenager."
CASE 18
   PRINT "You're old enough to join the military and"
   PRINT "fire an automatic rifle, but you still can't"
   PRINT "buy beer legally. Figure that one out."
CASE 17
   PRINT "You can see R-rated movies on"
   PRINT "your own (but you've probably done that for years)."
END SELECT
END
```

If the user types 21, the program prints, "Congratulations! You may be able to rent a car in some states." If the user types 19, the program prints, "You're still officially a teenager." If the user types 17, the program prints, "You can see R-rated movies on your own (but you've probably done that for years)."

Of course, if the user types any value not listed in the SELECT CASE statement, such as 22 or 16, the SELECT CASE statement won't run any instructions.

To make sure that at least one set of instructions is followed in a SELECT CASE statement, just add a CASE ELSE command at the very end, like this:

```
CLS
INPUT "How old are you"; Answer
SELECT CASE Answer
CASE 21
   PRINT "Congratulations! You may be able to rent a"
   PRINT "car in some states."
CASE 20
   PRINT "You can't rent a car, but you're pre-approved
   PRINT "for 20 different credit cards."
CASE 19
   PRINT "You're still officially a teenager."
CASE 18
   PRINT "You're old enough to join the military and"
   PRINT "fire an automatic rifle, but you still can't"
   PRINT "buy beer legally. Figure that one out."
CASE 17
   PRINT "You can see R-rated movies on"
   PRINT "your own (but you've probably done that for years)."
CASE ELSE
   PRINT "This sentence prints out if the user does NOT"
   PRINT "type numbers 17, 18, 19, 20, or 21."
END SELECT
END
```

Checking a range of values

The SELECT CASE statement is often used to check whether a variable happens to exactly match a specific value, such as the number 21 or the string "yes". But sometimes you may want to run a set of instructions if a variable falls within a range of values, such as any number between 3 and 18. In that case, you have to use the TO command, as in this example:

```
CASE 1 TO 10
```

This checks whether a variable represents a number between 1 and 10, as shown in the following program:

```
CLS
INPUT "How many water balloons do you have"; Answer
SELECT CASE Answer
```

```
CASE 1 TO 10
   PRINT "You need more water balloons."
CASE 11 TO 1000
   PRINT "Now you need a target."
CASE ELSE
   PRINT "What are you? A peace-loving hippie freak?"
END SELECT
END
```

In this example, if the user types a number from 1 to 10, the program prints, "You need more water balloons." If the user types a number from 11 to 1000, the program prints, "Now you need a target." If the user types zero, a negative number, or any number greater than 1000, the program prints, "What are you? A peace-loving hippie freak?"

Make sure that the ranges don't overlap another part of the SELECT CASE statement, as in this example:

```
SELECT CASE Answer
CASE 1 TO 10
   PRINT "This always prints."
CASE 5 TO 10
   PRINT "This never prints."
END SELECT
```

In the preceding SELECT CASE statement, the program will print "This always prints" if the user types a number from 1 to 10, but the program will never print the instructions under the second CASE statement (CASE 5 TO 10). That's because the first CASE statement will run first, preventing the second CASE statement from getting a chance to run at all.

Checking a relational operator

Sometimes, checking for an exact value or a range of values may still be too limiting. For example, you may compare a variable to another value using one of those friendly symbols called relational operators. A relational operator lets the SELECT CASE statement determine whether a variable is greater than (>), less than (<), greater than or equal to (>=), less than or equal to (<=), or not equal to (<>) a specific value.

To use a relational operator, you have to use the IS command, as in this example:

```
CASE IS <= 5
```

This checks whether a variable is less than or equal to 5, as the following program shows:

```
CLS
INPUT "How many cats do you own"; Answer
SELECT CASE Answer
CASE IS <= 5
   PRINT "You need more cats."
CASE IS > 5
   PRINT "Are you out of your mind?"
END SELECT
END
```

If the user types any number equal to or less than 5, the program prints, "You need more cats." If the user types any number greater than 5, the program prints, "Are you out of your mind?"

Make sure that your relational operators don't overlap another part of the SELECT CASE statement, as in this example:

```
SELECT CASE Answer
CASE IS < 10
   PRINT "This always prints."
CASE IS < 12
   PRINT "This only prints if the user types in 11."
END SELECT
```

In this SELECT CASE statement, the program will print "This always prints" if the user types any number less than 10, but the program will print the instructions under the second CASE statement (CASE IS < 12) only if the user types **11**.

TECHNICAL STUFF

Beware of the SELECT CASE statement in C/C++ and Java

In QBASIC, the SELECT CASE statement runs only one set of instructions the moment that it finds a match, such as printing "You need a fake picture ID" in the QBASIC example in the section, "Working with SELECT CASE Statements," when the user types the number 20.

However, C/C++ and Java programs behave much differently. With these languages, you must specifically tell the computer to stop following instructions in a SELECT CASE statement (technically called a *switch statement* in C/C++ and Java) by using a command called break.

For example, consider this C program:

```
#include <stdio.h>
main ()
{
  char akey;
  printf ("Type a lower case
    letter ");
  scanf(" ");
  scanf ("%c", &akey);
  switch (akey) {
    case 'a': printf ("You
    pressed the A key.\n");
    case 'b': printf ("You
    pressed the B key.\n");
  }
}
```

If you run this program and type the "a" key, this C program prints the following:

You pressed the A key.

You pressed the B key.

With C/C++ and Java, the computer follows every set of instructions in the switch statement from the first match that it finds to the end. To make sure that a C/C++ or Java program stops following any instructions in a switch statement, you have to insert the break command as follows:

```
#include <stdio.h>
main ()
{
  char akey;
  printf ("Type a lower case
    letter ");
  scanf(" ");
  scanf ("%c", &akey);
  switch (akey) {
    case 'a': printf ("You
    pressed the A key.\n");
          break;
    case 'b': printf ("You
    pressed the B key.\n");
  }
}
```

If you eventually plan to program in C/C++ or Java, remember this subtle difference, or you may find your C/C++ or Java programs acting different from a similar QBASIC program.

Chapter 10

Repeating Yourself with Loops

. . . .

. . . .

*I*n general, programmers try to get the computer to do as much as possible so that they can do as little as possible. Ideally, you want to write the smallest programs possible, not only because small programs are easier to debug and modify, but also because smaller programs require less typing.

One way that programmers write as little as possible is by using something called *loops*. The idea behind a loop is to make the computer repeat one or more instructions. For example, consider this program that prints the numbers 1 through 5 on the screen:

```
CLS
PRINT 1
PRINT 2
PRINT 3
PRINT 4
PRINT 5
END
```

If you wanted to expand this program to print out 5 million numbers, guess what? You'd have to type out 5 million instructions. Because this is something you really don't want to do, you use loops to make the computer repeat the same instructions multiple times. The computer does the hard work. Consider this example:

```
CLS
FOR I = 1 TO 5
PRINT I
NEXT I
END
```

If you run this program, it does exactly the same thing as the previous QBASIC program. However, the loop version of this program can print out 5 numbers or 5 million numbers (by changing the number 5 in the program to 5000000). Loops make the computer do more without forcing you to type additional instructions.

Although loops can help create shorter programs, the trade-off is that loops are also harder to read and understand than a straightforward list of instructions. When you create a loop, write a comment in the program to explain exactly what the loop is supposed to do.

Conditional Looping

A loop forces the computer to run the same instructions over and over, but eventually the computer needs to know when to stop. To tell the computer when to stop looping, you use a *condition* (a Boolean expression that represents either true or false).

One of the most common problems with loops is something called an *endless loop*, which means that the computer follows a set of instructions but never stops. When a program gets caught in an endless loop, the program may appear to freeze on the screen. Usually, the only way to get out of an endless loop is to turn the computer off and then on again.

To create a loop that repeats one or more instructions, QBASIC provides four methods:

- DO LOOP UNTIL
- DO LOOP WHILE
- DO UNTIL LOOP
- DO WHILE LOOP

The DO LOOP UNTIL loop

The DO LOOP UNTIL loop looks like this:

```
DO
   ' One or more instructions
LOOP UNTIL (condition)
```

To repeat one or more instructions, you just sandwich them between the DO and LOOP UNTIL commands. Look at this example:

```
CLS
I = 1
DO
    PRINT "The square of "; I; "is "; I * I
    I = I + 1
LOOP UNTIL I > 5
END
```

If you run this program (you are typing these QBASIC programs into your computer and testing them, aren't you?), the program does the following:

1. The first line clears the screen.

2. The second line creates a variable called I and sets its value to 1.

3. The third line tells the computer that this is the start of a loop.

4. The fourth line tells the computer to print, "The square of 1 is 1."

5. The fifth line tells the computer to add one to the value of the variable I, so now I represents the number 1 + 1, or 2.

6. The sixth line tells the computer to check whether the Boolean expression (I > 5) is true. If it is true, the program skips to the seventh line. If it is not true (if I represents the number 1, 2, 3, 4, or 5), the program returns to the top of the loop on the third line. The computer repeats the loop five times to print out the following:

```
The square of 1 is 1
The square of 2 is 4
The square of 3 is 9
The square of 4 is 16
The square of 5 is 25
```

7. The seventh line tells the computer that this is the end of the program.

The DO LOOP UNTIL loop makes the computer follow at least once any instructions sandwiched between the DO and LOOP commands. A DO LOOP UNTIL loop stops looping only when its condition (a Boolean expression) becomes true.

To prevent an endless loop, you must include at least one instruction that changes the Boolean expression. The DO LOOP UNTIL command checks the Boolean expression to know when to stop repeating the loop.

Pascal's REPEAT UNTIL loop

If you decide to transfer your QBASIC programming skills to learning Pascal (the native language of Delphi), be aware that Pascal doesn't have a DO LOOP UNTIL loop. Instead, Pascal uses something similar called a REPEAT UNTIL loop, as shown in the following program:

```
program LoopComparison;
var
  I : integer;
begin
  I := 1;
  repeat
```

```
    writeln ('The square of ',
    I, ' is = ', I * I);
    I := I + 1;
  until I > 5;
end.
```

Pascal's REPEAT UNTIL loop is equivalent to QBASIC's DO LOOP UNTIL loop in this way:

```
DO
  PRINT "The square of "; I;
    "is "; I * I
  I = I + 1
LOOP UNTIL I > 5
```

The DO LOOP WHILE loop

The DO LOOP WHILE loop looks and acts exactly like the DO LOOP UNTIL loop, as shown here:

```
DO
  ' One or more instructions
LOOP WHILE (condition)
```

To repeat one or more instructions, you just sandwich them between the DO and LOOP WHILE commands, like this:

```
CLS
Answer$ = "N"
DO
  INPUT "Do you want to stop spending other people's money?
         (Y = Yes, N = No)"; Answer$
  IF Answer$ <> "Y" THEN
    PRINT "Good, that means as a politician, you can keep"
    PRINT "spending money for your benefit, regardless of"
    PRINT "what's good for the public welfare."
  END IF
LOOP WHILE Answer$ <> "Y"
END
```

This loop keeps running until the Boolean expression (Answer$ <> "Y") becomes false. (In other words, this loop stops the moment the Answer$ variable equals Y.)

The DO LOOP WHILE loop makes the computer follow at least once any instructions sandwiched between the DO and LOOP commands. A DO LOOP WHILE loop stops looping only when its condition (a Boolean expression) becomes false.

To prevent an endless loop, you must include at least one instruction that changes the Boolean expression. The DO LOOP WHILE loop command checks the Boolean expression to know when to stop repeating the loop.

The DO UNTIL LOOP loop

The DO UNTIL LOOP loop looks like this:

```
DO UNTIL (condition)
   ' One or more instructions
LOOP
```

Because the DO UNTIL LOOP loop checks a condition (a Boolean expression that's either true or false) first, it's possible that none of the instructions sandwiched between the DO UNTIL and LOOP commands will run.

A typical DO UNTIL LOOP loop looks like this:

```
CLS
Age = 18
DO UNTIL Age > 25
   PRINT "You're perfect for Hollywood at age"; Age
   Age = Age + 1
LOOP
PRINT "You're now a has-been. Time for plastic surgery!"
END
```

This program keeps looping until the Boolean expression (Age > 25) becomes true, which happens when Age equals 26. If you run this program, you'll see this on the screen:

```
You're perfect for Hollywood at age 18
You're perfect for Hollywood at age 19
You're perfect for Hollywood at age 20
You're perfect for Hollywood at age 21
You're perfect for Hollywood at age 22
You're perfect for Hollywood at age 23
You're perfect for Hollywood at age 24
You're perfect for Hollywood at age 25
You're now a has-been. Time for plastic surgery!
```

The DO UNTIL LOOP loop makes the computer follow zero or more times any instructions sandwiched between the DO and LOOP commands. A DO UNTIL LOOP loop stops looping only when its condition (a Boolean expression) becomes true.

To prevent an endless loop, you must include at least one instruction that changes the Boolean expression. The DO UNTIL LOOP loop command checks the Boolean expression to know when to stop repeating the loop.

The DO WHILE LOOP loop

The DO WHILE LOOP loop looks like this:

```
DO WHILE (condition)
   ' One or more instructions
LOOP
```

Because the DO WHILE LOOP loop checks a condition (a Boolean expression that's either true or false) first, it's possible that none of the instructions sandwiched between the DO WHILE and LOOP commands will run.

A typical DO WHILE LOOP loop looks like this:

```
CLS
Calories = 100
DO WHILE Calories < 1600
   PRINT "Keep eating! You've only consumed"; Calories;
          "calories."
   Calories = Calories * 2
LOOP
PRINT "Time to start dieting."
END
```

This program keeps looping until the Boolean expression (Calories < 1600) becomes true, which happens when Calories equals 1600. If you run this program, you'll see this on the screen:

```
Keep eating! You've only consumed 100 calories.
Keep eating! You've only consumed 200 calories.
Keep eating! You've only consumed 400 calories.
Keep eating! You've only consumed 800 calories.
Time to start dieting.
```

The DO WHILE LOOP loop makes the computer follow zero or more times any instructions sandwiched between the DO and LOOP commands. A DO WHILE LOOP loop stops looping only when its condition (a Boolean expression) becomes false.

To prevent an endless loop, you must include at least one instruction that changes the Boolean expression. The DO WHILE LOOP loop command checks the Boolean expression to know when to stop repeating the loop.

Choosing the right loop

With four types of loops to choose from, you can use any loop at any given time. Table 10-1 tells you how each loop behaves so that you can choose the one that you think is best for your program.

Table 10-1	The Four Conditional Loops	
Loop	*How many times it runs*	*It stops looping when its condition becomes*
DO ' Instructions here LOOP UNTIL (condition)	1 or more times	True
DO ' Instructions here LOOP WHILE (condition)	1 or more times	False
DO UNTIL (condition) ' Instructions here LOOP	0 or more times	True
DO WHILE (condition) ' Instructions here LOOP	0 or more times	False

Looping a Fixed Number of Times

A conditional loop stops repeating itself only when a certain condition becomes true or false. So the number of times that a loop repeats can vary from one moment to the next.

However, sometimes you may need to loop a specific number of times. Although you could still use a conditional loop, you may prefer to use another type of loop called the FOR NEXT loop, which looks like this:

```
FOR counter = start TO end
   ' One or more instructions
NEXT
```

This loop tells the computer, "Repeat a fixed number of times the instructions sandwiched between the FOR and NEXT commands. The number of repeats is determined by the start and end values." A typical FOR NEXT loop looks like this:

```
CLS
FOR I = 1 TO 10
   PRINT "The square of "; I; " is "; I * I
NEXT
END
```

If you run this program, this is what happens:

1. The first line clears the screen.

2. The second line creates a variable called I and tells the computer to keep repeating the command 10 times.

3. The third line tells the computer to print, "The square of 1 is 1." Each time this line runs, the value of I is different, so the final output from the program looks like this:

```
The square of 1 is 1
The square of 2 is 4
The square of 3 is 9
The square of 4 is 16
The square of 5 is 25
The square of 6 is 36
The square of 7 is 49
The square of 8 is 64
The square of 9 is 81
The square of 10 is 100
```

4. The fourth line tells the computer to go back to the second line.

5. The fifth line tells the computer that this is the end of the program.

If the start value is less than the end value, the FOR NEXT loop will not run at all, as in this example:

```
FOR counter = 8 TO 2
   ' This won't work at all
NEXT
```

Counting with different numbers

Most FOR NEXT loops count from 1 to another fixed value, such as 10. However, the FOR NEXT loop can count from any number to any other number, as in this example:

```
CLS
FOR I = 8 TO 14
  PRINT "The value of I ="; I
NEXT
END
```

This loop repeats seven times and prints the following:

```
The value of I = 8
The value of I = 9
The value of I = 10
The value of I = 11
The value of I = 12
The value of I = 13
The value of I = 14
```

You can also use negative numbers for the start and end values, like this:

```
FOR counter = -5 TO 3
  ' One or more instructions
NEXT
```

Unless you have a good reason for choosing different numbers to start and end, it's a good idea to always start at number 1. Using 1 as the starting point simply makes it easier for you or someone else to tell how many times the FOR NEXT loop repeats.

Counting in increments

A FOR NEXT loop counts by one. In this example, the loop runs four times:

```
FOR counter = 1 TO 4
  ' One or more instructions
NEXT
```

If you like, you can use the following STEP command to make the FOR NEXT loop count in any increments other than one:

```
FOR counter = 1 TO 4 STEP increment
  ' One or more instructions
NEXT
```

If you want to count by twos, you can use this FOR NEXT loop:

```
FOR counter = 1 TO 8 STEP 2
  "PRINT "The value of I = "; I
NEXT
```

Mimicking the FOR NEXT loop with a DO WHILE LOOP loop

Instead of using the FOR NEXT loop, you can use a DO WHILE LOOP loop:

```
Counter = start
DO WHILE counter <= end
  ' One or more instructions
  Counter = Counter + 1
LOOP
```

Suppose that you had a FOR NEXT loop that looked like this:

```
FOR I = 1 TO 5
  PRINT I
NEXT
```

You could rewrite this FOR NEXT loop as a DO WHILE LOOP loop like this:

```
I = 1
DO WHILE I <= 5
  PRINT I
  I = I + 1
LOOP
```

However, the FOR NEXT loop is much easier to read than the slightly clumsier and more confusing DO WHILE LOOP loop. You have multiple ways to accomplish the same task, so you should always choose the simplest method to make your program easier to read now and easier to understand later.

If you run this program, the FOR NEXT loop doesn't repeat eight times. It repeats four times and prints this:

```
The value of I = 1
The value of I = 3
The value of I = 5
The value of I = 7
```

You can make a FOR NEXT loop count backward by using a negative number for the increment value. This is the only time that the start value can be greater than the end value, as shown in this example:

```
FOR counter = 6 TO -8 STEP -3
  "PRINT "The value of I = "; I
NEXT
```

If you run this program, the FOR NEXT loop repeats five times, printing these results:

```
The value of I = 6
The value of I = 3
The value of I = 0
The value of I = -3
The value of I = -6
```

Exiting a Loop

Normally, a loop ends when its condition becomes true or false, or (in the case of the FOR NEXT loop) when it finishes looping a fixed number of times. But sometimes you may need to prematurely exit a loop. To do that, you use the special EXIT command.

To exit a DO LOOP loop, use the EXIT DO command in this way:

```
CLS
Counter = 1
DO WHILE Counter < 25
  PRINT "The value of counter = "; counter
  Counter = Counter + 1
  IF Counter = 3 THEN
    EXIT DO
  END IF
LOOP
END
```

This program repeats the DO WHILE LOOP loop only two times before the EXIT DO command stops the DO WHILE LOOP loop.

To exit a FOR NEXT loop, use the EXIT FOR command in this way:

```
CLS
FOR I = 1 TO 14
  PRINT "The value of I ="; I
  IF I = 5 THEN
    EXIT FOR
  END IF
NEXT
END
```

This program repeats the FOR NEXT loop only five times before the EXIT FOR command stops the FOR NEXT loop.

What the FOR NEXT loop looks like in a C Program

Because many people eventually graduate to programming in C, here's a glimpse at how the FOR NEXT loop appears in a C program:

```
main ()
{
  int counter;
  for (counter = 1; counter <=
  5; counter++) {
    printf ("The square of %d
  is %d\n", counter, counter
  * counter);
  }
}
```

This FOR NEXT loop tells the computer, "Create an integer variable called counter and set its value to 1 (counter = 1). Then keep incrementing the value of counter by 1 (counter++) until the Boolean expression (counter <= 5) becomes false. Then stop looping." (This FOR NEXT loop repeats itself exactly five times.)

If the C version of the FOR NEXT loop looks a bit cryptic, that's because it is. So now you know why learning the fundamentals of programming is much easier using QBASIC than C.

Use the EXIT command sparingly. Throwing the EXIT command inside a loop means that you have to worry about two different ways that the loop can end (instead of one), essentially doubling the possible problems that could mess up your program.

Part III

Advanced QBASIC Programming

The 5th Wave — By Rich Tennant

"...AND THESE ARE OUR OBJECT-ORIENTED PROGRAMMING SPECIALISTS."

In this part . . .

*T*his part shows you all the fancy features buried in QBASIC — creating graphics, making sounds, saving data on a floppy or hard disk, and much more. When you understand these more advanced features of QBASIC, you can create useful and interesting programs that rival the features found in commercial-quality software.

For maximum understanding, be sure to type and run the many QBASIC programs sprinkled throughout each chapter. And keep your eyes open for QBASIC programs displayed along with equivalent programs written in other languages, such as C/C++ or Java. The more you use QBASIC to help you master general programming principles now, the easier you will be able to migrate to another language such as C/C++ later.

Chapter 11

Writing Large Programs Using Subroutines and Functions

● ●

In This Chapter

▶ Introducing structured programming

▶ Writing modular programs

▶ Using subroutines

▶ Using functions

▶ Viewing and editing subroutines and functions

● ●

*P*rogramming is not so much a hard science as it is a creative art form. The ultimate goal of programming is to write the smallest possible program that uses the least amount of computer resources (memory, hard disk space, and so on) while accomplishing as much as possible.

Although some people are naturally talented at writing small, tight, fast code (to use the lingo of the programming community), most people need guidelines to help them write programs.

Small programs are easy to write and read. But if you're writing a large program that consists of several thousand lines of instructions, guess what? You'd better organize your program carefully from the start, or you could waste lots of time writing a large program that doesn't work.

Breaking the Bad Programming Habits of the Past

You can write a program in a million different ways. No two people will write the same program in exactly the same way, just as no two people will write exactly the same term paper on the same topic (unless they copy from each other, that is).

In the old days, people wrote programs without any advance planning, which is like trying to write a novel by sitting down at a word processor and typing continuously until you're done. You could possibly write a decent novel that way, but you're more likely to create an unreadable mess.

Similarly, programmers used to write programs by typing commands into the computer just to get something to work. After they had a simple program that worked, they started typing new instructions into the program.

Unfortunately, programmers often didn't add new instructions with any planning or organization. Some programmers added new instructions in the beginning of a program, others put new instructions at the end, and still others sprinkled new instructions throughout the program's existing instructions, making it nearly impossible to tell where the new instructions began and the old ones ended.

This practice of writing programs without organization often created unreliable programs that were nearly impossible to modify or fix (but companies still made money selling their programs anyway).

Programmers used to write programs that were hard to read because they used a special programming command called the GOTO command. The GOTO command tells the computer to jump to another part of the program. For example, GOTO LabelOne tells the computer to suddenly jump to the part of the program identified by a label called LabelOne.

The GOTO command encouraged programmers to write programs that told the computer to jump from one place in the program to another to find instructions. Programs that use the GOTO command are like a novel in which page 2 tells you to jump to page 349, page 349 tells you to jump to page 34, page 34 tells you to jump to page 125, and so on.

Because bouncing from one part of a program to another could be as confusing as trying to untangle strands of spaghetti, writing programs in this manner became known as *spaghetti coding*.

For example, consider the following BASIC program:

```
GOTO LabelOne

LabelFour:
  INPUT "How much money do you have"; MyCash
  GOTO LabelThree

LabelTwo:
  END

LabelOne:
  CLS
  GOTO LabelFour
```

```
LabelThree:
  PRINT "You owe me = "; MyCash * .95
  GOTO LabelTwo
```

Trying to figure out what this program does is confusing because the instructions are jumbled. But the following breakdown shows you how the program works:

1. The first line tells the computer to jump to the part of the program identified by a label called `LabelOne` (which happens to be on the seventh line of the program).

2. The computer jumps to the seventh line in the program that has a label called `LabelOne`.

3. The eighth line in the program clears the screen.

4. The ninth line in the program tells the computer to jump to the part of the program identified by a label called `LabelFour` (which happens to be the second line of the program).

5. The computer jumps to the second line in the program that has a label called `LabelFour`.

6. The third line prints, "How much money do you have?" on the screen and waits for the user to type a number, which will be stored in a variable called `MyCash`.

7. The fourth line tells the computer to jump to the part of the program identified by a label called `LabelThree` (which happens to be the tenth line in the program).

8. The computer jumps to the tenth line in the program that has a label called `LabelThree`.

9. The eleventh line prints, "You owe me = " followed by the value of `MyCash` multiplied by `.95`.

10. The twelfth line tells the computer to jump to the part of the program identified by a label called `LabelTwo` (which happens to be the fifth line of the program).

11. The computer jumps to the fifth line of the program that has a label called `LabelTwo`.

12. The sixth line tells the computer that this is the end of the program.

The preceding GOTO program is equivalent to the following simple program:

```
CLS
INPUT "How much money do you have:"; MyCash
PRINT "You owe me ="; MyCash * .95
PRINT
END
```

In the early days of computer programming, structures such as IF THEN and SELECT CASE statements didn't exist. For many years the GOTO command was the only way programmers could tell the computer to skip over certain instructions or follow a different set of instructions. Although you can still use the GOTO command, a good programming practice is to avoid it whenever possible.

Introducing Structured Programming

You'll never find one "right" way to write a program, but programmers have created different ways to write programs that are at least well organized. One popular way to write a program is called *structured programming*, and its main idea is to organize your program using only three types of instructions (none of which resembles the GOTO command). If you use only the following three instructions, you ensure that you and other people can easily read and understand your program:

- ✔ Sequential instructions
- ✔ Branching instructions
- ✔ Looping instructions

Sequential instructions

The simplest way to organize instructions in a program is to place them sequentially, one after another, as in the following example:

```
CLS
INPUT "How much stuff did you steal last year"; Amount
TaxesOwed = Amount * .95
PRINT "This is how much tax you owe ="; TaxesOwed
END
```

Unfortunately, not every program can be written as one big list of instructions. When the computer needs to make a decision, your program may need to choose between two or more different sets of instructions. When you write a program that must make a choice, this is called *branching*. Other times the computer may need to follow the same instructions over and over, so using a loop (such as a FOR NEXT loop) is much easier than typing nearly identical instructions multiple times.

Branching instructions

Branching instructions (such as the IF THEN statement) provide two or more different instructions for the computer to follow, based on a certain condition. (For more information about IF THEN statements and other types of branching statements, see Chapter 8.) For example, the following program calculates two different taxes owed, depending on whether or not you're a politician:

```
CLS
INPUT "How much stuff did you steal last year"; Amount
TaxesOwed = Amount * .95
INPUT "Are you a professional criminal (Y or N)"; Answer
IF (Answer = "N") THEN
    PRINT "This is how much tax you owe ="; TaxOwed
ELSE
    PRINT "Lawyers and politicians don't need to pay tax."
END
```

Branching instructions offer two or more alternate sets of instructions for the computer to follow. As a result, branching instructions are harder to read than sequentially organized instructions because you have to determine which set of instructions the computer may follow at any given time.

Looping instructions

Sometimes the computer may need to repeat certain instructions. Rather than type the same instructions over and over, you can use a loop, such as a FOR NEXT or a DO WHILE LOOP.

A FOR NEXT loop repeats a fixed number of times. A DO WHILE LOOP loop repeats itself while a certain condition remains true. Thus the number of times a DO WHILE LOOP loop repeats itself can range from zero to infinity.

For example, the following program asks for a password, checks to see whether the user typed the correct password (which is the string "open"), and keeps repeating these instructions until the user types the correct password:

```
CLS
INPUT "What is the password"; Password$
DO WHILE Password$ <> "open"
    PRINT "Wrong password, moron. Try again."
    INPUT "What is the password"; Password$
LOOP
PRINT "You typed the correct password!"
END
```

Loops can be harder to read than sequential instructions and branching instructions, because you can't always tell how many times a loop repeats itself. Essentially, a loop is a shortcut so that you don't have to type a long series of sequential instructions in your program. (For more information about loops, see Chapter 10.)

Putting structured programming into practice

The reason for organizing your program in chunks of sequential, branching, and looping instructions is to make it easier for others to understand how your program works. When they can understand how your program works, they can modify and improve upon it later.

Just because you wrote the program, don't be so sure that you'll be able to understand it later. If you write a program made up of several thousand lines of instructions, you'll probably forget how certain parts of the program work — especially if you put the program aside and work on another project for awhile. So writing programs that are easy to understand is crucial for your own benefit and for the benefit of any other programmer who has the job of fixing or modifying programs that you wrote.

To see how structured programming can make a program easier to read, look at the following program, which consists of sequential, branching, and looping instructions:

```
'Sequential instructions
CLS
PRINT "This program prints a message, of your"
PRINT "choosing, on the screen."
INPUT "What message do you want to appear"; Message$
PRINT "Would you like the message to appear in all"
PRINT "UPPERCASE (type U) or lowercase (type l)?"
INPUT WhatCase$

'Branching instructions
IF WhatCase$ = "U" THEN
  Message$ = UCASE$(Message$)
ELSEIF WhatCase$ = "l" THEN
  Message$ = LCASE$(Message$)
END IF

'Looping instructions
FOR I = 1 TO 15
  PRINT SPC(I + 4); Message$
NEXT
END
```

Think of sequential, branching, or looping instructions as the building blocks of any program. When you write a program that uses only sequential, branching, and looping instructions, your program is easier for you (or anyone else) to read and edit at a later date.

Writing Modular Programs

If you plan to write large, complicated programs that control the trajectory of a satellite or search the oceans for oil deposits, chances are pretty good that such programs will be fairly large. (Programs consisting of several thousand lines of instructions are common in commercial quality software. In fact, really big programs like Windows 2000 consist of several million lines of instructions, which makes ridding the programs of bugs very difficult.)

If you're really ambitious, you could write a large program as one huge list of instructions. However, the larger your program is, the harder reading, writing, and understanding the program will be. Writing a large program as one set of instructions is like trying to build a house out of sand. Most likely, one part of the structure (such as a wall) will be weaker than the rest of the structure and will cause the whole thing to collapse.

Rather than create one huge program, programmers create a bunch of smaller programs and paste them together (sort of like using bricks to build a house). That way, if one part of the program doesn't work, you can unplug that portion, rewrite or replace it, and leave the rest of your program unaffected.

In the computer world, little programs that make up part of a larger program are called *subprograms*. Subprograms are also called *modules*, hence the term *modular programming*.

Every modular program has at least one subprogram, called the *main program*. The main program usually does nothing more than tell the computer which subprograms to use next to accomplish a specific task.

A subprogram typically solves a single task, such as multiplying two numbers or verifying that the user typed a correct password. For really complicated programs, you may have several subprograms that are themselves broken up into several smaller subprograms.

For example, suppose that you wanted to write a program to break into another computer. The overall task is simply this:

```
Break into another computer.
```

Of course, you can't tell the computer, "Break into another computer" because it won't know how to do it. You have to tell the computer, in specific detail, exactly what you want it to do. This means defining the overall goal of the program using smaller tasks, like this:

Break into the computer.

Find the phone number of the target computer.

Guess a password to access the system.

When access is gained, beep to notify the user.

Ideally, each task can be solved by a separate subprogram that is completely independent of any other part of the program. After you get each subprogram to work properly, you can paste all the subprograms together to create a larger working program.

QBASIC provides two ways to create subprograms:

- ✔ **Subroutines** contain instructions for performing certain tasks, such as verifying that the user typed in a correct password or moving the cursor when the user moves the mouse.
- ✔ **Functions** calculate a single value, such as calculating the cube of a number or counting the number of words in a sentence.

When you use subprograms (subroutines and functions) in a QBASIC program, you're essentially dividing a larger program into smaller parts, although everything still gets saved in a single file with a name such as PACMAN.BAS or BLACKJAK.BAS.

Be aware that programming languages often use similar terms to represent different items. For example, when you divide a large program into smaller parts, QBASIC calls these smaller parts *subprograms*. But what QBASIC calls a subprogram, the C language calls a *function*. Similarly, what QBASIC calls a *subroutine*, Pascal calls a *procedure*. So when you use a different language, make sure that you use the correct terms for that particular language; otherwise, you may get confused when talking to other programmers.

Using Subroutines

Subroutines have two purposes:

- ✔ To store frequently used instructions in a single location.
- ✔ To isolate instructions (that perform a specific task) from other parts of the program.

The main reason to store frequently used instructions in a subroutine is to

Modular programming in other languages

When you use subprograms in QBASIC, you have to store your subprograms in the same file as your main program. This is like printing the Encyclopedia Britannica in a single book and then wondering why it's so bulky and difficult to find what you want.

Unlike QBASIC, most other programming languages, such as Pascal, C/C++, Java, and Visual Basic, allow you to store subprograms in separate files. So rather than have a single large file

divided into small subprograms, other languages let you create several files containing one or more subprograms.

Storing subprograms in separate files isolates the different parts of a program. That way, teams of programmers can work on different parts of a program. When everyone's done, they can compile all the separate files into a single working program, much like putting building blocks together.

avoid typing nearly identical instructions over and over. For example, notice the repetition in the following program:

```
CLS
INPUT "What is your name"; MyName$
FOR I = 1 TO 10
   PRINT SPC(I + 4); "Hello " + MyName$
NEXT
INPUT "What is the name of your boss"; BossName$
FOR I = 1 TO 10
   PRINT SPC(I + 4); BossName$ + " sounds like the name of a
            loser to me."
NEXT
END
```

This program uses two nearly identical FOR NEXT loops to accomplish a similar task (printing a message on the screen). A larger program might use the same nearly identical FOR NEXT loop several hundred or several thousand times.

Typing several thousand nearly identical instructions would be tiresome and possibly error-prone, but what would happen if you needed to modify the way the FOR NEXT loop worked? You would have to modify several thousand nearly identical FOR NEXT loops, which would again be tedious and error-prone.

As an alternative to typing nearly identical instructions multiple times, you can just type them once and store them in a subroutine.

Defining a subroutine

A subroutine consists of two or three parts:

- ✔ A name
- ✔ One or more instructions that you want the subroutine to follow
- ✔ Any data that you want the subroutine to use (optional)

A typical subroutine looks like this:

```
SUB SubroutineName (Data)
   ' One or more instructions
END SUB
```

If a subroutine doesn't need to accept data from the main program or another subprogram, you can omit the parentheses, as in the following example:

```
SUB SubroutineName
   ' One or more instructions
END SUB
```

To create a subroutine in QBASIC, follow these steps:

1. Choose Edit⇨New SUB.

A New SUB dialog box appears, as shown in Figure 11-1.

Figure 11-1:
The New SUB dialog box for creating a new subroutine.

2. Type a name for your subroutine and press Enter.

QBASIC creates an empty subroutine that looks like this:

```
SUB SubroutineName
END SUB
```

3. Create variable names, and add the data type that the subroutine may need in parentheses, as in the following example:

```
SUB SubroutineName (Message AS STRING)
END SUB
```

4. Type any instructions between the SUB **and** END SUB **lines:**

```
SUB SubroutineName (Message AS STRING)
   PRINT Message
END SUB
```

Ideally, you should strive to make all your subprograms small enough to fit on a single screen. The smaller your subprograms are, the easier they will be to understand, debug, and modify.

Passing data to a subroutine

A subroutine acts like a miniature program that performs one or more tasks. Even though a subroutine is part of a bigger program, some subroutines can act independently from the rest of the program. For example, you may have a subroutine that does nothing but display a message on the screen. When a subroutine can act independently from the rest of the program, you need to define only a name for your subroutine and any instructions you want the subroutine to follow, as in the following example:

```
SUB SubroutineName
   PRINT "This subroutine doesn't use any data."
END SUB
```

When your program runs the preceding subroutine, the subroutine merrily follows its instructions without using any data from any other part of the program.

But in many cases, a subroutine requires outside data to accomplish a given task, such as checking to see whether the user typed a valid password. If your subroutine needs data from another part of your program, you need to create a variable to store this data, as in the following example:

```
SUB SubroutineName (Variable)
   ' One or more instructions here
END SUB
```

When another part of the program tells this subroutine to run, it "passes" data to this subroutine, in much the same way that a person might pass a baton to another person. When a subroutine receives data passed to it from another part of the program, the subroutine uses variables (trapped inside parentheses) to "hold" any data sent to it from another part of the program.

The list of variables inside the parentheses of a subroutine is called a *parameter list*.

Each variable inside a subroutine's parentheses specifies one chunk of data, such as a number or string. If your subroutine is passed two chunks of data, the subroutine's parameter list must contain exactly two variables to hold this data. The following subroutine example uses three variables in its parameter list:

```
SUB SubroutineName (Variable1, Variable2, Variable3)
   ' One or more instructions here
END SUB
```

When you declare variables, always define the type of data that they represent — for example, strings, integers, single-precision numbers, and so on. A complete declaration of variables looks like this:

```
SUB SubroutineName (Name AS STRING, Age AS INTEGER)
   ' One or more instructions here
END SUB
```

The first line of the preceding subroutine defines the name of the subroutine (which is SubroutineName) and creates two variables called Name and Age. The Name variable represents a string, and the Age variable represents an integer.

To shorten the amount of typing that you need to do, substitute symbols for the data type declarations. Use the dollar sign ($) for a string, the percentage sign (%) for an integer, the ampersand (&) for long integers, the exclamation mark (!) for single-precision numbers, and the pound sign (#) for double-precision numbers. Here is an example:

```
SUB SubroutineName (Name$, Age%)
   ' One or more instructions here
END SUB
```

Calling a subroutine

After you have created a subroutine, the final step is to actually run the instructions trapped inside the subroutine. Normally, the subroutine sits around and does absolutely nothing (much like a politician) until the computer specifically tells the subroutine to run its instructions. In technical terms, when you tell the subroutine to run its instructions, you're *calling a subroutine*. Essentially, you're saying, "Hey, stupid subroutine! Start running your instructions now!"

If you want to call a subroutine named `BurnOutMonitor`, you can use one of two methods:

- ✔ `CALL BurnOutMonitor`
- ✔ `BurnOutMonitor`

If the `BurnOutMonitor` subroutine needs an integer to run, the two methods to call the subroutine look like this:

- ✔ `CALL BurnOutMonitor (45)`
- ✔ `BurnOutMonitor 45`

If you omit the `CALL` command, you don't have to use parentheses to surround any data that you're passing to the subroutine.

Although QBASIC gives you two different ways to call a subroutine, your best approach is to stick to one method throughout your program. That just makes your program easier to read.

If all this babble about subroutines still doesn't make sense to you, follow these steps to see for yourself how to create and call a subroutine from within your main program:

1. **Type the following program in the QBASIC window:**

```
CLS
INPUT "What is your name"; MyName$
CALL PrintMessage ("Hello " + MyName$)
INPUT "What is the name of your boss"; BossName$
PrintMessage BossName$ + " sounds like the name of a
         loser to me."
END
```

   Note: This program shows two different methods to call a subroutine named `PrintMessage`, so that you can see how both methods work:

   - `CALL PrintMessage ("Hello " + MyName$)`

   - `PrintMessage BossName$ + " sounds like the name of a loser to me."`

2. **Choose Edit⇨New SUB.**

   A New SUB dialog box appears.

3. **Type** PrintMessage **in the Name text box, and press Enter.**

   QBASIC creates an empty subroutine for you, as shown in Figure 11-2.

Figure 11-2:
QBASIC
creates an
empty
subroutine
for you
to modify.

4. **Type the following code into your empty subroutine, so that the entire subroutine looks like the following:**

```
SUB PrintMessage (InString$)
FOR I = 1 TO 10
   PRINT SPC(I + 4); InString$
NEXT
END SUB
```

5. **Press F2.**

A SUBs dialog box appears, listing all the different subprograms that make up your single program. Figure 11-3 shows the SUBs window for this example program. You see a subprogram called `PrintMessage` and a main program called `Untitled`. (When you save a QBASIC program, the actual file name appears instead of the word `Untitled`.)

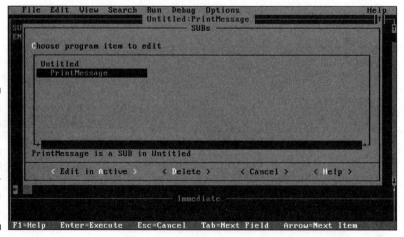

Figure 11-3:
QBASIC lists
all the sub-
programs
that make
up your
entire
program.

6. **Double-click on *Untitled* to view the main program.**

   The main program, which you typed in Step 1, appears again.

7. **Press F5.**

   The program types on the screen, "What is your name?".

8. **Type a name, and press Enter.**

   The program displays ten times on the screen the name that you typed. Then it asks, "What is the name of your boss?"

9. **Type a name, and press Enter.**

   Again, the program displays ten times the name that you typed on the screen.

10. **Press any key (such as the space bar) to view your program again.**

No matter how many subprograms you create, QBASIC always stores them in a single file. When you're editing a program, QBASIC normally shows only one subprogram at a time.

Using Functions

A function is a specialized subprogram that does nothing but calculate and return a single value. For example, if you want to calculate the cube of a number (which is the same number multiplied by itself three times), you can use the following instructions:

```
Cube = Number * Number * Number
```

But if you have to calculate the cube of a number in several places throughout your program, you have to type the formula Number * Number * Number in each place in your program. As you know, this would be tedious and error-prone, especially if you want to modify the program later.

Defining a function

Rather than type similar instructions multiple times (using slightly different numbers), you can store instructions in a function. Then you pass data to the function, and the function spits back a single value. A function consists of four parts:

  ✔ A name
  ✔ One or more instructions for the function to calculate a single value

✔ One line that assigns a value (or an expression that represents a value) to the function name

✔ Any data that you want the function to use

A typical function looks like this:

```
FUNCTION FunctionName (Data)
  ' One or more instructions
  FunctionName = value
END FUNCTION
```

To create a function, follow these steps:

1. **In the QBASIC window, choose Edit⇨New FUNCTION.**

   A New FUNCTION dialog box appears.

2. **Type a name for your function and press Enter.**

   QBASIC creates an empty function that looks like this:

   ```
   FUNCTION FunctionName
   END FUNCTION
   ```

3. **Create variable names, and add the data type that the function may need in parentheses, as in the following example:**

   ```
   FUNCTION FunctionName (Number AS INTEGER)
   END SUB
   ```

4. **Type any instructions between the FUNCTION and END FUNCTION lines. Make sure that at least one line in the function assigns a value to the function name:**

   ```
   FUNCTION FunctionName (Number AS INTEGER)
     FunctionName = Number * Number * Number
   END SUB
   ```

Passing data to a function

Nearly all functions need to receive data from another part of your program. When another part of a program runs (or *calls*) a function, it needs to send (or *pass*) data to that function. To make sure that the function receives any data passed to it, you need to specify one or more variables in parentheses, as in the following example:

```
FUNCTION FunctionName (Variable)
  ' One or more instructions here
  FunctionName = value
END FUNCTION
```

The preceding function can receive one chunk of data (such as a string or number) that another part of the program passes to it.

If your function needs to receive two or more chunks of data passed to it from another part of the program, just separate the variable names with commas, as in this example:

```
FUNCTION FunctionName (Variable1, Variable2, Variable3)
  ' One or more instructions here
  FunctionName = value
END FUNCTION
```

When you declare variables, define the type of data that they represent — for example, strings, integers, single-precision numbers, and so on. A complete declaration of variables looks like this:

```
FUNCTION FunctionName (Note AS STRING, Salary AS SINGLE)
  ' One or more instructions here
  FunctionName = value
END FUNCTION
```

The first line of the preceding function defines the name of the function (which is `FunctionName`) and creates two variables called `Note` and `Salary`. The `Note` variable represents a string, and the `Salary` variable represents a single-precision value such as 3.14.

You can substitute symbols for the data type declarations. Use the dollar sign ($) for a string, the percentage sign (%) for an integer, the ampersand (&) for long integers, the exclamation mark (!) for single-precision numbers, and the pound sign (#) for double-precision numbers. Here is an example:

```
FUNCTION FunctionName (Note$, Salary!)
  ' One or more instructions here
  FunctionName = value
END FUNCTION
```

Calling a function

Of course, you want to use the function that you create in your program. A function represents a single value such as an integer or a double-precision number, so you can treat the function name as a variable.

For example, suppose that you have a function called `Cube`:

```
FUNCTION Cube (Number AS INTEGER)
  Cube = Number * Number * Number
END FUNCTION
```

You could treat this function like any other variable, as in the following examples:

```
PRINT Cube (3)
```

or

```
MyValue = Cube (3)
```

The following breakdown shows how the computer interprets the first example, `PRINT Cube (3)`:

1. The `PRINT Cube (3)` line tells the computer, "Print the value represented by the function called `Cube`, when the `Cube` function uses the number 3 as data."

2. Right away, the computer searches for a function called `Cube`. The first line in the `Cube` function tells the computer, "The function name is `Cube` and it needs an integer, which is represented by the variable called `Number`, which in this case represents the number 3."

3. The second line in the `Cube` function tells the computer, "Multiply the value represented by the `Number` variable three times and assign this value to the function name of `Cube`." In this case, the value represented by the `Number` variable is 3, so the value of `Cube` is 3 * 3 * 3, or 27.

4. The third line in the `Cube` function tells the computer, "This is the end of the function. Go back to the part of the program that originally called the `Cube` function." In this case, the computer goes back to the instruction `PRINT Cube (3)`.

5. Because the value of `Cube (3)` is actually 27, the computer reinterprets the instruction `PRINT Cube (3)` to actually mean `PRINT 27`. Thus, the number 27 appears on the screen.

To see how QBASIC uses functions, follow these steps:

1. **In the QBASIC window, type the following program:**

   ```
   CLS
   INPUT "Give me a whole number such as 2 or 8"; MyNum%
   PRINT Cube (MyNum%)
   END
   ```

2. **Choose Edit⇨New FUNCTION.**

   A New FUNCTION dialog box appears.

3. **Type Cube, and press Enter.**

   QBASIC creates an empty function.

4. **Type the following:**

```
FUNCTION Cube (Number AS INTEGER)
    Cube = Number * Number * Number
END FUNCTION
```

5. **Press F2.**

A SUBs dialog box appears, listing all the different subprograms that make up your single program. In this example, you see a subprogram called Cube and a main program called Untitled.

6. **Double-click** Untitled **to view the main program.**

The main program, which you typed in Step 1, appears again.

7. **Press F5.**

The program types on the screen, "Give me a whole number such as 2 or 8.".

8. **Type a number (such as 4), and press Enter.**

The program displays the cube of the number that you typed. (For example, the program displays 64 if you typed the number 4.)

9. **Press any key (such as the space bar) to view your program again.**

Viewing and Editing Subroutines and Functions

Normally QBASIC displays only a single subprogram at a time to decrease the chance that you'll get mixed up looking at two or more subprograms simultaneously. To view a different subprogram, follow these steps:

1. **Press F2.**

A SUBs dialog box appears, listing all the different subprograms that make up your single program.

2. **Double-click the name of the subprogram that you want to view.**

Your chosen subprogram appears on the screen.

To view two subprograms at the same time, choose View⇨Split, press F2, and double-click the subprogram that you want to view. Figure 11-4 shows how you can view two subprograms at once. To close one subprogram window, click in the close box (which looks like a small box with an up arrow inside it) that appears in the upper-right corner of the window. You can also choose View⇨Split again to close one window.

Close boxes

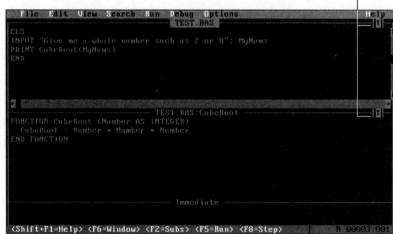

Figure 11-4:
QBASIC can
display two
subprograms
at once.

Deleting a Subroutine or Function

You may write a subroutine or function and then realize later that you no longer need it. To delete a subroutine or function, follow these steps:

1. Press F2.

A SUBs dialog box appears, listing all the different subprograms that make up your single program.

2. Click the name of the subprogram that you want to delete.

3. Click Delete.

A dialog box appears, asking whether you really want to delete the subprogram.

4. Click OK.

The SUBs window appears again.

5. Press Esc.

Chapter 12

Making Pretty Graphics and Obnoxious Noises

. . . .

In This Chapter

▶ Creating ASCII graphics

▶ Drawing points, lines, and circles

▶ Painting what you've drawn

▶ Making music

. . . .

*I*n the old days, people typed information into a computer using a keyboard, and the computer responded by printing data on a piece of paper. When computers eventually got monitors so that the computer could display data directly on the screen, many programs still displayed data as letters and numbers, just as if the data were still being printed on a piece of paper.

Eventually programmers realized that computer screens could allow their programs to display data in more colorful ways than previously possible with a piece of paper. That's when programs started adding fancy graphics such as icons, pull-down menus, and windows.

Unfortunately, QBASIC was designed to run under the ancient MS-DOS operating system, which wasn't designed to display fancy graphics. Nevertheless, Microsoft managed to cram enough features into QBASIC to make it display fairly simple graphics and offer limited sound.

What you discover in this chapter are different ways to make QBASIC programs more colorful and visually appealing. After you add graphics and sound to your program, people will naturally find your program more interesting and (sometimes) easier to use.

Playing with ASCII Graphics

In the early days of computers, monitors couldn't display the fancy graphics that you see on today's computers. Instead, old-fashioned computers could display only ASCII characters, which include letters, numbers, symbols (such as #, %, and *), and simple graphic characters (such as lines and shaded rectangles).

To view all the ASCII characters that your computer can display, choose Help⇨ Contents and then double-click ASCII Character Codes under the Quick Reference group. The main ASCII graphics characters are numbered 169 to 223.

To draw an ASCII character on the screen, you use the PRINT and CHR$ commands:

```
PRINT CHR$(X)
```

In this example, X represents the ASCII character number (such as 169 or 188) that you want to draw on the screen. To tell the computer an exact screen position where you want to draw an ASCII character, use the LOCATE command:

```
LOCATE X, Y
```

Here, X represents the row and Y represents the column of the screen. (Row 1 represents the top of the screen, and Row 24 represents the bottom. Column 1 represents the left of the screen, and Column 80 represents the right.

To see how you can use ASCII graphics to draw a simple box on the screen (like the box shown in Figure 12-1), run the following program:

Figure 12-1:
Multiple
QBASIC
commands
are necessary
just to draw
a simple box
on the screen.

```
CLS
LOCATE 10, 35
PRINT CHR$(201)
LOCATE 10, 36
PRINT CHR$(205)
LOCATE 10, 37
PRINT CHR$(203)
```

```
LOCATE 10, 38
PRINT CHR$(205)
LOCATE 10, 39
PRINT CHR$(187)

LOCATE 11, 35
PRINT CHR$(186)
LOCATE 11, 37
PRINT CHR$(186)
LOCATE 11, 39
PRINT CHR$(186)

LOCATE 12, 35
PRINT CHR$(204)
LOCATE 12, 36
PRINT CHR$(205)
LOCATE 12, 37
PRINT CHR$(206)
LOCATE 12, 38
PRINT CHR$(205)
LOCATE 12, 39
PRINT CHR$(185)

LOCATE 13, 35
PRINT CHR$(200)
LOCATE 13, 36
PRINT CHR$(205)
LOCATE 13, 37
PRINT CHR$(202)
LOCATE 13, 38
PRINT CHR$(205)
LOCATE 13, 39
PRINT CHR$(188)
END
```

Drawing Fancier Graphics

Using ASCII characters to draw images on the screen can be like using black and white crayons to draw a rainbow. In both cases, no matter how creative you may be, the ultimate outcome is limited by your choice of tools.

To create fancier graphics that don't rely on a limited choice of ASCII characters, QBASIC provides a range of additional commands for drawing lines, circles, and points, as well as choosing different colors.

Using different graphics modes

During the evolution of the original IBM PC, computer monitors went from being able to display only simple ASCII characters to being able to display crude graphics, and then to the current ability to display three-dimensional helicopters hovering over a computer-generated town.

But because QBASIC is still rooted in the past, it contains commands for displaying graphics only on older, more limited computer monitors. Although your monitor can probably display fancier graphics, QBASIC won't be able to take advantage of your monitor's capabilities. For example, many monitors can now display text and pictures on the screen at a resolution of 1024 by 768 (the higher the resolution, the sharper the picture), but the highest resolution that QBASIC can use is 720 by 348.

Because older computer monitors could display only limited resolution, QBASIC can display graphics using all the older graphics standards or modes. To switch between different graphics modes, QBASIC offers the SCREEN command, which you can use as follows:

```
SCREEN X
```

In this example, X represents the specific graphics mode that you want to use. The modes available are listed in Table 12-1.

Table 12-1 The Graphics Modes for QBASIC		
X value	*Resolution*	*Number of Colors Available*
1	320 x 200	16
2	640 x 200	16
3	720 x 348	1
7	320 x 200	16
8	640 x 200	16
9	640 x 350	64
10	640 x 350	9
11	640 x 480	256
12	640 x 480	256
13	320 x 200	256

To find out more about the specific details of each graphic mode, choose Help⇨Index; then double-click the SCREEN statement and double-click Screen Modes.

In case you're wondering, several graphics modes, such as 11 and 12, appear to be identical. However, they offer subtle differences. For example, graphics mode 11 works with monochrome monitors, but graphics mode 12 doesn't. Because few people use monochrome monitors, these differences are more a technical curiosity than anything crucial to remember.

To see the graphics modes that QBASIC can use, try the following program:

```
DO
  CLS
  INPUT "Type in a screen mode number"; ThisMode%
  SCREEN ThisMode%
  PRINT "This is screen mode"; ThisMode%
  INPUT "Do you want to see another screen mode(Y or N)";
        Answer$
LOOP UNTIL UCASE$(Answer$) = "N"
END
```

When you type different screen mode values from Table 12-1, you can see how ugly screen mode 1 looks (320 x 200 resolution) compared to screen mode 11 (640 x 480 resolution).

Before drawing any graphic image, such as a point, a line, or a circle, you must choose a specific screen mode using the SCREEN command.

In Table 12-1, the lower X values (such as 1 and 2) are designed for older graphics standards, such as monochrome color graphics adapter (MCGA), color graphics adapter (CGA), and enhanced graphics adapter (EGA). The higher X values (such as 12 and 13) take advantage of new graphics standards, such as video gate array (VGA). Knowing the capabilities of different video graphics standards used to be important in the world of MS-DOS, but graphics adapter standards can be ignored in the world of Microsoft Windows.

Drawing a point

The simplest graphic to draw is a single point, which you can draw using the PSET command like this:

```
PSET (X, Y)
```

In this example, X represents the X-coordinate and Y represents the Y-coordinate.

Depending on the graphics mode you choose, the resolution can vary from 320 x 200 to 720 x 348. If you choose a resolution of 320 x 200, the maximum X-coordinate is 320 and the maximum Y-coordinate is 200.

To see the PSET command draw a bunch of points at random locations on your screen, run the following program:

```
CLS
SCREEN 1 '320 by 200 resolution
INPUT "How many points do you want"; Answer%
RANDOMIZE TIMER
FOR I = 1 TO Answer%
  X = INT(RND * 250) + 1
  Y = INT(RND * 250) + 1
  PSET (X, Y)
NEXT I
END
```

The preceding program uses two commands that you may want to know more about:

- RANDOMIZE TIMER
- INT(RND * 250) + 1

The RANDOMIZE TIMER command tells the computer, "Get ready to create a random number based on the current time of the computer." The INT(RND * 250) + 1 command tells the computer, "Create a random number between 0 and 249 (such as 58.93), add 1 to the result (to get 59.93), and turn the number into an integer (59)."

Drawing lines

Drawing a dot on the screen may not look very impressive, so QBASIC offers another command that draws lines on your screen. Not surprisingly, this command is called LINE and is used as follows:

```
LINE (X1, Y1) - (X2, Y2)
```

In this example, (X1, Y1) represents the location of one end of the line, and (X2, Y2) represents the location of the other end of the line. To see how incredibly useful the LINE command can be, run the following program:

```
CLS
SCREEN 1 '320 by 200 resolution
RANDOMIZE TIMER
X1 = INT(RND * 320) + 1
Y1 = INT(RND * 200) + 1
X2 = INT(RND * 320) + 1
Y2 = INT(RND * 200) + 1
LINE (X1, Y1) - (X2, Y2)
END
```

Each time you run this program, it randomly draws a line using different X and Y coordinates.

Drawing circles

In addition to drawing points and lines, QBASIC also has the incredible ability to draw circles, using the magical CIRCLE command like this:

```
CIRCLE (X, Y), Radius
```

Here, X represents the X-coordinate and Y represents the Y-coordinate of the center of the circle, and Radius represents the distance between the circle and the center X and Y coordinates.

To see how to draw a face using the PSET and CIRCLE commands, run the following program:

```
CLS
SCREEN 1 '320 by 200 resolution
RANDOMIZE TIMER
CIRCLE (100, 100), 75
PSET (100, 100)      ' Nose
PSET (75, 75)        ' Eye
PSET (125, 75)       ' Eye
LINE (75, 125) - (125, 125)
END
```

Using the DRAW command

Drawing simple points, lines, and circles can be fairly limited, so QBASIC also includes a special DRAW command. Unlike the LINE command (which requires exact X and Y coordinates), the DRAW command draws a line relative from the center of the screen.

To use the DRAW command, you have to give it a string, like this:

```
DRAW "u15 g55 r55 u40"
```

This command tells the computer, "Starting from the center of the screen, draw a line going up for 15 units, draw a line diagonally down and to the left for 55 units, draw another line to the right for 55 units, and then draw another line up for 40 units." This string draws a triangle on the screen. Figure 12-2 shows the directions in which you can draw a line using the DRAW command.

To draw a triangle using the DRAW command, run the following program:

```
CLS
SCREEN 1 '320 by 200 resolution
DRAW "u15 g55 r55 u40"
END
```

Drawing graphics in Microsoft Windows

If you want to draw graphics in Microsoft Windows, you usually have two options. One, you can use your favorite programming language's drawing commands, which are similar to QBASIC's `LINE`, `PSET`, and `CIRCLE` commands. Unfortunately, using a language's drawing commands is often a slow process.

For faster graphics performance, most programmers use something called Windows Application Programming Interface (API).

Essentially Windows API provides graphics functions that can create graphics quickly.

Because games need near instantaneous graphics drawing capabilities, Microsoft has created a special library of graphics functions called DirectX. DirectX is an attempt by Microsoft to make Windows more suitable for creating games. Microsoft hopes that having more games available for Windows will lead more people to buy Windows.

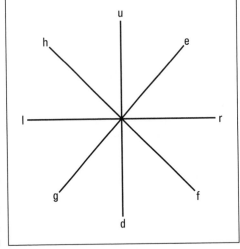

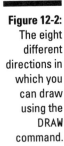

Figure 12-2:
The eight different directions in which you can draw using the DRAW command.

Using color

To add interest to graphics, QBASIC can also display color. The choices of available colors depend on the graphics mode that you choose. To choose a color, you have to use the `COLOR` command. Table 12-2 shows ways that you can use the `COLOR` command.

Table 12-2	The COLOR Command Screen Modes
Screen mode	*COLOR command*
SCREEN 1	COLOR background, palette
SCREEN 4	COLOR foreground
SCREEN 12	COLOR foreground
SCREEN 13	COLOR foreground
SCREEN 7 – 10	COLOR foreground, background

If you use the SCREEN 1 mode, you can define both a background color and a palette. A palette provides different colors to choose from, and the background color defines a specific color.

For example, if you want to display a blue background with the SCREEN 1 command, use the COLOR 1, 1 command, as shown here:

```
CLS
SCREEN 1 '320 by 200 resolution
COLOR 1, 1
DRAW "u15 g55 r55 u40"
END
```

The COLOR 1, 1 command says, "Use background color 1 using palette 1." Experiment with different numbers to see what colors they create.

If you were using the SCREEN 7 mode with the COLOR 1, 1 command, this would tell the computer, "Use foreground color 1 (blue) and background color 2 (green)."

Making Sounds

QBASIC provides several different ways to make sounds, ranging from simple beeps to synthesized music. At the simplest level, QBASIC can make a simple (and annoying) beeping noise by using a special BEEP command like this:

```
CLS
INPUT "How many beeps do you want to hear"; Answer
FOR I = 1 TO Answer
   BEEP
   SLEEP 2
NEXT
END
```

The BEEP command is often used as a warning message to the user, such as when the user presses the wrong key.

In the preceding program, the SLEEP command causes the program to pause for two seconds between beeps. The SLEEP command looks like this:

```
SLEEP X
```

In this example, X represents the number of seconds that you want the computer to wait and do nothing.

You can use the SLEEP command with all of QBASIC's noise-making functions to provide silence between any computer-generated sounds that your program may make.

Playing sound frequencies

Because the BEEP command is simplistic and relatively limited, QBASIC also provides the SOUND command, which can create specific frequencies of sound for short periods of time. The SOUND command looks like this:

```
SOUND frequency, duration
```

In this example, frequency is a value (in hertz) ranging from 37 to 32,767 and duration is the number of system clock ticks for which you want the sound to last. The duration can range from 0 to 65,535 clock ticks; 18.2 clock ticks equal one second.

If you want to create specific musical notes, take a look at Table 12-3, which shows the specific frequencies of different notes.

Table 12-3	Frequencies of Musical Notes		
Musical Note	*Frequency*	*Musical Note*	*Frequency*
C	261.63	F#	369.99
C#	277.18	G	392.00
D	293.66	G#	415.30
D#	311.13	A	440.00
E	329.63	A#	466.16
F	349.23	B	493.88

If you wanted to play a G note for eight seconds, you would use the SOUND command like this:

```
SOUND 392.00, (8 * 18.2)
```

To define how many seconds you want the SOUND command to play, multiply the duration value by 18.2. (18.2 clock ticks equals one second, so 18.2 clock ticks multiplied by 8 equals eight seconds.)

Playing music with the PLAY command

The PLAY command is a more flexible command for making noise. To use the PLAY command, give it a string like this:

```
PLAY musicstring$
```

The string musicstring$ contains one or more of the commands shown in Tables 12-4, 12-5, 12-6, and 12-7.

Table 12-4   Octave and Tone Commands for the PLAY Command

String Command	What It Does
O	Sets the current octave (0 – 6)
< or >	Moves up or down one octave
A - G	Plays the specified note in the current octave
N	Plays a specific note (0 – 84) in the seven-octave range (where 0 is a rest)

Table 12-5 Duration and Tempo Commands for the PLAY Command

String Command	What It Does
L	Sets the length of each note (1 – 64) where L1 is a whole note, L2 is a half note, and so on
ML	Sets music legato
MN	Sets music normal
MS	Sets music staccato
P	Specifies a pause (1 – 64) where P1 is a whole note pause, P2 is a half note pause, and so on.
T	Sets the tempo in quarter notes per minute (32 – 255)

Table 12-6	Mode Commands for the PLAY Command
String Command	**What It Does**
MF	Plays music in the foreground
MB	Plays music in the background

When you tell QBASIC to play music in the foreground, your program waits until the music is done playing before it continues running the rest of the instructions in your program. When you tell QBASIC to play music in the background, the computer plays the music and runs the rest of the program instructions at the same time.

Table 12-7	Suffix Commands for the PLAY Command
String Command	**What It Does**
# or +	Turns the preceding note into a sharp
−	Turns the preceding note into a flat
. (period)	Plays the preceding note 3/2 as long as specified

To see how you can use strings to define the way QBASIC plays music, try running the following program, which plays the beginning of the song "Deck the Halls."

```
CLS
PLAY "L4 C"
PLAY "L8 B"
PLAY "L4 AGFGAF"
END
```

The following list shows you how the preceding program works:

1. The first line clears the screen.

2. The second line plays a quarter C note.

3. The third line plays an eighth B note.

4. The fourth line plays quarter notes of A, G, F, G, A, and F in rapid succession.

5. The fifth line ends the program.

Chapter 13

Saving and Retrieving Stuff in Files

· ·

In This Chapter

▶ Storing text

▶ Using random access files

▶ Using directories

· ·

*E*very program needs to accept data from an outside source (such as from a person banging away on the keyboard) and then spit it back out again in some useful format (such as in a neatly printed report). To store data temporarily, programs use variables, which store data in the computer's memory. As soon as the program ends, the computer wipes out the data in memory to make room for another program.

But what if you want to store data on a more permanent basis? For example, many computer games save the highest score to give future players a goal to beat. When a program stores data on a hard (or floppy) disk, the program saves the data in a file separate from the program file.

Storing Stuff in Text Files

The simplest data that a program can save is text, which consists of nothing more exciting than letters, numbers, and symbols from the keyboard (such as #, ~, <, or &). Any file that contains only text is called a *text file*. If you want to store, write, or retrieve data from a text file, you always have to start reading the text file from the beginning. As a result, text files are sometimes called *sequential files*.

Because text files contain only letters, numbers, and symbols, text files can be shared between different computers, such as a Macintosh and any computer running Windows 95/98/NT/2000. If you use the Save As command in your favorite word processor, you'll find an option to save your document as a text file. Just remember that saving a word-processing document as a text file loses all the document's formatting, such as underlining or fonts.

Creating a new text file

Before you can store any data in a text file, you (obviously) have to create that text file first. To create a text file, you use the following QBASIC command:

```
OPEN "Filename" FOR OUTPUT AS #Filenumber
```

1. The OPEN command tells the computer, "Create a new text file, and give it the name specified by "Filename", which can represent a filename (such as STUFF.TXT) or a drive, directory, and filename (such as C:\WINDOWS\STUFF .TXT)."

2. The FOR OUTPUT command tells the computer, "Get ready to start outputting data into the newly created text file identified by "Filename"."

3. The #Filenumber can be any number between 1 and 255. Even though you just defined a name for your text file, QBASIC makes you identify the file by a number as well.

If you want to create a file called STUFF.TXT and save it on your floppy disk (the A: drive), you use the following command:

```
OPEN "A:\STUFF.TXT" FOR OUTPUT AS #1
```

This tells QBASIC to create a text file called STUFF.TXT on the A: drive and assign it file number 1.

Any time you use the OPEN command to create a new text file or to open an existing text file, you must eventually use the CLOSE command to shut the text file. If you don't use the CLOSE command eventually, your program may cause the computer to crash.

Putting stuff in a text file

After you've created a text file, you can use the PRINT command to stuff data into that text file. When you use the PRINT command, QBASIC normally displays that data on the screen, so you have to tell QBASIC to store the data in your text file instead by using the file number of the text file, as in the following command:

```
PRINT #3, "This line gets stored in the text file."
```

This command tells QBASIC, "Look for a text file identified by the number 3, and stuff that text file with the line, "This line gets stored in the text file."."

Putting it all together, you have a program like this:

```
CLS
OPEN "A:\STUFF.TXT" FOR OUTPUT AS #3
PRINT #3, "This line gets stored in the text file."
CLOSE #3
END
```

This QBASIC program tells the computer to do the following:

1. The first line clears the screen.

2. The second line tells the computer, "Open a text file on the A: drive, and call this text file STUFF.TXT. Then give it the file number 3."

3. The third line tells the computer, "Look for a file identified as number 3, and stuff it with the line, `"This line gets stored in the text file."`."

4. The fourth line tells the computer, "Close the text file identified as number 3."

5. The fifth line tells the computer that this is the end of the program.

To see whether this program really stored the line `"This line gets stored in the text file"` inside a text file called STUFF.TXT, run the Windows Explorer program from within Windows 95/98/NT/2000 and double-click on the STUFF.TXT file to see its contents. If you're using MS-DOS, you can type the command **TYPE A:\STUFF.TXT** and then press Enter to see the contents of the STUFF.TXT file.

Adding new stuff to an existing text file

When you use the OPEN command, QBASIC knows that you are ready to store data.

```
OPEN "A:\STUFF.TXT" FOR OUTPUT AS #1
```

This line of code tells QBASIC, "Make a new text file called STUFF.TXT on the A: drive, and get ready to store data in it."

But what happens if the STUFF.TXT file already exists? Then the OPEN command tells QBASIC, "Wipe out any data currently stored in the STUFF.TXT text file, and get ready to store new data in it."

If you want to save any data currently stored in a text file, but you still want to add new data to the text file, use the APPEND command:

```
OPEN "A:\STUFF.TXT" FOR APPEND AS #1
```

If you've already run the previous QBASIC program that created a file called STUFF.TXT, try running this program to see how you can add new data to a text file without wiping out any existing data:

```
CLS
OPEN "A:\STUFF.TXT" FOR OUTPUT AS #1
PRINT #1, "This line gets stored in the text file."
CLOSE #1
OPEN "A:\STUFF.TXT" FOR APPEND AS #1
PRINT #1, "New data gets appended to existing data."
CLOSE #1
END
```

Retrieving data from a text file

Of course, storing data inside a text file is nice just as long as you need to use that data again. Fortunately, QBASIC includes a command to retrieve any data stored in a text file. That way, you can display it on the screen again.

To retrieve data from a text file, you use the INPUT command with the OPEN command, like this:

```
OPEN "A:\STUFF.TXT" FOR INPUT AS #21
```

Then you use the LINE INPUT command to read each line stored in the text file:

```
LINE INPUT #Filenumber, Variable$
```

In this example, #Filenumber represents the file number previously used with the OPEN command, and Variable$ is the name of a string variable that temporarily stores the line retrieved from the text file.

If all this sounds too complicated, just run the following program to see how this works:

```
CLS
OPEN "A:\STUFF.TXT" FOR OUTPUT AS #1
INPUT "What is your name"; Name$
PRINT #1, Name$
CLOSE #1
OPEN "A:\STUFF.TXT" FOR INPUT AS #2
LINE INPUT #2, YourName$
PRINT "This is the name you stored in the text file = ";
          YourName$
CLOSE #2
END
```

The LINE INPUT command retrieves only one line at a time, starting from the first line stored in the text file. Because text files usually have two or more lines of data, you use a loop and a special EOF (which stands for End Of File) command to retrieve every line stored inside a text file.

To see how this works, try running the following program, which stuffs three lines of text in a text file and then retrieves it:

```
CLS
OPEN "A:\STUFF.TXT" FOR OUTPUT AS #1
PRINT #1, "Isn't this exciting?"
PRINT #1, "Another line bites the dust."
PRINT #1, "The last line in the text file."
CLOSE #1
OPEN "A:\STUFF.TXT" FOR INPUT AS #2
I% = 1
DO WHILE NOT EOF(2)
   LINE INPUT #2, OneLine$
   PRINT "Line #" + STR$(I%) + ": " + OneLine$
   I% = I% + 1
LOOP
CLOSE #2
END
```

The DO WHILE LOOP loop may look a bit strange to you. Take a closer look to see how it works:

```
OPEN "A:\STUFF.TXT" FOR INPUT AS #2
I% = 1
DO WHILE NOT EOF(2)
   LINE INPUT #2, OneLine$
   PRINT "Line #" + STR$(I%) + ": " + OneLine$
   I% = I% + 1
LOOP
CLOSE #2
```

1. The first line of the preceding code tells the computer, "Open up a text file called STUFF.TXT, assign it a file number of 2, and get ready to read data from it."

2. The second line tells the computer, "Create a variable called I% (the percentage sign defines it as an integer data type), and set its value to 1."

3. The third line tells the computer, "This is the start of a DO WHILE LOOP," which tells the computer to keep looping until it reaches the end of the file (EOF) for file number 2 (which is the STUFF.TXT file identified as file number 2 in the first line).

4. The fourth line tells the computer, "Read a line from a file identified as file number 2, and store this line in a variable called OneLine$." After the LINE INPUT command, the computer automatically jumps to the next line in the text file.

5. The fifth line tells the computer, "Print the line stored in the `OneLine$` variable." To make the printed output look nice, this fifth line prints the text `"Line #: "` followed by the value of `I%` and the text stored in the `OneLine$` variable.

6. The sixth line tells the computer, "Take the value stored in the variable called `I%` and add 1 to it."

7. The seventh line tells the computer, "This is the end of the `DO WHILE LOOP`."

8. The eighth line tells the computer, "Close file number 2."

Storing Stuff in Random Access Files

Text files are handy for storing and retrieving one line of text at a time, but you may not want to store just text. Sometimes you may want to store discrete chunks of information such as a person's name, address, and phone number. Although you could store this type of information in a text file, QBASIC gives you the option of storing organized chunks of data in something called a *random access file* instead.

The main advantage of a random access file is that it can store data more efficiently (and thus create a smaller file than a text file). A second advantage is that a random access file can retrieve data from the middle of a file without having to read the entire file from start to finish, like a text file requires.

Creating a new random access file

Before you can create a random access file, you need to define something called a *record*. (Chapter 16 explains more about records and how they work.) Essentially a record consists of one or more chunks of related data, such as a person's name, address, employee ID, and phone number.

To create a record, you have to define one or more variables and their data types. The following BASIC code defines a single record that consists of variables for `DroneName`, `EmployeeID`, and `Phone`:

```
TYPE Drones
  DroneName AS STRING * 10
  EmployeeID AS INTEGER
  Phone AS STRING * 13
END TYPE
```

When defining a variable as a string data type in a record that you want to store in a random access file, you must specify a fixed length for all string variables.

After you've defined a record, the second step is to create a variable to represent that record:

```
DIM Employees AS Drones
```

After you have defined a record type and assigned a variable to represent that record type, you can create a random access file by using the following QBASIC command:

```
OPEN "Filename" FOR RANDOM AS #Filenumber LEN = LEN(Record)
```

1. The OPEN command tells the computer, "Create a new random access file and give it the name specified by "Filename", which can represent a filename (such as TRASH.DAT) or a drive, directory, and filename (such as C:\WINDOWS\TRASH.DAT)."

2. The FOR RANDOM command tells the computer, "Get ready to start shoving data into the newly created random access file identified by "Filename"."

3. The #Filenumber can be any number between 1 and 255. Even though you just defined a name for your random access file, QBASIC needs to identify the file by a number as well.

4. The LEN = LEN (Record) command tells the computer, "Calculate the length of each record." (When the computer knows the exact length of each record, it knows how many records to skip over when trying to retrieve a record from the middle of a random access file.)

To create a file called TRASH.DAT that stores data saved in the Drones record type, you use the following command:

```
OPEN "A:\TRASH.DAT" FOR RANDOM AS #1 LEN = LEN(Employees)
```

This command tells the computer to create a random access file called TRASH.DAT on the A: drive, assign it file number 1, and use the length of a variable named Employees, which represents a record data type called Drones.

When you use the OPEN command to create a new random access file or open an existing random access file, you have to eventually use the CLOSE command to shut the text file. If you don't use the CLOSE command after using an OPEN command, your program may cause the computer to crash.

Saving data into a random access file

After you've gone through the three-step hassle of defining a record type, creating a variable to represent that record type, and then (finally) creating a random access file, the next step is knowing how to stuff data into that random access file.

To put something inside a random access file, use this command:

```
PUT #Filenumber, Recordnumber, Variable
```

In this example, #Filenumber represents the number assigned to the random access file with the OPEN command, Recordnumber is the order in which you want to store the data in the random access file (record number 1 is the first chunk of data in the file, record number 2 is the second, and so on), and Variable is the actual data that you want to stuff into the random access file.

The data that you can store into a random access file must represent a record data type.

Putting it all together, you have a program like this:

```
CLS
TYPE Drones
   DroneName AS STRING * 10
   EmployeeID AS INTEGER
   Phone AS STRING * 14
END TYPE

DIM Employees AS Drones

Employees.DroneName = "Bob Smith"
Employees.EmployeeID = 4
Employees.Phone = "555-1234"

OPEN "A:\TRASH.DAT" FOR RANDOM AS #1 LEN = LEN(Employees)
PUT #1, 1, Employees
CLOSE #1
END
```

This QBASIC program tells the computer to do the following:

1. The first line clears the screen.

2. The second line tells the computer, "Create a record data type called Drones."

3. The third line tells the computer, "As part of the Drones record data type, create DroneName, which is a string variable that can hold up to 10 characters."

4. The fourth line tells the computer, "As part of the Drones record data type, create EmployeeID, which is an integer variable."

5. The fifth line tells the computer, "As part of the Drones record data type, create Phone, which is a string variable that can hold up to 14 characters."

6. The sixth line tells the computer, "This is the end of the definition for the Drones record."

7. The seventh line tells the computer, "Create a variable named Employees, which represents the Drones record data type."

8. The eighth line tells the computer, "Store the name "Bob Smith" in the Employees variable. Because the Employees variable represents three additional variables (DroneName, EmployeeID, and Phone), this line says to store the "Bob Smith" string in the DroneName variable."

9. The ninth line tells the computer, "Store the number 4 in the EmployeeID variable of the Employees record variable."

10. The tenth line tells the computer, "Store the string "555-1234" in the Phone variable of the Employees record variable."

11. The eleventh line tells the computer, "Open a random access file called TRASH.DAT on the A: drive, identify it as file number 1, and get ready to store records of a fixed length as defined by the Employees record variable."

12. The twelfth line tells the computer, "Look for file number 1, and store the data from the Employees record variable into the position of record number 1 in the random access file."

13. The thirteenth line tells the computer, "Close file number 1."

14. The fourteenth line tells the computer, "This is the end of the program."

If you run this program, nothing will appear on the screen. To see whether this program really did store any data into the random access file called TRASH.DAT, you need to eventually retrieve the data from the random access file, which you'll find out how to do in the following section.

Retrieving data from a random access file

After storing data in a random access file, you can yank it back out again using the following command:

```
GET #Filenumber, Recordnumber, Variable
```

In this command, #Filenumber represents the file number previously used with the OPEN command, Recordnumber represents the record that you want to retrieve (which can be 1 to retrieve the first record in the random access file, 2 to retrieve the second record, and so on), and Variable represents a record data type identical to the record data type originally stored in the random access file.

If you try to retrieve data from a random access file using a variable that represents a different record, the GET command won't work.

The previous statements will make sense after you run the following program and see for yourself how to yank out data stored in a random access file. Add commands near the bottom of the previous QBASIC program as follows:

```
CLS
TYPE Drones
   DroneName AS STRING * 10
   EmployeeID AS INTEGER
   Phone AS STRING * 14
END TYPE

DIM Employees AS Drones

Employees.DroneName = "Bob Smith"
Employees.EmployeeID = -4
Employees.Phone = "555-1234"

OPEN "A:\TRASH.DAT" FOR RANDOM AS #1 LEN = LEN(Employees)
PUT #1, 1, Employees

DIM Losers AS Drones
GET #1, 1, Losers
PRINT "Loser Name = " + Losers.DroneName
PRINT "Loser ID = "; Losers.EmployeeID
PRINT "Loser Phone = " + Losers.Phone
CLOSE #1
END
```

If you want to delete a record stored in a random access file, you have to store new information in the record's location. For example, if you want to delete record number 3, you store new information in record number 3's position using the PUT command:

```
PUT #1, 3, NewData
```

Making and Deleting Directories

Every time a program saves data to a disk, it stores that file in a directory. All disks have at least one directory called the *root directory*. If your hard disk is called the C: drive, the root directory of that hard drive is called C:\. If you're using Windows, chances are good that you have a directory on your hard disk called C:\WINDOWS. Figure 13-1 shows a typical hard drive divided into multiple directories.

The word "directories" means the same thing as the Windows term "folders." For some odd reason when people used the ancient MS-DOS operating system, they divided disks into directories. Nowadays with Windows 95/98/NT/2000, people divide disks into directories but Windows calls them folders in an attempt to make computers seem easier to understand.

Making a directory

Many programs save data in a file and store that file in an existing directory. However, you may need to create a new directory so that your program can store its data safely in a location where it won't risk messing up any existing files. To create a new directory, use this command:

```
MKDIR Directoryname
```

Directoryname is the actual drive and directory you want to create. For example, if you want to create a new directory on the A: drive and call it TEMP, you use this command:

```
MKDIR "A:\TEMP"
```

Changing to an existing directory

Whenever you create a text or random access file using the OPEN command, you should always specify the drive and directory in which to store the file. If you don't specify a drive (such as the C: drive), QBASIC simply uses the default directory, which is the directory in which the QBASIC program is stored. If you're using Windows 95/98/NT/2000, that default directory will probably be C:\WINDOWS\COMMAND.

To define a new default directory, you tell QBASIC to switch to another directory. To do this, you can use the following command:

```
CHDIR Directoryname
```

Directories

Subdirectories

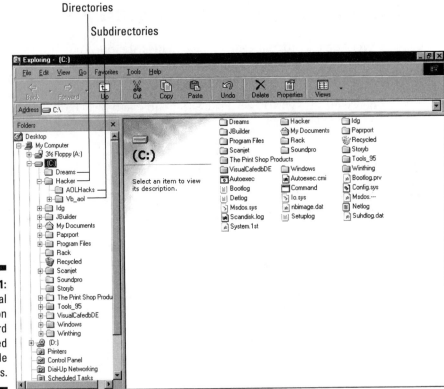

Figure 13-1:
The typical
organization
of a hard
disk divided
into multiple
directories.

In this command, Directoryname is the actual drive and directory that you want to define as the new default directory. For example, if you want to define a new default directory on drive A: called TEMP, you use this command:

```
CHDIR "A:\TEMP"
```

The CHDIR command can switch only to an existing directory. If you give it the name of a directory that doesn't exist, the CHDIR command will get confused and fail.

Deleting a directory

If you have a directory that you don't want anymore, you can delete it.

Before you can delete a directory, you must delete all files and subdirectories stored inside the directory that you want to delete.

To delete a directory, you use this command:

```
RMDIR Directoryname
```

In this command, Directoryname is the actual name of the drive and directory that you want to delete. For example, if you want to delete a directory on drive A: called KITTY, you use this command:

```
RMDIR "A:\KITTY"
```

Deleting a file

Because you can delete a directory only after you delete all files from it, QBASIC offers a special command to delete individual files as well.

Deleting the wrong files on your hard disk can really mess up your computer, so use this command sparingly:

```
KILL Filename
```

In this command, Filename defines the drive, directory, and file that you want to delete. For example, if you want to delete a file called RAMFILE.BAS stored on drive A: in the TEMP directory, you use this command:

```
KILL "A:\TEMP\RAMFILE.BAS"
```

You can use wildcards with the KILL command. Wildcards are the characters ? and *. For example, to wipe out all files in the A:\ directory, you could use this command:

```
KILL "A:\*.*"
```

To wipe out all files that end in the .EXE file extension on the A: drive, you could use this command:

```
KILL "A:\*.EXE"
```

Chapter 14

Debugging Your QBASIC Programs

- -

In This Chapter

▶ Understanding computer bugs

▶ Checking your program line by line

▶ Setting breakpoints in your program

▶ Trapping errors

- -

*N*obody writes programs that work 100 percent correctly all the time. The problem is that programming means giving the computer extremely detailed instructions. Insert one wrong instruction or one misplaced instruction or omit one necessary instruction, and the computer has no idea what to do next, which can cause your program to fail or, in programming lingo, to *crash*.

If a program doesn't work correctly, programmers never say, "My program has a problem." Instead, programmers use their own lingo and say, "My program has a *bug*." Most people find bugs distasteful, so the idea of a bug infesting your program creates a more visually appealing image than simply saying, "My program has a problem."

No matter how large or small your programs may be, you always need to look for bugs that may keep your program from working correctly. Although eliminating all bugs from a program is impossible, QBASIC (and many other language compilers) provides special features to help you track down the obvious bugs and wipe them out so that your program works well enough for people to actually use.

The process of looking for bugs in a program is called *debugging*.

Anatomy of a Computer Bug

Computer bugs tend to fall into three categories:

- **Syntax errors:** This type of error occurs when you spell something wrong, such as a variable or BASIC command (for example, misspelling PRINT as PRRINT).

- **Run-time errors:** These occur when your program runs into something unexpected, such as when you ask the user to input an age and the user types a negative number.

- **Logic errors:** These bugs occur when your instructions don't work as you expected but the computer performs these flawed instructions anyway, creating unpredictable results.

Even though every program is riddled with bugs, most bugs are relatively harmless or cause only minor problems, such as displaying a pull-down menu incorrectly at unpredictable times. The bugs that keep a program from working at all are more serious. Any bug that keeps a company from shipping (and selling) a program is called a *showstopper*.

Dealing with Syntax Errors

If you misspell a BASIC command such as PRINT or CLS, QBASIC is usually smart enough to find the misspelling. QBASIC highlights the command and displays a dialog box, as shown in Figure 14-1.

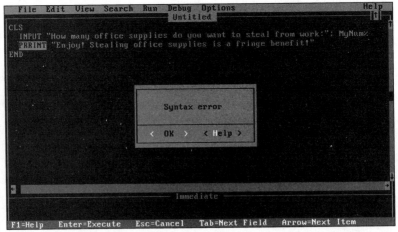

Figure 14-1:
If you run a program with a misspelled BASIC command, QBASIC highlights the error.

More troublesome are times when you misspell a variable name. For example, consider the following program:

```
CLS
INPUT "How many times do I have to tell you no"; Answeer$
PRINT Your reply = "; Answer$
END
```

The preceding program asks the user, "How many times do I have to tell you no?" Then the program stores whatever the user typed into a variable called `Answeer$` (the misspelling of `Answer$`). Because QBASIC considers `Answer$` and `Answeer$` to be two completely different variable names, the `Answer$` variable does not contain any data. If you run this program, it doesn't print out what the user typed in, simply because of a single misspelling.

Because a single misspelling of a variable name can mess up your program, many programmers take shortcuts and choose short, cryptic variable names. Don't do this! The time that you save in using short variable names is lost in comparison to the time you need to decipher what those short variable names represent.

Syntax errors can be hard to detect because a misspelling can still enable the program to run, albeit incorrectly. Anytime your program runs but doesn't seem to work right, start looking for misspellings or missing things such as quotation marks, commas, and parentheses that may be causing the program to fail.

Stopping Run-Time Errors

Run-time errors are sneaky little bugs that hide in programs. A program may work correctly right up until it receives data that the programmer never expected, such as a negative number that the user typed for his year of birth. Unfortunately, the only time that you can find run-time errors is when they cause the program to crash.

That's why software companies always test their programs with the general public by releasing beta copies of the program. A beta copy is a version of the program that the company hopes to sell soon, but the company wants special people (called *beta-testers*) to play with the program and see whether they can find bugs that the company's own internal testers may have missed.

Because run-time errors occur only when your program receives data that it doesn't know how to handle, the best way to hunt down run-time errors is to run your program over and over, feeding the program extreme values of different data each time.

For example, if your program asks the user to input an age, type a huge number (such as 60,000). Then type zero. Finally, type a negative number such as –9,489. By testing extreme ranges of values, you can often smoke out run-time errors before you release your program for actual use.

Error Trapping

You probably can't eliminate every single bug from your program (but that doesn't mean that you shouldn't try). Bugs can often keep your program from working, so consider using QBASIC's special error-trapping commands.

Error trapping tells QBASIC, "Any time a problem arises, follow these special instructions to avoid causing the entire program to crash." (Of course, you still need to write these special error-handling instructions.)

Error trapping can trap only run-time errors. It can't help find logic errors.

To use error trapping, QBASIC offers several commands:

- ✔ ON ERROR GOTO: This command tells QBASIC where to look for special instructions to handle a run-time error.

- ✔ RESUME and RESUME NEXT: The RESUME command tells QBASIC to again run the instruction in the program that caused the run-time error. The RESUME NEXT command tells QBASIC to skip the instruction in the program that caused the error and go to the next instruction.

- ✔ ERR: This variable stores a numeric value that (if you know how to decipher it correctly) tells you exactly what causes the run-time error, such as dividing by zero. Table 14-1 lists all possible run-time errors along with their corresponding numeric values.

Table 14-1   Run-Time Errors That the ERR Function Can Detect

Value	Error	Value	Error
1	NEXT without FOR	37	Argument-count mismatch
2	Syntax error	38	Array not defined
3	RETURN without GOSUB	40	Variable required
4	Out of DATA	50	FIELD overflow
5	Illegal function call	51	Internal error
6	Overflow	52	Bad file name or number
7	Out of memory	53	File not found

Value	Error	Value	Error
8	Label not defined	54	Bad file mode
9	Subscript out of range	55	File already open
10	Duplicate definition	56	FIELD statement active
11	Division by zero	57	Device I/O error
12	Illegal in direct mode	58	File already exists
13	Type mismatch	59	Bad record length
14	Out of string space	61	Disk full
16	String formula too complex	62	Input past end of file
17	Cannot continue	63	Bad record number
18	Function not defined	64	Bad file name
19	No RESUME	67	Too many files
20	RESUME without error	68	Device unavailable
24	Device timeout	69	Communication-buffer overflow
25	Device fault	70	Permission denied
26	FOR without NEXT	71	Disk not ready
27	Out of paper	72	Disk-media error
29	WHILE without WEND	73	Feature unavailable
30	WEND without WHILE	74	Rename across disks
33	Duplicate label	75	Path/File access error
35	Subprogram not defined	76	Path not found

The ON ERROR GOTO command tells the computer to jump to a special part of your program to handle errors. For example, the following shows a typical program that uses error trapping:

```
ON ERROR GOTO HandleMe
CLS
'Instructions for main program
END
```

```
HandleMe:
'Instructions for handling errors
RESUME 'or RESUME NEXT
```

This QBASIC program tells the computer to do the following:

1. The first line tells the computer, "Any time that you find a run-time error, immediately jump to the part of the program that begins with the word HandleMe." (This word can be any word that you make up; it doesn't need to be called HandleMe.)

2. The second line clears the screen.

3. The third line contains one or more instructions that make your program do something useful.

4. The fourth line tells the computer, "This is the end of the program."

5. The fifth line tells the computer, "This is the start of the special instructions to deal with run-time errors."

6. The sixth line tells the computer, "These are the special instructions that run only when a run-time error occurs."

7. The seventh line tells the computer, "After running the special error-handling instructions, go back to the original program where the run-time error occurred and either run the line that caused the error (RESUME) or run the line following the line that caused the error (RESUME NEXT)."

If you want to see a real-life example, try the following program:

```
ON ERROR GOTO ErrorCode
CLS
  CHDIR "X:\TEMP"
  PRINT "This is the end of the program."
END

ErrorCode:
  PRINT "Error number = "; ERR
RESUME NEXT
```

This is how the computer runs the program:

1. The first line tells the computer, "Any time that you find a run-time error, immediately jump to the part of the program that begins with the word ErrorCode."

2. The second line clears the screen.

3. The third line tells the computer, "Change directories to the X: drive and the X:\TEMP directory." Because your computer probably doesn't have an X: drive, this immediately causes a run-time error, which forces the computer to jump to the sixth line containing the ErrorCode: label.

The bug in Apollo 11

Before the United States launched Apollo 11 to land on the moon, the programmers made a surprising discovery. The lunar module's program contained a slight error, which could have been catastrophic to the crew. Instead of assuming that the moon's gravity would pull the lunar module to its surface, the program had been mistakenly written to assume that gravity would *push* the lunar module *away* from the moon's surface. Fortunately, the programmers fixed this crucial error before launch time, and the lunar module landed just fine on the surface of the moon.

4. The computer jumps to the `ErrorCode:` label, which is on the sixth line.

5. Now the computer runs the seventh line, which prints the message `"Error number = "` followed by the value of `ERR`. In this case, the value of `ERR` is 76, which tells you that the computer could not find the path of X:\TEMP.

6. The eighth line tells the computer to `RESUME NEXT`, which means "Go back to the original line that caused the run-time error, and run the next instruction."

7. The computer jumps to the fourth line and prints, "This is the end of the program."

8. The computer jumps to the fifth line, which ends the program.

Fun with Logic Errors

Of all the types of bugs that can infest your program, none is more insidious than a logic error. Syntax errors can be fairly easy to find, because you just need to look for misspellings or places where you forgot to type a character, such as a closing parenthesis. Similarly, you can often find run-time errors by testing your program by using extreme values of data.

However, logic errors occur when you've written instructions perfectly — except that they're the wrong instructions. Because you assume that the instructions you've written are correct, you need to examine them line by line to see whether your instructions are missing a step or simply solving the wrong problem altogether.

Because logic errors can be so difficult to find, you must examine your program line by line to see how the computer interprets each line. This can be tedious, so QBASIC provides special debugging features to help make this task a little easier.

The two main ways to examine a program for logic errors are by using *stepping* and *breakpoints*.

Stepping line by line

Stepping involves running through your program line by line and watching to see how your program works. The moment that you spot the program doing something wrong, you know exactly which line in your program is making the mistake.

QBASIC provides several keys to press so that you can step through your program line by line:

- **F8:** Each time you press F8, QBASIC highlights the next line to run in your program.

- **F4:** When you press F4, QBASIC shows what your program has displayed on-screen. If you press F8 to run a line in your program, you can then press F4 to see how that line may have affected any data the program prints on-screen. Press F4 again to return to the QBASIC editor.

- **F10:** Pressing F10 causes QBASIC to highlight the next line to run in your program. The difference between the F8 key and the F10 key is that pressing F10 causes QBASIC to skip any lines of code stored inside a *subprogram*. (A subprogram is a procedure or a function.)

Press the F8 key if you need to examine your entire program, line by line. If you know that your BASIC code inside a procedure or function already works, press the F10 key whenever you reach a line in your program that calls a procedure or function.

Using breakpoints

Stepping through an entire program line by line can be tedious and time-consuming, especially if you already have an idea of which part of your program may be hiding a bug. Instead of stepping through your whole program, line by line from the beginning, you can use breakpoints.

A breakpoint tells QBASIC, "Run the entire program until you reach a certain line in the program (designated as a breakpoint). Then stop and wait for further instructions."

If you're trying to debug a large program, you can set a breakpoint in the middle of the program. When you press the F8 key or F10 key to step through your program line by line, you can start from the breakpoint, not from the very beginning.

To set and use a breakpoint in your program, follow these steps:

1. **Move the cursor to the line in your program where you want to start stepping through your program line by line.**

2. **Press F9.**

   QBASIC highlights the entire line so that you know it's a breakpoint, as shown in Figure 14-2.

3. **Press Shift+F5.**

   QBASIC runs your entire program and then stops at the breakpoint you chose in Step 2.

4. **Press F8 or F10 to step through the rest of your program line by line.**

You can set as many breakpoints in a program as you want. To skip from one breakpoint to another, just press F5.

If you want to remove a breakpoint, move the cursor to the breakpoint and press F9. QBASIC removes the highlighting of the entire line.

Figure 14-2:
QBASIC
displays a
breakpoint
by
highlighting
the entire
line.

```
 File  Edit  View  Search  Run  Debug  Options                       Help
                           SHELSORT.BAS
   MyArray(I) = INT(RND * 100) + 1
   PRINT MyArray(I);
 NEXT I
 PRINT "(Initial array)"

 X = MaxSize \ 2
 DO WHILE X >,0
   Limit = MaxSize - X
   DO
     Switch = 0
     FOR K = 0 TO Limit
       IF MyArray(K) > MyArray(K + X) THEN
         SWAP MyArray(K), MyArray(K + X)
       END IF
       Switch = K
     NEXT K
     Limit = Switch - X
   LOOP WHILE Switch <> 0

                           Immediate

 <Shift+F1=Help> <F6=Window> <FZ=Subs> <F5=Run> <F8=Step>      N 00020:001
```

Part IV
Dealing with Data Structures

The 5th Wave   By Rich Tennant

WITH OBJECT-ORIENTED PROGRAMMING, I UNDERSTAND THE "ENCAPSULATION" AND "INHERITANCE" PART PRETTY WELL. IT'S THAT DARN "CLUTTERMORPHISM" THAT STUMPS ME.

In this part . . .

*W*hen you write a program, your program needs to store data in the computer's memory. Of course, your program can't just toss data anywhere in the computer's memory; if it did that, the memory would become as disorganized as a closet where you randomly throw clothes onto a heap.

To help organize the computer's memory, programs store data in something called a data structure. A data structure is nothing more than a way to organize data so that you can easily store and retrieve information. The simplest data structure is a simple variable that holds one chunk of information. More complicated data structure are arrays, records, linked lists, and objects. You get to know all of them in this part of the book.

Chapter 15

Storing Stuff in Arrays

· ·

In This Chapter

▶ Making an array

▶ Storing data in an array

▶ Making a multidimensional array

▶ Creating dynamic arrays

· ·

*W*hen you want to store data temporarily, you have to use a variable with a descriptive name such as PhoneNumber, MovieRating, or FirstName. After you create a variable name to hold data, you should also define what type of data the variable can hold, such as a string, integer, or single-precision number.

But sometimes you may want to store a list of nearly identical data. For example, if you write a program to store the names of all the people in your class, you may have to create a series of nearly identically named variables just to hold their names:

```
Name1$ = "Patrick DeGuire"
Name2$ = "Dat Phan"
Name3$ = "Mike Elizondo"
Name4$ = "Mark Wiberg"
```

Naturally, this is clumsy, and any time programmers run into a problem that threatens to make programming harder than it needs to be, they come up with a solution to avoid the problem. In this case, the solution that programmers have developed is called an *array*. Think of an array as a list like the one in Figure 15-1.

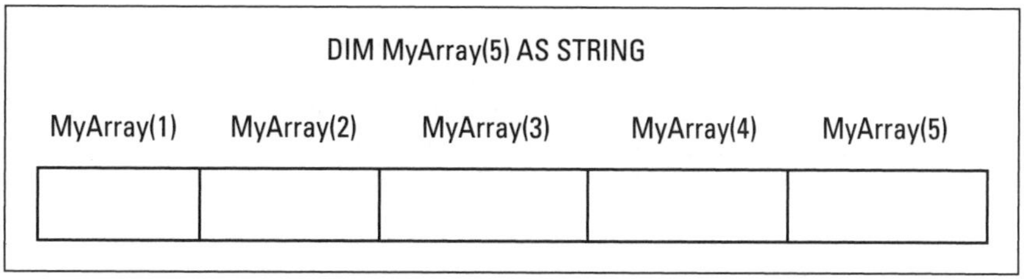

Figure 15-1:
An array stores items identified by array name and position number.

DIM MyArray(5) AS STRING				
MyArray(1)	MyArray(2)	MyArray(3)	MyArray(4)	MyArray(5)

Making an Array

An ordinary variable can hold only one chunk of data at a time, such as a number or a name. The moment you try to store another chunk of data in a variable, the variable immediately erases the old data and saves the new data.

Unlike ordinary variables, an array is a single variable name that can hold one or more chunks of data, as long as each chunk of data represents the same data type, such as string, integer, single-precision, and so on. To make an array, you have to define it:

```
DIM ArrayName(Number) AS Type
```

In this example, `ArrayName` is any valid variable name, `Number` represents the total number of items that you want to store in the array, and `Type` defines the data type that will be stored in the array, such as integers, strings, and so on.

You can create two types of arrays: static and dynamic. *Static arrays* are a fixed size. *Dynamic arrays* can change size as the program runs.

If you want to store four names in an array, you can use the following:

```
DIM Classmates(4) AS STRING
```

This tells QBASIC to create an array called `Classmates` that can hold four strings.

An array consists of three parts:

- ✔ A name.
- ✔ A number that defines how many elements the array can hold. (A single element can hold one chunk of data.) This number is sometimes called the *array index*.
- ✔ A data type that defines the only type of data the array can hold, such as strings or integers.

You can define the size of an array using a single number, like this:

```
DIM CatArray(45) AS STRING
```

This creates an array that can hold 45 items, in locations starting with number 1, such as `CatArray(1)`, and ending with number 45, such as `CatArray(45)`. If you don't like the idea of starting the array with number 1, you can define your own starting number like this:

How C/C++ and Java define arrays

When you define the size of an array in languages such as QBASIC and Pascal, the array locations are numbered starting with 1. For example, an array is defined in QBASIC this way:

```
DIM AgeArray(3) AS INTEGER
```

In QBASIC, the AgeArray consists of three locations: AgeArray(1), AgeArray(2), and AgeArray(3).

But when you define the size of an array in C/C++ or Java, the array locations are numbered starting with 0. For example, consider an array as defined in C:

```
int agearray(3)
```

In C, this array consists of three locations: agearray(0), agearray(1), and agearray(2). If you eventually decide to learn C/C++ or Java, be aware of this subtle difference so

that your arrays in C/C++ or Java will work the way you expect.

If you want, you can use the following command in the beginning of your program to make QBASIC arrays work like C/C++ and Java arrays:

```
OPTION BASE 0
```

This command tells QBASIC, "Number all arrays starting with zero." You can combine these commands to create an array with numbers starting at zero:

```
OPTION BASE 0
DIM AgeArray(2) AS INTEGER
```

The first line tells QBASIC, "Start numbering all arrays with zero." The second line tells QBASIC, "Create an array called AgeArray that can store three integers in locations AgeArray(0), AgeArray(1), and AgeArray(2).

```
DIM ArrayName(Lower TO Upper) AS Datatype
```

This tells QBASIC to start the first array location with the number defined by Lower and end with the last array location with the number defined by Upper:

```
DIM WeaponArray(52 TO 75) AS INTEGER
```

This command creates an array called WeaponArray that can hold 14 integers starting with the first array location at WeaponArray(52), the second array location at WeaponArray(53), and continuing to the fourteenth array location at WeaponArray(75).

Unless you have a good reason for numbering your array locations with weird numbers, it's usually best to start with number 1 to make it easy to see exactly how many items a specific array can hold.

Storing (And Retrieving) Data in an Array

When you first create an array, it's completely empty. Because an array can hold multiple chunks of data, you need to specify the location in the array in which you want to store your data.

For example, suppose that you created an array to hold five different integers:

```
DIM IQArray(5) AS INTEGER
```

Then to stuff the number 93 into a variable, use a command like this:

```
MyVariable = 93
```

But because an array can hold multiple chunks of data, you have to specify the location in the array in which you want to store the data. If you want to store data in the first location in the array, use this command:

```
IQArray(1) = 93
```

If you try to store data in a location in the array that already contains data, QBASIC simply wipes out the old data and replaces it with the new data.

To retrieve data out of an array, you assign a variable of the proper data type to a specific array location, in this way:

```
YourIQ = IQArray(3)
```

If you had previously stored the number 93 in the third location of IQArray, the value of the YourIQ variable would be 93 as well.

Arrays can store multiple chunks of data, so programmers use loops to make storing and retrieving data from an array easy. Without a loop, you would have to specify the exact location in an array to store (or retrieve) data:

```
NameArray(1) = "Mike Ross"
NameArray(2) = "Bill McPherson"
NameArray(3) = "John Smith"
```

You can specify the array location using the loop counting variable:

```
FOR I% = 1 TO 3
   NumberArray(I%) = 125
NEXT I%
```

The FOR NEXT loop stores the number 125 in the first, second, and third location of NumberArray.

To see how to store and retrieve data in an array, try the following program:

```
CLS
DIM NameArray(2) AS STRING
FOR I% = 1 TO 3
  INPUT "Type the name of someone you hate:"; Enemy$
  NameArray(I%) = Enemy$
NEXT I%
PRINT
FOR I% = 1 TO 3
  PRINT NameArray(I%) + " sounds like the name of a moron."
NEXT I%
END
```

This is how the computer runs the program:

1. The first line clears the screen.

2. The second line creates an array called `NameArray` that can hold three different strings.

3. The third line starts a `FOR NEXT` loop that runs three times.

4. The fourth line tells the user, "Type the name of someone you hate." Whatever name the user types gets stored in the `Enemy$` string variable.

5. The fifth line tells the computer, "Store the value of the `Enemy$` string variable into the `NameArray`. The first time that this `FOR NEXT` loop runs, store the value of the `Enemy$` string variable in `NameArray(1)`. The second time, store the `Enemy$` string variable in `NameArray(2)`. The third time, store the `Enemy$` string variable in `NameArray(3)`."

6. The sixth line marks the end of the `FOR NEXT` loop.

7. The seventh line prints a blank line.

8. The eighth line starts a second `FOR NEXT` loop that runs three times.

9. The ninth line prints the value of `NameArray` plus the string `"sounds like the name of a moron."` The first time it prints the value stored in `NameArray(1)`, the second time it prints the value stored in `Name-Array(2)`, and the third time it prints the value stored in `NameArray(3)`.

10. The tenth line marks the end of the `FOR NEXT` loop.

11. The eleventh line tells the computer that this is the end of the program.

Making a Multidimensional Array

The simplest arrays are nothing more than a single list of items, as in this example:

```
DIM PetArray(5) AS STRING
```

This command creates an array that can hold five strings (refer to Figure 15-1). In programming lingo, any array that holds a single list of data is called a *one-dimensional array*. A one-dimensional array uses a single number to define its size:

```
DIM ArrayName(X) AS Datatype
```

QBASIC can also create two-dimensional arrays and three-dimensional arrays by defining two or three sizes. The code looks like this:

```
DIM ArrayName(X, Y) AS Datatype
```

This creates a two-dimensional array, as shown in Figure 15-2.

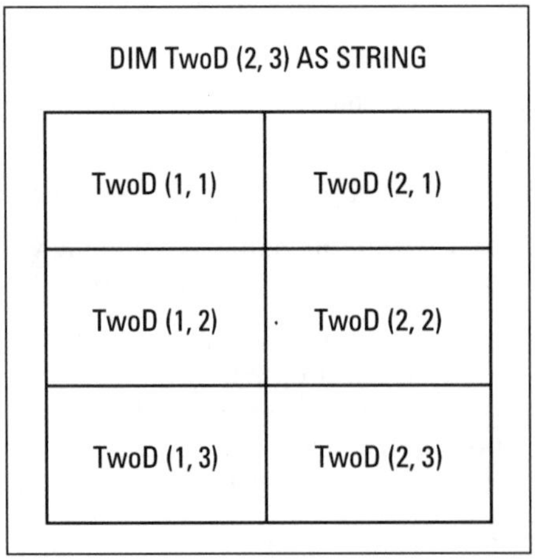

Figure 15-2:
A two-dimensional array uses two numbers to define its total size.

```
DIM TwoD (2, 3) AS STRING
```

TwoD (1, 1)	TwoD (2, 1)
TwoD (1, 2)	TwoD (2, 2)
TwoD (1, 3)	TwoD (2, 3)

Here's an example of a two-dimensional array:

```
DIM VictimArray(10, 9) AS STRING
```

This creates a two-dimensional array that can hold 90 (or 10 * 9) strings.

To create a three-dimensional array, you have to define three sizes, as in the following array. Figure 15-3 illustrates this array.

```
DIM ArrayName(X, Y, Z) AS Datatype
```

Storing and retrieving data with multidimensional arrays requires identifying the X, Y, and Z locations of the array in which you want to store your data. To see a two-dimensional array that can store up to six strings, try the following program:

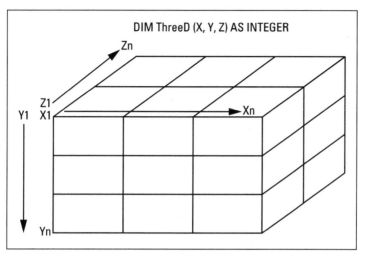

DIM ThreeD (X, Y, Z) AS INTEGER

```
CLS
DIM VictimArray(2, 3) AS STRING
FOR I% = 1 TO 2
  FOR J% = 1 TO 3
    INPUT "Who do you want to hurt"; Enemy$
    VictimArray(I%, J%) = Enemy$
  NEXT J%
NEXT I%
PRINT
  INPUT "Type X and Y locations of the array item that you
         want to print, such as 1, 3"; X%, Y%
PRINT VictimArray(X%, Y%) + " deserves to be hurt the most."
END
```

This program asks you to type six names. Suppose that you typed the following six names:

```
Mike Ross
Bill McPherson
Jon Markey
Bobby Lee
Tom Clark
Roger Smith
```

This is the order in which the program would store these names:

```
VictimArray (1, 1) = Mike Ross
VictimArray (1, 2) = Bill McPherson
VictimArray (1, 3) = Jon Markey
VictimArray (2, 1) = Bobby Lee
VictimArray (2, 2) = Tom Clark
VictimArray (2, 3) = Roger Smith
```

If the program said, "Type X and Y locations of the array item that you want to print, such as 1, 3" and you typed **2, 1**, the program would print:

```
"Bobby Lee deserves to be hurt the most."
```

Because storing and retrieving data in a multidimensional array can be confusing, consider using multidimensional arrays only when absolutely necessary.

Creating Dynamic Arrays

Normally, when you create an array, you create something called a *static array*. Static arrays are easy to use but pose two potential problems:

✔ After you've defined the array size, you can't change the array size later to make it smaller (if you made the array too big) or larger (if you made the array too small).

✔ A static array always requires a certain amount of memory, regardless of whether the array contains any data.

Despite these problems, static arrays are often suitable for most programs. However, if you want the ability to resize an array while your program is running or to completely erase all data in an array to free up memory, you may want to consider creating something called a *dynamic array*.

The main advantage of a dynamic array is that you can resize it or completely erase it (thus freeing up memory) while the program is running. The disadvantage is that you have to write specific commands to do this and the nuisance of writing these commands may make a static array easier to use.

Defining a dynamic array

To tell QBASIC that every array you define should be a dynamic array, put this command in your program:

```
REM $DYNAMIC
```

Or

```
' $DYNAMIC
```

This command tells the computer, "The next time you see a command to create an array, make it a dynamic array."

Normally, QBASIC treats anything that appears after the REM or ' (apostrophe) commands as a comment — and, thus, ignores it. The REM $DYNAMIC command is a special case where QBASIC does not ignore what appears after the REM command.

The only difference between creating a dynamic array and a static array is the REM $DYNAMIC command. If you want to create a dynamic array that can hold five strings, use the following two commands:

```
REM $DYNAMIC
DIM LoserArray(5) AS STRING
```

QBASIC lets you switch between creating a static array and a dynamic array by using the REM $DYNAMIC and the REM $STATIC commands.

Erasing an entire dynamic array

Before you can resize a dynamic array, you have to erase any data stored inside it. To erase a dynamic array, use the ERASE command:

```
ERASE ArrayName
```

When you erase an array, the array contains either null strings (if the data type of the array is STRING) or zeroes (if the data type of the array is INTEGER, SINGLE, LONG, or DOUBLE).

A *null string* is a special string that contains nothing. A null string is different from a space because a space represents a single character (and thus takes up space), while a null string does not represent a single character (and thus requires no space at all).

After you erase a dynamic array, you can resize it and then stuff it with data all over again.

Resizing a dynamic array

Only after you've erased a dynamic array can you change its size by using the REDIM command, like this:

```
REDIM ArrayName(Number) AS Datatype
```

Resizing a dynamic array allows you to change the size of the array, but not the data type. If your original array held strings, your newly resized array must also hold strings.

After you've resized a dynamic array, you can stuff new data into it. To see how dynamic arrays can work, try the following program:

```
REM $DYNAMIC
CLS
DIM LoserArray(3) AS STRING
FOR I% = 1 TO 3
  INPUT "Who is incompetent"; MyBoss$
  LoserArray(I%) = MyBoss$
NEXT I%
PRINT
ERASE LoserArray
REDIM LoserArray(7) AS STRING
LoserArray(7) = "Bobby Lee"
PRINT LoserArray(7) + " is a pathetic character."
END
```

This is how the computer runs the program:

1. The first line tells QBASIC, "Every time you see a command creating an array, make it a dynamic array."

2. The second line clears the screen.

3. The third line creates an array called `LoserArray` that can hold three different strings.

4. The fourth line starts a `FOR NEXT` loop that runs three times.

5. The fifth line asks the user, "Who is incompetent?" Any name that the user types is stored in the `MyBoss$` string variable.

6. The sixth line tells the computer, "Store the value of the `MyBoss$` string variable into `LoserArray`."

7. The seventh line marks the end of the `FOR NEXT` loop.

8. The eighth line prints a blank line.

9. The ninth line erases everything in `LoserArray`. At this point, `LoserArray` contains nothing.

10. The tenth line resizes `LoserArray` to hold seven strings instead of the original three strings.

11. The eleventh line stores the string `"Bobby Lee"` into the seventh location in `LoserArray`.

12. The twelfth line prints the contents of `LoserArray(7)`, which is the string `"Bobby Lee"`, and combines it with the string, `" is a pathetic character."` The entire `PRINT` statement displays, `"Bobby Lee is a pathetic character."`

13. The thirteenth line tells the computer that this is the end of the program.

You can resize multidimensional arrays, but you can't change the number of dimensions. For example, if you create a two-dimensional array, you can't resize it to a one-dimensional array or a three-dimensional array.

Chapter 16

Lumping Related Data in Records

· ·

In This Chapter

▶ Making records

▶ Adding data to and retrieving data from records

▶ Combining records and arrays

· ·

*A*n array can be handy for storing the same type of data (such as strings or integers) in a list, but sometimes you may need to store a variety of related data that consists of strings and numbers. Because you can't store different data types in an array, you have to use a different data structure called a *record*.

Data structure is a fancy term for something that can hold information such as words or numbers. The simplest data structure is a variable, which can hold one chunk of data. A more complicated data structure is an array, which can hold a list of data, as long as all the information shares the same data type (such as integers or strings).

A record stores related data under a single variable name. For example, if you want to store the names, addresses, and phone numbers of all your friends (and enemies), you create several different variables:

```
Name1$ = "Bo Katz"
Address1$ = "123 Main Street"
Phone1$ = "555-1234"
Salary1 = 55000
Name2$ = "Roger Wilco"
Address2$ = "948 Manchester Road"
Phone2$ = "555-4587"
Salary2 = 29000
```

The more names, addresses, and phone numbers you need to store, the more separate variables you'll have to create. Because this is cumbersome, complicated, and ultimately confusing, programmers created records as a way to simplify storing related data under a single variable name.

Creating a Record

A record consists of a name and one or more variables.

For example, if you want to create a record to store names, addresses, and phone numbers, you use the following code:

```
TYPE RecordName
   FullName AS STRING * 15
   Address AS STRING * 25
   Phone AS STRING * 14
   Salary AS SINGLE
END TYPE
```

This record definition tells the computer to do the following:

1. The first line tells the computer, "This is the beginning of a record called RecordName."

2. The second line creates a FullName variable that can hold a string up to 15 characters long.

3. The third line creates an Address variable that can hold a string up to 25 characters long.

4. The fourth line creates a Phone variable that can hold a string up to 14 characters long.

5. The fifth line creates a Salary variable that can hold a single-precision number.

6. The sixth line tells the computer, "This is the end of the record called RecordName."

When you first create a record, you can't use it immediately. In technical terms, a record is a *user-defined data type*. Before you can use a record, you have to create a variable to hold the information stored in your record, in much the same way that you create a variable to hold an integer or string.

The following bit of code shows that you must first define your record and then create a variable to represent your record:

```
TYPE EmployeeRecord
   FullName AS STRING * 15
   Address AS STRING * 25
   Phone AS STRING * 14
   Salary AS SINGLE
END TYPE
DIM Workers AS EmployeeRecord
```

The DIM command tells the computer, "Create a variable called Workers that can hold data defined by the record called EmployeeRecord."

Only after you have defined a variable to represent your record can you start stuffing data into the record.

Manipulating Data in Records

To add data to and retrieve data from a record, you need to specify two items:

- ✔ The variable name that represents the record
- ✔ The variable name inside the record in which you want to store data or from which you want to take data

Storing data in a record

To store data in a record, you need to specify both the variable name (that represents a record) and the specific record variable to use, like this:

```
RecordVariable.Variable = Data
```

Suppose that you had a record definition like this:

```
TYPE BomberInfo
   NickName AS STRING * 16
   MissionsFlown AS INTEGER
   Crew AS INTEGER
END TYPE
```

You would define a variable to represent this record like this:

```
DIM B17 AS BomberInfo
```

Then if you want to store a string in the NickName variable, use this command:

```
B17.NickName = "Brennan's Circus"
```

This command tells the computer, "Look for the variable named B17, and store the string "Brennan's Circus" in the NickName variable."

Retrieving data from a record

You can retrieve stored data by specifying both the record variable name and the specific variable that contains the data you want to retrieve:

```
Variable = RecordVariable.Variable
```

See how C creates records

You should know that different languages use different ways to create identical data structures. The C programming language creates a record (called a *structure* in the C language), as shown in the following example:

```
struct bomberinfo {
    char nickname[15]
    int missionsflown
    int crew
} B24;
```

This bit of C code creates a structure (or record) called bomberinfo. The bomberinfo structure can store a nickname up to 15 characters, an integer in a variable called missionsflown, and another integer in a variable called crew. In addition, this code also creates a variable called B24 that represents this structure.

For example, suppose that you had the following record definition and a variable to represent that record:

```
TYPE BomberInfo
   NickName AS STRING * 15
   MissionsFlown AS INTEGER
   Crew AS INTEGER
END TYPE

DIM B24 AS BomberInfo
```

If you had already stored data in the B24 record, you could retrieve it by using these commands:

```
GetName = B24.NickName
GetHistory = B24.MissionsFlown
GetCrew = B24.Crew
```

For a real-life example to stare at, try the following program, which stores data in and retrieves data from a record:

```
TYPE EmployeeRecord
   FullName AS STRING * 15
   Address AS STRING * 25
   Phone AS STRING * 14
   Salary AS SINGLE
END TYPE
```

```
DIM Workers AS EmployeeRecord

CLS
Workers.FullName = "Joe Smith"
Workers.Address = "9097 West Haven Drive"
Workers.Phone = "555-9893"
Workers.Salary = 45000

PRINT Workers.FullName
PRINT Workers.Address
PRINT Workers.Phone
PRINT Workers.Salary
END
```

Using Records with Arrays

Although a record can store several related chunks of data under a single variable name, records by themselves aren't very good at storing lists of related data such as a list of names, addresses, and phone numbers. To solve this problem, you can create an array that contains a record:

```
DIM ArrayName(Number) AS RecordType
```

Refer to Chapter 15 for more information about arrays.

Because an array is nothing more than a list representing a specific data type, you can define an array to represent a record as follows:

```
TYPE GulliblePeople
   FullName AS STRING * 15
   CashAvailable AS SINGLE
END TYPE
```

```
DIM PotentialVictims(3) AS GulliblePeople
```

This chunk of code tells the computer to do the following:

1. The first line creates a record called GulliblePeople.

2. The second line creates a FullName string variable that can hold up to 15 characters.

3. The third line creates a CashAvailable variable that can hold a single-precision number.

4. The fourth line marks the end of the GulliblePeople record.

5. The fifth line creates an array that can hold three records based on the GulliblePeople record. Figure 16-1 shows a representation of this array.

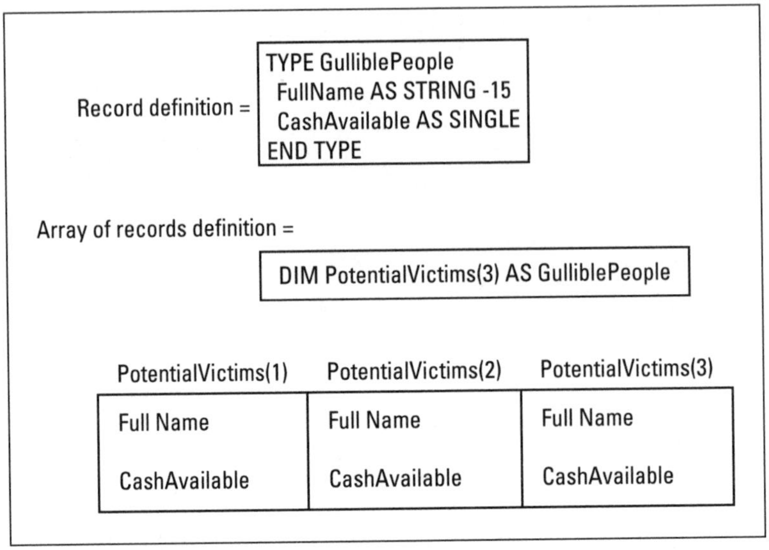

Figure 16-1:
An array
can hold a
list of
records.

To see a real-life example, type and run the following program:

```
TYPE GulliblePeople
   FullName AS STRING * 15
   CashAvailable AS SINGLE
END TYPE

DIM PotentialVictims(2) AS GulliblePeople

FOR I% = 1 TO 2
   PRINT "Type the name of someone you want to con:"
   INPUT PotentialVictims(I%).FullName
   PRINT "How much money do you think you can get?"
   INPUT PotentialVictims(I%).CashAvailable
NEXT I%

PRINT
PRINT "Here is your list of future con victims:"
FOR I% = 1 TO 2
   PRINT PotentialVictims(I%).FullName
   PRINT PotentialVictims(I%).CashAvailable
NEXT I%
END
```

When you run this program, it asks that you type in two names and two numbers. The first name is stored in `PotentialVictims(1).FullName`, and the first number is stored in `PotentialVictims(1).CashAvailable`. The second name is stored in `PotentialVictims(2).FullName`, and the second number is stored in `PotentialVictims(2).CashAvailable`.

Chapter 17

Linked Lists and Pointers

• •

In This Chapter

▶ Pointing at data

▶ Understanding how linked lists work

▶ Creating linked lists

▶ Making data structures with linked lists

• •

When you create an array you have to specify a size for it. If you make your array too small, you have to increase its size. Make the array too large, and you waste your computer's valuable memory.

As a compromise, programmers have developed something called a *linked list*. Like an array, a linked list can store a list of items. But unlike an array, a linked list can grow or shrink as you need it to, so you never have to decide how much space to allocate ahead of time.

Some languages, such as BASIC, can't create a linked list. Even though you can't make or use linked lists in QBASIC, you should still learn about them. Linked lists are a common data structure used in many other programming languages, such as Pascal and C/C++.

It All Starts with a Pointer

An array contains a fixed number of storage units for holding data. If you have an array designed to hold five numbers but it holds only two numbers, you're wasting space in the computer's memory. For small arrays, this isn't much of a problem. But if you're using a large, multidimensional array, the large amount of memory consumed could actually keep your program from working on computers that don't have enough memory.

Another problem is that you can't easily rearrange data in an array. For example, suppose that you had an array with a list of first names, like the array shown in Figure 17-1. If you wanted to rearrange the names alphabetically, you'd have to take all the data out and put it back in the array in alphabetical order.

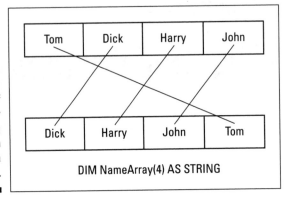

Figure 17-1:
Rearranging
data in an
array means
taking all
data out of
the array
and putting
it back in
again in a
new order.

DIM NameArray(4) AS STRING

To solve both of these problems, programmers created linked lists. A linked list can grow and shrink depending on the amount of data stored in it, so it uses memory more efficiently than an array.

In addition, although an array is like a box divided into sections that can hold data, a linked list is more like a collection of separate boxes (called *nodes*) that you can tie together, as shown in Figure 17-2. Each node contains the following two items:

- ✔ A record to hold data
- ✔ A pointer that tells the computer where to find the next node in the linked list

Figure 17-2:
A linked list
consists of
one or more
nodes that
contain data
and a
pointer that
points to the
next node
of the
linked list.

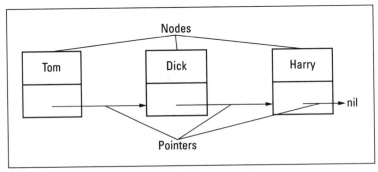

The pointer stored in the last node of a linked list points to a special value called *nil*. A nil value represents the end of the linked list.

Unlike an array, you don't have to remove data just to rearrange it. Instead, you can rearrange data in a linked list by simply rearranging the order of the pointers, as illustrated in Figure 17-3.

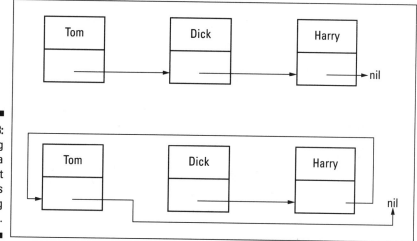

Figure 17-3: Rearranging data in a linked list means rearranging the pointers.

Although variables normally contain numbers or strings, a pointer contains a memory address, which works much like a mailing address. By reading the memory address, the computer can find its way to the next chunk of data stored in a node.

Pointers are a main part of C/C++ programming. Because a pointer represents a memory address, you can really mess up your C/C++ programs if even one pointer contains the wrong memory address. If this happens, your program can directly manipulate your computer's memory, which is like randomly probing your brain with a long, sharp needle (yipe!). Using pointers incorrectly (like using brain surgery incorrectly) can mess up your computer's memory, causing it to crash, freeze up, or simply act erratically.

Defining the parts of a linked list

A linked list consists of one or more nodes, where each node contains the following:

- ✔ A pointer that points to the next node in your linked list
- ✔ A record for storing data in the linked list

QBASIC does not offer commands for creating pointers, so the following code examples use the Pascal programming language, which looks enough like BASIC that you should understand how it works. If this looks too confusing, just browse over the Pascal programs and look at the pictures to get a general idea of how linked lists work.

To create a linked list in Pascal, you must first create a pointer:

```
TYPE
  PointerName = ^RecordType;
```

This tells the computer, "Create a data type called `PointerName`. This data type can hold the memory address that defines the location of a record type called `RecordType`."

After creating a pointer to a record, you now create the actual record itself. For example, the following record stores a string variable called `FullName`, a second string variable called `Address`, and a pointer variable called `Next`:

```
TYPE
  PointerName = ^RecordType;

  RecordType = RECORD
    FullName : string[15];
    Address : string[25];
    Next : PointerName;
  END;
```

After you've defined a pointer and a record, the third step is to define a variable to represent your record. This variable creates each node of your linked list:

```
VAR
  Node : PointerName;
```

Putting this all together, you have a program that looks like this:

```
PROGRAM LinkedLists;
TYPE
  PointerName = ^RecordType;

  RecordType = RECORD
    FullName : string[15];
    Address : string[25];
    Next : PointerName;
  END;

VAR
  Node : PointerName;
```

The preceding Pascal program tells the computer to perform the following tasks:

1. The first line tells the computer, "This is the beginning of my program called LinkedLists."

2. The second line contains just the word TYPE, which tells the computer, "Get ready to define a pointer and a record."

3. The third line defines a data type called PointerName, which points to any record called RecordType.

4. The fourth line defines the name of a record called RecordType.

5. The fifth line tells the computer, "Create a variable called FullName that can hold up to 15 characters."

6. The sixth line tells the computer, "Create a variable called Address that can hold up to 25 characters."

7. The seventh line tells the computer, "Create a variable called Next that can point to another record defined by RecordType."

8. The eighth line tells the computer, "This is the end of the record definition called RecordType."

8. The ninth line contains just the word VAR, which tells the computer, "Get ready to define one or more variables."

10. The tenth line tells the computer, "Create a variable called Node that represents a pointer to a record defined by RecordType." (This variable pointer defines a single node in your linked list.)

Don't worry if linked lists look confusing at this point. Soon, you'll see some pictures to clarify how linked lists work.

Creating a linked list

After you've defined a record to hold your data, a pointer to point to each record, and a variable to represent each node in your linked list, you still need to create your linked list. You need to follow three additional steps to create a linked list. These steps are illustrated in Figure 17-4:

1. **Create a node.**

2. **Store data in that node.**

3. **Set the pointer of each node to the next node of the linked list.**

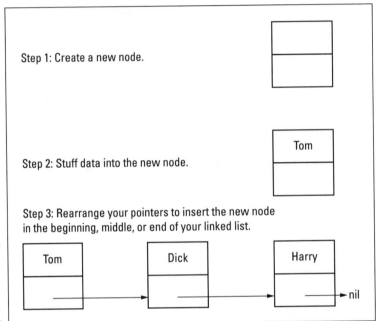

To see how a Pascal program creates a node and stores data in it, take a look at the following bit of code:

```
PROGRAM LinkedLists;
TYPE
  PointerName = ^RecordType;

  RecordType = RECORD
    FullName : string[15];
    Address : string[25];
    Next : PointerName;
  END;

VAR
  Node : PointerName;

BEGIN
  New(Node);
  Node^.FullName := 'Jonathan Blake';
  Node^.Address := '837 Dead-End Avenue';
  Node^.Next := nil;
END.
```

Starting from the word BEGIN, this program tells the computer to do the following:

1. The BEGIN line tells the computer, "This is the start of the instructions to follow."

2. The second line creates a new node. At this point, the node contains nothing.

3. The third line stores the name 'Jonathan Blake' in the FullName variable of the node record.

4. The fourth line stores the address '837 Dead-End Avenue' in the Address variable of the node record.

5. The fifth line stores the value nil in the Next pointer. A nil value means that the pointer doesn't point to anything. Using a nil value keeps the pointer from accidentally pointing to another part of the computer's memory. If you create a second node, you would want the value of Node^.Next to point to this second node.

Managing a linked list

When you store data in an array and you delete a chunk of data in the middle of the array, you wind up with an empty spot in your array. Even though nothing is stored in that particular location in the array, the computer must still allocate memory for that empty part of the array. Even worse, now your array contains an empty gap that you must skip over to find the next chunk of data in the array, as shown in Figure 17-5.

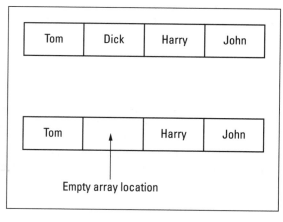

Figure 17-5: Deleting data in the middle of an array leaves a gap in the array.

Deleting data from a linked list is easy — just follow two steps:

1. **Rearrange the pointers of the nodes so that they ignore the node containing the data that you want to erase.**

2. **Delete the node containing the data that you want to erase.**

Figure 17-6 illustrates the process of deleting data in a linked list.

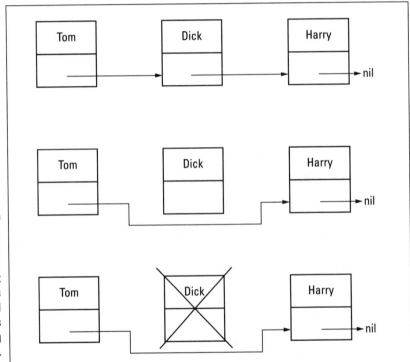

Figure 17-6:
Deleting
data in a
linked list
saves
memory and
avoids
storing
empty gaps.

Writing the actual instructions to tell the computer to rearrange pointers and delete a node can be fairly lengthy. So although arrays can be inefficient in terms of memory storage, arrays are much simpler to use and manage. On the other hand, linked lists are more efficient in storing data in memory, but they can be really troublesome to manage because you have to write many instructions just to accomplish something as seemingly simple as rearranging pointers.

Making Data Structures with Linked Lists

The simplest linked list is a single-linked list, in which each node contains data and one pointer that points to another node in the linked list (refer to Figure 17-2).

The trouble with a single-linked list is that each node points only to the next node. If you want to find the previous node, you can't. In Figure 17-2, the middle node (containing the name "Dick") points only to the node containing the name "Harry." But you can't tell which name appears before "Dick." In this case, an array is much simpler because an array can identify which data appears before and which data appears after a specific array location.

You can arrange linked lists in a variety of ways to create different types of data structures. Because data structures do nothing more than hold data, choosing the right data structure can make your program easier to write. (And choosing the wrong data structure can make your program harder to write.)

For example, a personal organizer program that stores names and addresses might use a linked list of records. The program could expand or shrink the linked list, depending on the number of names and addresses the user stores. The type of program you're writing can determine the type of data structure you need (or should use). That's what makes linked lists so powerful — they can create a variety of different data structures.

Don't worry about the details of creating different data structures with linked lists. Just be aware that different data structures exist, because you'll run into these different data structures later if you continue learning about computer programming.

Double-linked lists

The problem with a single-linked list is that each node can identify only the next node but not the preceding node. To solve this problem, you can create a double-linked list, in which each node contains data and two pointers. One pointer points to the next node in the linked list, and the second pointer points to the previous node in the linked list, as illustrated in Figure 17-7.

A personal organizer program would probably use a double-linked list to allow the user to scroll forward and backward through the linked list to view all the names and addresses stored in the personal organizer program.

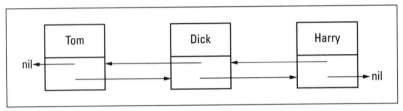

Figure 17-7:
A double-
linked list
uses two
pointers to
track nodes
both before
and after.

Creating a double-linked list means writing instructions to manage twice as many pointers, which essentially doubles the chances that you could leave a pointer *dangling* (pointing to a non-existent node) or pointing to the wrong node. In either case, incorrect pointers can cause subtle, yet serious bugs in your program, so use pointers sparingly.

Circular-linked lists

A typical double-linked list looks like a long rectangle with a beginning and an end (refer to Figure 17-7). But instead of creating an artificial end and beginning, you can link both ends of a single-linked list or a double-linked list to create a circular-linked list, as shown in Figure 17-8.

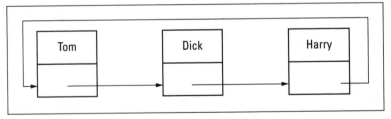

Figure 17-8:
A circular-
linked list
has no
beginning or
end and
resembles
a circle.

A circular-linked list may be useful for a presentation program that needs to display information continuously, such as a presentation in a museum kiosk. In this case, the presentation program may display information one screen at a time and then begin again when it reaches the end.

Stacks

A stack is a special single-linked list that allows you to add and remove nodes only at the beginning of the linked list. In the real world, the most common implementation of a stack is when you stack plates. When you want to store a new plate, you add it to the top of the stack. When you want to remove a plate, you take it off the top of the stack as well.

One common use for stacks is for calculating formulas using a method called Reverse Polish Notation (RPN), which is a method of calculation used in many Hewlett-Packard calculators. If you wanted to calculate the formula (1 + 2) * 3 using RPN, you would type the following:

```
1 2 + 3 *
```

Figure 17-9 shows how a stack can be used to calculate Reverse Polish Notation.

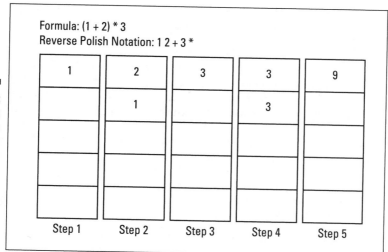

Figure 17-9: A stack adds data to and removes data from the beginning of the stack (or linked list).

Figure 17-9 shows how a stack stores the five steps needed to calculate the formula (1 + 2) * 3 using Reverse Polish Notation. Here's how it works:

1. The first step pushes the number 1 on the top of the stack.

2. The second step pushes the number 2 on the top of the stack and pushes the number 1 underneath.

3. The third step pops the number 2 off the stack, pops the number 1 off the stack, and adds the numbers together to get the number 3. Then it stores the number 3 back on top of the stack.

4. The fourth step pushes the number 3 (from the formula) on the top of the stack, and pushes the calculated value of 3 further down the stack.

5. The fifth step pops the first number 3 off the stack, pops the second number 3 off the stack, and multiplies the two number 3s to get the number 9. Then it stores the number 9 back on top of the stack.

Stacks are often called *LIFO* (which stands for *Last In, First Out*) linked lists. This means that the last data stored in a stack is the first data that gets removed from the stack (just like stacking and removing plates).

Don't worry if you don't understand the logic behind Reverse Polish Notation. Just understand how stacks work and leave Reverse Polish Notation for the engineers at Hewlett-Packard.

Queues

A queue is a special linked list that has two rules. The first rule is that you can add nodes only to the end of the linked list. The second rule is that you can remove nodes only from the beginning of the linked list.

Queues are often called *FIFO* (which stands for *First In, First Out*) linked lists. This means that the first data stored in the queue is the first data that gets removed from the queue. A queue mimics a line of people waiting to board an airplane or see a science-fiction movie. In both cases, the first person (data) put in the queue is the first person (data) removed, as illustrated in Figure 17-10.

The following steps (along with the illustration in Figure 17-10) explain how a queue stores and removes data:

1. The first step shows a queue in which the name "John" was first, the name "Harry" was second, the name "Dick" was third, and the name "Tom" was fourth and last.

2. The second step removes "John" from the queue. Now all the remaining names move closer to the front of the queue.

3. The third step removes "Harry" from the queue. All the remaining names move closer to the front of the queue.

4. The fourth step adds a new name, "Mike," to the queue. Because "Mike" is the newest data added to the queue, it is placed in the back of the queue.

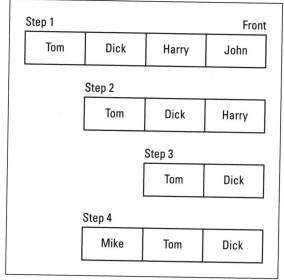

Figure 17-10:
A queue
stores new
data at the
end and
removes the
oldest data
from the
front.

Trees

Linked lists don't always have to resemble a linear or circular shape. The most common nonlinear shape for a linked list is called a *tree*, in which one node (called *the root*) represents the top of the tree with the rest of the nodes (called *leaves*) stored underneath the root, as shown in Figure 17-11.

In a tree, a node can point to zero or more nodes. For simplicity, many programmers use a special tree called a *binary tree*, in which each node can link only to zero, one, or two other nodes.

Trees are often used to mimic artificial intelligence in programs, such as chess-playing programs. A chess-playing program might use a tree in which the root represents a possible move for the first player and the leaf nodes underneath (at level 1) represent potential moves that the second player could make. Then the leaf nodes at level 2 represent potential moves for the first player, and the leaf nodes at level 3 represent potential moves for the second player, and so on.

Graphs

A graph is a linked list in which each node can point to one or more nodes without regard to mimicking a certain shape, such as a list. Figure 17-12 shows what a typical graph looks like.

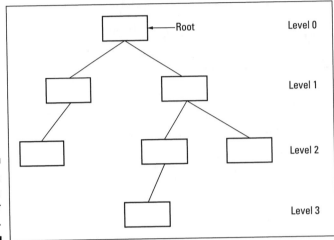

Figure 17-11:
A tree is a
nonlinear
linked list.

Graphs are often used in something called a *neural network* — a special program that can mimic the way the brain thinks. In a neural network, each node represents a neuron and the links between them represent the synapses linking the neurons together.

Graphs, trees, queues, stacks, circular-linked lists, and double-linked lists are just different ways to arrange and use a linked list. The more complicated your programs, the more you're likely to need these advanced data structures.

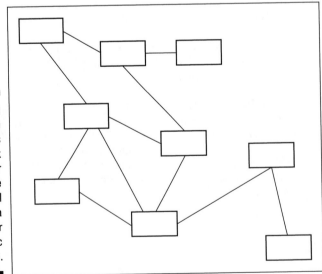

Figure 17-12:
A graph
allows
nodes to link
to one or
more
additional
nodes in a
rather
chaotic
pattern.

Chapter 18

Playing with Object-Oriented Programming

In This Chapter

▶ Understanding the problem with software

▶ Making programming easier

▶ Breaking programs into objects

▶ Choosing an object-oriented language

*O*bject-oriented programming is the latest fad (or to use proper programming lingo, the latest *methodology*) for pursuing the following Holy Trinity of characteristics that programmers want for their software:

- ✔ Simple and fast to create
- ✔ Easy to understand and modify
- ✔ Reliable and error-free

Object-oriented programming is often abbreviated as OOP as in "Oops, I don't think that object-oriented programming alone will magically make programming any easier."

QBASIC is not an object-oriented language, which means you can't experiment with using objects in QBASIC. Although BASIC doesn't support objects, Microsoft has tortured Visual Basic to offer some (but not all) features of object-oriented programming. If you want to learn about object-oriented programming using BASIC, pick up a copy of Visual Basic and a copy of *Visual Basic For Dummies* (IDG Books Worldwide, Inc.) today. Otherwise, you'll have to use a different programming language such as C++ or Java.

The Problem with Software

No matter how powerful a computer may be, the software that controls it limits its power. Unfortunately, advances in computer hardware occur more rapidly than advances in computer software. That explains why today's personal computers are still using Microsoft Windows, which is a 32-bit operating system, while companies such as Nintendo and Sony are busy selling video games that use 64-bit and 128-bit operating systems. Essentially, a $150 dedicated video game is more powerful than a $1,000 personal computer.

The biggest problem with software is reliability. Reliability means that software works without crashing, freezing up, or acting erratically. Software reliability is especially critical with real-time systems, such as airplane navigation systems, computers that host corporate Web sites, and financial trading programs where losing a single number could mean the loss of billions of dollars. Software reliability is so important because human lives and (more importantly from a corporate point of view) millions of dollars depend on computers working.

Of course, reliable software is useless if it isn't written in time. Programmers face the conflicting demands of delivering software on time and making sure that it is reliable.

Because of the conflicting demands that software be done on time and work reliably, most software is rushed out before it can be fully tested (which means it won't work right), or (more likely) the software is delayed so long that people switch to a competing product. (Then there's still no guarantee for those who wait that the software will work correctly even if it's several years late.)

Whatever fancy new technology, programming language, or programming style may appear, software will always face the twin challenge of working right while being written as quickly as possible. This means all software will likely have bugs that keep it from working as efficiently as it could work.

Ways to Make Programming Easier

To help you understand the headaches involved in designing software, you may like to know how programming has evolved over the years. In the early days of computers, most programs were fairly small. As a result, programmers often wrote programs with little planning and organization. After finishing the program, they would run it to see whether it worked. If it didn't work, they rewrote the program and tried again.

Such a trial-and-error approach worked fine when writing small programs, but when programs became larger and more complicated, rewriting the program over and over made programming tedious and error-prone. The larger the program, the more places bugs could hide, making it more likely that the program would not work at all.

With today's programs often consisting of a million or more lines of code, the trial-and-error method of writing programs no longer worked. Writing a large program without planning or organization is like trying to build a skyscraper without blueprints.

Programmers adopted a new strategy. Instead of trying to write one huge program, they decided to write a bunch of little programs (called *subprograms*).

The idea was that small programs are easier to write and debug, so you just had to write a bunch of small programs, paste them together, and have a larger program that works reliably, as illustrated in Figure 18-1.

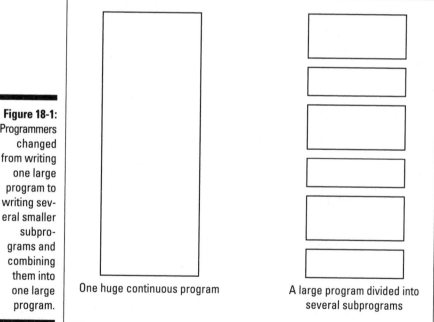

Figure 18-1: Programmers changed from writing one large program to writing several smaller subprograms and combining them into one large program.

One huge continuous program

A large program divided into several subprograms

Although the idea of writing small subprograms and pasting them together like building blocks was a sound idea, problems still existed. A large program might be divided into smaller subprograms, but the instructions stored in one subprogram could still manipulate data used by another subprogram.

This interaction between subprograms inevitably caused problems. If you

The Department of Defense and Ada

Back in the late 1970s, the United States Department of Defense realized that it was spending too much money on software. (At the same time, the Department of Defense officials also realized that they were paying $400 for toilet seats and $750 for screwdrivers, but that's another story altogether.)

Not only was the DOD spending more money to modify and update existing programs than it was spending to develop new programs, but the new software was taking too long to write and tended not to work when it was done.

Compounding the problems was the fact that much of the military's software was written in a variety of computer languages. This meant that the Department of Defense had to spend even more money to train programmers on all these programming languages.

So, in a rare moment of budget consciousness, the Department of Defense decided to standardize around a single programming language. The theory was that if everyone used the same programming language, programmers would just need to learn that one programming language. Better yet, older programs could be salvaged to reuse in new programs, and if everyone used the right language, programs could be developed faster and more reliably than ever before.

After spending millions of dollars to study existing programming languages, the Department of Defense decided to spend more millions of dollars to develop their own programming language, rather than use an existing language

that millions of people already knew how to use. Even stranger was that the Department of Defense based its new programming language (dubbed Ada, in honor of Ada Lovelace, considered to be the world's first programmer) on Pascal without even considering the more popular C programming language.

Predictably, the Ada programming language was complicated, slow, and difficult to learn. Even more predictable was that almost nobody adopted Ada for widespread use among military projects. One reason for the lack of popularity was the cost of training programmers to use Ada. Another reason was that other programming languages were easier to use and more appropriate for specific projects. Instead of using Ada, some programmers used C, some used Pascal, and some used a variety of other programming languages, essentially defeating the purpose of standardizing around a single programming language.

Today, many people use the Ada programming language, but it never achieved the widespread popularity that the Department of Defense had hoped. And to this day, the Department of Defense is still spending too much money to update existing programs rather than paying for new software, and most new software is perpetually late, doesn't work right, and is hard to modify. So decades and millions of dollars later, nothing much has changed, except that everyone realizes that if you want to write large, reliable software quickly and easily, choosing a new programming language isn't going to be the answer.

modified one subprogram, it could potentially affect the data used by another subprogram, as shown in Figure 18-2.

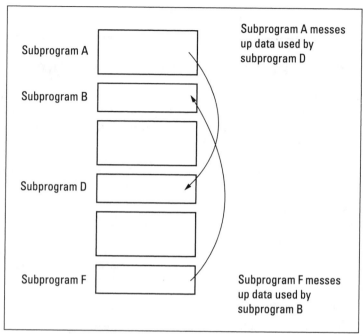

Figure 18-2:
Instructions
from one
subprogram
could often
affect the
data used
by another
subprogram.

To solve this problem (and solving problems is something that programmers continually strive to do), programmers developed the idea of isolating subprograms in separately compiled files. In this way, subprograms could not mess around with each other's data, and yet they could still work together to create one larger program.

Taking the idea of isolating subprograms into separate and isolated parts (called *modules* in programming lingo), programmers eventually developed the idea for objects, and hence the term object-oriented programming.

Breaking Programs into Objects

After programmers succeeded in breaking a large program into smaller sub-programs, the next logical step was to isolate both data and the instructions that manipulate that data into an individual unit — in other words, an object.

A program consists of one or more objects in which each object is a self-contained unit that contains two items:

✔ Data (also called *properties*)

✔ Instructions (also called *methods*) for manipulating that data.

Getting an inheritance from an object

Objects encourage reliability and reusability through something called *inheritance*. The main idea behind inheritance is to encourage programmers to reuse existing code.

In the old days of programming, a large program could be divided into several subprograms. After studying one of your subprograms, you might realize that with a little modification, you could adapt it to work in a second program. Unfortunately, any time you modify a program, you take the risk of messing it up so that it won't work at all.

To prevent the problem of modifying an existing subprogram and wrecking it by mistake, objects

use something called inheritance. Inheritance allows you to copy an existing object and then add new code to this new copy without ever modifying any of the existing code inside. Thus the new copy of your object "inherits" all the old data and code, while still allowing you to tack on new code to modify the object for a slightly different purpose.

Inheritance not only protects you from ruining a perfectly good chunk of code by mistake, but it also helps you create programs faster. Copying and modifying an existing object is easier than creating a brand new object from scratch.

Because an object has no dependence on any other part of your program, designing a program using objects provides the following benefits:

- **Reliability:** If your program doesn't work, you just need to isolate the bug in a single object and debug that one object, instead of trying to debug an entire program that may contain a million lines of code.

- **Reusability:** Because objects are self-contained units, you can (theoretically) copy an object from one program and plug it into another program much like making a structure using building blocks. Not only does this simplify creating new programs, but it also helps create new programs faster because you can reuse objects that already work.

In a traditionally designed program, data is often stored in one location and the instructions that manipulate that data are stored in another location, as illustrated in Figure 18-3. In comparison, an object-oriented program lumps data and the instructions that manipulate that data in a single location (known by its official programming term as *encapsulation*). Encapsulation simply keeps one part of a program from messing with data used by another part of the program.

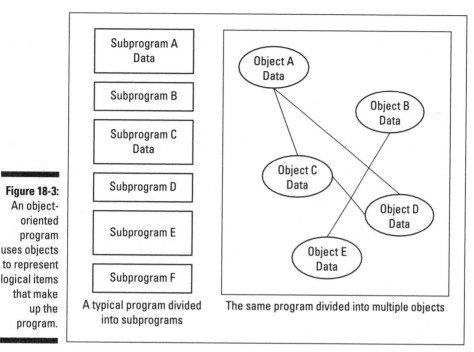

Figure 18-3:
An object-oriented program uses objects to represent logical items that make up the program.

Subprogram A Data

Subprogram B

Subprogram C Data

Subprogram D

Subprogram E

Subprogram F

A typical program divided into subprograms

Object A Data

Object B Data

Object C Data

Object D Data

Object E Data

The same program divided into multiple objects

How to use objects

One of the biggest problems with programming is the need to constantly modify existing programs. Most programs are used for years, if not decades. Rather than write a brand new program to replace an existing one, most companies prefer to modify the existing program. The theory is that modifying an existing program (that already works) takes less time and creates a more reliable program than creating a brand new program.

Unfortunately, constantly modifying an existing program can create a program as confusing to read as a book written one page at a time by three hundred different people. In both cases, the overall structure has been patched together in so many different ways that it can be hard to tell where one part ends and another part begins.

That's why object-oriented programming looks so appealing. To modify an object-oriented program you just unplug the object containing the program features you want to change, rewrite or replace it, and plug it back into the original program.

Best of all, objects make easy work of identifying which part of the program you want to update. For example, suppose that a video game displays aliens that pop up on the screen so that you can shoot them in the head. Your job is to modify the way the aliens look and move on the screen.

TECHNICAL STUFF

Hiding and exposing data in an object

Because objects need to communicate with one another, objects can classify their data and instructions into one of three categories: *private, public,* and *protected.*

If an object defines data and instructions as private, only that particular object can use that data and instructions. Private data and instructions can never be used by any other object. (That's why it's called private.)

On the other hand, public data and instructions can be used by other objects. Objects use public data and instructions to communicate and share data with other objects.

Protected data and instructions work just like private data and instructions, with one important exception. When you use inheritance to copy an existing object and create a new object, the new object only inherits public and protected data and instructions. Any private data and instructions remain with the old object.

If the video game were written in the traditional way of programming (dividing the program into smaller subprograms), you'd have to figure out which subprogram controls the way the alien looks and which subprogram controls the way the alien moves. Even if you manage to find which subprograms control the alien's appearance and movement, you still have to worry whether these subprograms rely on other subprograms buried somewhere deep within the bowels of your million-line program. Sound complicated? It is, especially if you're the one whose job relies on modifying a million-line video game program in less than two weeks.

But if the video game were written using object-oriented programming techniques, your job would be much easier. All you'd have to do is find the object that represents the alien. Inside that object would be all the subprograms you'd need in order to modify the way the alien looks and moves. Change this single object, plug it back into the original program, and you're done.

How to create an object

The first part to creating an object is to define a *class*, which is similar to a record. (See Chapter 16 for more information about records.) A class defines data and instructions to manipulate that data. After you have created a class, you can create one or more objects based on that class to use in your program.

QBASIC does not offer commands for creating objects, so the following code examples use the C++ programming language. Don't worry about trying to understand the syntax of C++; just browse the code to get a general idea of how the whole thing works.

The following example shows how to create a class in C++:

```
class monster
{
public:
    int x_coordinate;
    int y_coordinate;
    void moveme(int, int);
    void initialize(int, int);
};
```

The simple C++ code tells the computer to do the following:

1. The first line tells the computer, "This is a new class called monster."

2. The second line tells the computer, "This is the start of the class definition."

3. The third line tells the computer, "Any things that appears on the following lines are public, which means that they can be accessed by any part of the program."

4. The fourth line creates an integer variable called x_coordinate.

5. The fifth line creates an integer variable called y_coordinate.

6. The sixth line tells the computer, "The object has a subprogram (or method) called moveme that accepts two integer values."

7. The seventh line tells the computer, "The object has a subprogram called initialize that accepts two integer values."

8. The eighth line defines the end of the class definition.

A class is not an object. To create an object, you have to define a variable that represents your defined class.

Writing an object's methods

After you declare the subprograms (or methods) stored in a class, you still need to write the actual instructions that make that subprogram. I'll use the class definition that I defined in the preceding section:

```
class monster
{
public:
    int x_coordinate;
    int y_coordinate;
    void moveme(int, int);
    void initialize(int, int);
};
```

This class defines two subprograms (or methods) called moveme and initialize. To make these methods actually do something, you have to write the complete methods directly below the class definition, like this:

```
void monster::moveme(int new_x, int new_y)
{
    x_coordinate = x_coordinate + new_x;
    y_coordinate = y_coordinate + new_y;
}

void monster::initialize(int init_x, int init_y)
{
    x_coordinate = init_x;
    y_coordinate = init_y;
}
```

The initialize method defines the X-coordinate and Y-coordinate of any object derived from the class called monster. The moveme method is used to move an object's position a certain distance in the X (right and left) direction and Y (up and down) direction.

Creating an object

After you've defined a class and written any methods declared within that class, you still need to define a variable to represent that class. This variable represents the actual object in object-oriented programming.

To create an object, you declare a variable to represent that object. In this program, an object named zombie is defined to represent the monster class definition, as shown here:

```
#include <iostream.h>
class monster
{
public:
    int x_coordinate;
    int y_coordinate;
    void moveme(int, int);
    void initialize(int, int);
};
```

```
void monster::moveme(int new_x, int new_y)
{
   x_coordinate = x_coordinate + new_x;
   y_coordinate = y_coordinate + new_y;
}

void monster::initialize(int init_x, int init_y)
{
   x_coordinate = init_x;
   y_coordinate = init_y;
}

void main()
{
monster zombie;
   zombie.initialize(12, 15);
   cout << "The X-location of the zombie is " <<
                     zombie.x_coordinate << "\n";

   cout << "The Y-location of the zombie is " <<
                     zombie.y_coordinate << "\n";

   zombie.moveme (34, 9);

   cout << "The new X-location of the zombie is " <<
                     zombie.x_coordinate << "\n";

   cout << "The new Y-location of the zombie is " <<
                     zombie.y_coordinate << "\n";
}
```

The main C++ program starts with the void main() line. Just examining this portion line by line makes the computer do the following:

1. The first line tells the computer, "This is the start of the C++ program."

2. The second line tells the computer, "This is the start of all instructions inside the main C++ program."

3. The third line tells the computer, "Create an object called zombie, and base it on the class definition called monster."

4. The fourth line runs the method called initialize, which defines the X-coordinate (12) and Y-coordinate (15) of the object called zombie.

5. The fifth line prints the message, "The X-location of the zombie is 12."

6. The sixth line prints the message, "The Y-location of the zombie is 15."

7. The seventh line runs the method called moveme, which moves the object called zombie 34 units of measurement in the X-direction and 9 units in the Y-direction.

8. The eighth line prints the message, "The new X-location of the zombie is 46." (That's 12, the original X-location of the zombie as defined in step 4, plus 34 as defined in step 7, which equals 46.)

9. The ninth line prints the message, "The new Y-location of the zombie is 24." (That's 15, the original Y-location of the zombie as defined in step 4, plus 9 as defined in step 7, which equals 24.)

10. The tenth line tells the computer, "This is the end of the C++ main program."

Although the C++ program may look confusing, remember these important points and you'll be fine:

✔ To create an object, you have to define a class first.

✔ A class contains data and instructions (methods) for manipulating the object's data.

Common terms associated with object-oriented programming

Although you aren't likely to become an expert in object-oriented programming from this brief introduction, you should at least understand the purpose behind objects, which is to make modifying and reusing programs easier.

If you plan to continue studying computer programming, you'll probably run into object-oriented programming over and over (or at least until a new programming methodology pops up to make programming easier). To add to your limited knowledge of object-oriented programming, remember these common object-oriented terms that you'll likely see at one time or another:

✔ **Encapsulation** means lumping all related data and instructions to manipulate that data in a single location.

✔ **Inheritance** means passing data and instructions from one object to a second object that is derived from the first object.

✔ **Message** is a subprogram (also called a method) that manipulates the data inside an object.

✔ **Object** is a collection of data and instructions for manipulating that data, grouped together in a self-contained unit.

Choosing an Object-Oriented Language

After you understand the general principles behind object-oriented programming, you may be anxious to start trying it out on your own. QBASIC doesn't support object-oriented programming, so you'll need to switch to a different programming language. The two types of programming languages that you can choose from are hybrid object-oriented languages and true (or pure) object-oriented languages.

A hybrid object-oriented language simply takes an existing language and slaps object-oriented features on top of it. Some of the more popular hybrid languages include Pascal (as implemented in Delphi), BASIC (as implemented in Visual Basic), and C++.

Unlike other hybrid languages, Visual Basic does not offer inheritance. If you really want to take advantage of all the features promised by object-oriented programming, you'll never be able to do it in Visual Basic.

The main advantage of using a hybrid language is that if you already know how to use a language such as Pascal, BASIC, or C, you can quickly learn to use the object-oriented features of these languages with a minimum of training, anguish, and experimentation. If you're not quite sure about the benefits of object-oriented programming, you can write a small part of your program using objects, and write the bulk of your program using old-fashioned programming methods.

Of course, the main disadvantage of hybrid languages is that they allow programmers to mix traditional and object-oriented programming techniques, which can become an untidy mess. Hybrid languages allow programmers to use none, some, or all object-oriented programming techniques, so hybrid languages often create programs that don't take full advantage of objects, destroying the advantage of using objects while making the program harder to read and understand.

That's why many people prefer pure object-oriented languages that force you to use objects right from the start. Some popular pure object-oriented languages include SmallTalk, Eiffel, and the popular Java.

Whether you decide to stick to a conventional language (and use its object-oriented hybrid) or jump straight into a pure object-oriented language, get used to the idea behind breaking your program into objects. Object-oriented programming techniques alone won't make software easier to write and more reliable, but they can make you more aware of the problems in writing software and how object-oriented programming can solve those problems.

In the long run, nobody really cares what language you use, whether you use any object-oriented programming techniques, or whether you write software while sitting in your underwear and listening to Barry Manilow albums at

3 a.m. The important point is to write software on time that works. If you can do that, you can focus on producing results and let your co-workers worry about trivial details like wearing a tie, dealing with corporate politics, and fighting each other for a cubicle near a window.

Part V
Algorithms: Telling the Computer What To Do

The 5th Wave   By Rich Tennant

THE GREAT THING ABOUT OBJECT-ORIENTED PROGRAMMING IS, IT'S MADE SOFTWARE DEVELOPMENT AS EASY AS PUTTING ONE FOOT IN FRONT OF THE OTHER.

In this part . . .

A program is nothing more than a list of instructions, but you can phrase your instructions in various ways to tell the computer to perform the same task. For example, if you want to give directions to tell someone how to get from the airport to your house, you probably can tell that person two or three different ways. Each way would eventually get the person to your house, but one way may be easier, another way may be faster during the day, and the third way may be more scenic.

In the world of computer programming, a specific way to accomplish a task is called an *algorithm*. By choosing the fastest set of instructions (the algorithm), you can make your program faster and more efficient. This part of the book introduces you to several common algorithms for accomplishing different tasks.

Chapter 19

Sorting

In This Chapter

▶ Sorting data in many ways

▶ Picking a sorting algorithm

*P*rograms typically accept data from the outside world (such as from someone typing on the keyboard), manipulate that data somehow, and spit that data back out in a format that someone finds useful.

Somewhere between accepting data and spitting it back out, the program has to store the data in its memory or on a hard disk using a data structure. (Browse through Chapters 15 through 18 for more information about data structures.) Before the program can spit out its useful result, it may need to sort and organize the data first.

For example, a database would be fairly useless if it let you store information without letting you do anything to rearrange that information. For example, you may want to rearrange your data alphabetically by last name, numerically by telephone area code, or by some other criterion, such as by those people who are single and earn $75,000 or more every year. So your program needs to know how to sort data.

Although sorting may seem like a fairly mundane topic, it can actually get rather complex. That's because whenever a program sorts data, it needs to do it as quickly as possible. After all, a program that sorts names and addresses is useless if it takes three hours just to sort 15 names.

So part of computer science has centered on studying and developing the most efficient sorting methods (called *algorithms*) possible. Because many types of programs need to sort data, nearly every programmer needs to know the different sorting algorithms available and how they work. Throughout this chapter, you can type in various QBASIC programs and see for yourself exactly how a particular sorting algorithm does its sorting magic.

Computer scientists have created a variety of sorting algorithms, but there is no single, perfect algorithm that your program should use all the time. The most efficient algorithm depends partly on the data that you want sorted and partly on the data structures that your program uses to store the data.

Measuring efficiency with Big-O notation

To measure the efficiency of specific algorithms, computer scientists have created something called Big-O notation. Essentially, Big-O notation measures the speed of a particular algorithm (such as a sorting algorithm) based on the number of items it has to manage.

For example, if you have an algorithm that sorts a list of names alphabetically, the speed of that algorithm depends on the number of names to be searched. In Big-O notation, this relationship would be expressed as O(N), where O stands for "order of magnitude" and N stands for the total number of items the algorithm has to manage.

The way that programmers determine the Big-O notation of a particular algorithm depends on that algorithm's speed of execution and the number of items it has to handle. For example, if an algorithm's speed of execution and number of items (N) it can handle is expressed as N2 + N + 1, the Big-O notation for this algorithm would be O(N2).

When calculating the Big-O notation for an algorithm, you choose the fastest-growing item (in this case, N2) and ignore the rest of the expression. (Naturally, if you use the wrong expression to represent your algorithm, your Big-O notation will be wrong as well.)

Programmers often use Big-O notation to measure the average and worst-case scenarios when they study how an algorithm behaves while managing a typical number of items and how that same algorithm behaves while managing an extremely large number of items.

Not surprisingly, some algorithms are fast at managing relatively small numbers of items, but slow down rapidly when forced to manage a large number of items. Curiously, other algorithms are very fast and efficient when sorting items that are almost correctly sorted initially, but slow when sorting items randomly scattered in the list.

Programmers study the average and worst-case scenarios of an algorithm using Big-O notation to help them choose the algorithm that's best suited for their particular program.

Insertion Sort

Imagine that you're playing cards, and the dealer deals the cards to you. As soon as you get two cards, your first inclination is probably to sort those two cards in relation to one another (perhaps by suit or by number). When the dealer gives you a third card, you sort that card in relation to your previous two cards. You sort each additional card that you receive in relation to your previously sorted cards. This is how an insertion sort works. (See Figure 19-1.) From the computer's point of view, the insertion sort algorithm works as follows:

1. It compares the first two items in the list and sorts those two items.

2. It looks at the next item in the list and sorts that item in relation to the previously sorted items.

3. It repeats Step 2 for each additional item in the list until the entire list is sorted.

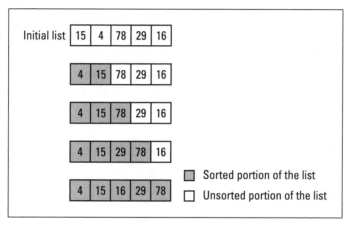

Figure 19-1:
An insertion sort removes one item at a time and sorts it in relation to the previous sorted items in the list.

To see for yourself how the insertion sort algorithm works, try the following program:

```
CLS
MaxSize = 5
DIM MyArray(MaxSize) AS INTEGER
RANDOMIZE TIMER
FOR I = 1 TO MaxSize
  MyArray(I) = INT(RND * 100) + 1
  PRINT MyArray(I);
NEXT I
PRINT "(Initial array)"

FOR ArrayPos = 2 TO MaxSize
  TempValue = MyArray(ArrayPos)
  StopNow = 0
  Count = 1
  DO
    IF TempValue < MyArray(Count) THEN
      FOR J = ArrayPos TO Count STEP -1
        MyArray(J) = MyArray(J - 1)
      NEXT J
      MyArray(Count) = TempValue
      StopNow = 1
      FOR I = 1 TO MaxSize
        PRINT MyArray(I);
      NEXT I
      PRINT
```

```
      END IF
      Count = Count + 1
   LOOP UNTIL (StopNow = 1 OR Count = ArrayPos)
NEXT ArrayPos

FOR I = 1 TO MaxSize
   PRINT MyArray(I);
NEXT I
PRINT "(Sorted array)"
END
```

A typical output for this program appears as follows:

```
57    89   77   3    21 (Initial array)
58    77   89   3    21
59    57   77   89   21
60    21   57   77   89
3     21   57   77   89 (Sorted array)
```

The insertion sort program works as follows:

1. The first through eighth lines clear the screen, create a variable called MaxSize that equals 5, create an array called MyArray to hold five integers, generate a random number based on the current time, create a random number between 1 and 100, store it in the array called MyArray, and then print the array on the screen along with the string, "(Initial array)".

2. The tenth line is the start of a FOR NEXT loop that starts counting from the second item in the array, using a variable called ArrayPos.

3. The eleventh line creates a variable called TempValue and stores the value in the array location designated by the ArrayPos variable. At the beginning of this FOR NEXT loop, the value of TempValue is equal to the second item in the array.

4. The twelfth line creates a variable called StopNow and sets its value to zero. The StopNow variable is used later in the program to tell the computer that it has already moved a number to its correctly sorted position in the array.

5. The thirteenth line creates a variable called Count and sets its value to one. The Count variable is used to locate where in the array to move the number stored in the TempValue variable.

6. The fourteenth line is the start of a DO LOOP UNTIL.

7. The fifteenth line is the start of an IF THEN statement that checks whether the value stored in the TempValue variable (which represents the number that you want to sort) is less than the value stored in the array position specified by the Count variable. The first time that this line runs, it checks whether the second item in the list is less than the first item.

8. The sixteenth through eighteenth lines form a FOR NEXT loop that moves each item in the array down (to the right) one position to make room for inserting the TempValue number in its sorted place in the array.

9. The nineteenth line moves the number stored in TempValue to its newly sorted position in the array location specified by the Count variable.

10. The twentieth line sets the value of the StopNow variable to 1. This tells the computer that it has correctly sorted the number stored in the TempValue variable.

11. The twenty-first through twenty-fourth lines print the partially sorted array on the screen so that you can see its progress.

12. The twenty-fifth line is the end of the IF THEN statement that started on the fourteenth line.

13. The twenty-sixth line increases the value of the Count variable.

14. The twenty-seventh line is the end of the DO LOOP UNTIL that tells the computer to stop looping only if the StopNow variable equals 1 (which means the computer has moved the number to its correctly sorted position), or until the value of Count equals the value of ArrayPos.

15. The twenty-eighth line is the end of the FOR NEXT loop that began on the ninth line.

16. The twenty-ninth through thirty-second lines print the final sorted array on the screen along with the message, "(Sorted array)".

17. The thirty-third line tells the computer that this is the end of the program.

To really study how this program works, press F8 to see how the program runs each line in the program, and then press F4 to see what it displays on the screen.

Bubble Sort

The bubble sort algorithm has that name because individual items in a list appear to "bubble up" to their proper location. The bubble sort algorithm examines a list of items repeatedly and sorts adjacent items until it has sorted the entire list. (See Figure 19-2.) Your computer handles a bubble sort algorithm like this:

1. It compares the first two items in the list and sorts those two items.

2. It moves to the next item in the list and sorts that item with the last item of the previously sorted pair.

3. It repeats Step 2 for each additional item in the list until the entire list has been examined.

4. It repeats Steps 1 through 3 until the entire list is sorted.

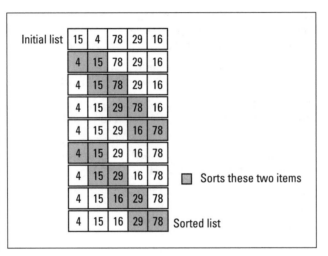

Figure 19-2:
A bubble sort examines each item in a list and sorts it in relation to its neighbor.

One drawback to the bubble sort algorithm is that it often has to reexamine a list two or more times before it has correctly sorted all items (refer to Figure 19-2).

To see for yourself how the bubble sort algorithm works, look at the following program:

```
CLS
MaxSize = 5
DIM MyArray(MaxSize) AS INTEGER
RANDOMIZE TIMER
FOR I = 1 TO MaxSize
  MyArray(I) = INT(RND * 100) + 1
  PRINT MyArray(I);
NEXT I
PRINT "(Initial array)"

Pass = 1
DO
  NoSwaps = 1
  FOR I = 1 TO (MaxSize - Pass)
    IF MyArray(I) > MyArray(I + 1) THEN
      TempValue = MyArray(I)
      MyArray(I) = MyArray(I + 1)
      MyArray(I + 1) = TempValue
      NoSwaps = 0
      FOR J = 1 TO MaxSize
        PRINT MyArray(J);
      NEXT J
      PRINT
    END IF
  NEXT I
LOOP UNTIL (NoSwaps = 1)
```

```
FOR I = 1 TO MaxSize
   PRINT MyArray(I);
NEXT I
PRINT "(Sorted array)"
END
```

Press F8 to see how the computer runs each line in the program, and then press F4 to see what it displays on the screen.

A typical output for this program looks like this:

```
5  19  61  26  27 (Initial array)
5  19  26  61  27
5  19  26  27  61
5  19  26  27  61 (Sorted array)
```

The following list breaks down the workings of the bubble sort program:

1. The first through ninth lines clear the screen, create a variable called MaxSize equal to 5, create an array called MyArray to hold five integers, generate a random number based on the current time, create a random number between 1 and 100, store it in the array called MyArray, and then print the array on the screen along with the string, "(Initial array)".

2. The tenth line creates a variable called Pass and sets its value to 1.

3. The eleventh line starts a DO LOOP UNTIL loop that continues until it reaches a variable called NoSwaps = 1.

4. The twelfth line creates a variable called NoSwaps and sets its value to 0.

5. The thirteenth line creates a FOR NEXT loop that repeats (5 - Pass) times. The first time the FOR NEXT loop runs, it repeats four times. The second time, it repeats three times, and so on.

6. The fourteenth line tells the computer, "Check the value of an array item with the item next to it." The first time this IF THEN statement runs, it checks the first item with the second item in MyArray.

7. The fifteenth through seventeenth lines switch two numbers stored next to each other in MyArray.

8. The eighteenth line sets the value of NoSwaps to zero. This tells the bubble sort algorithm that a swap has occurred somewhere in the list, so it has to repeat the DO LOOP UNTIL loop again.

9. The nineteenth through twenty-second lines print the array on the screen so that you can see how the computer has sorted the array so far.

10. The twenty-third line marks the end of the IF THEN statement that started on the thirteenth line.

11. The twenty-fourth line marks the end of the FOR NEXT loop.

12. The twenty-fifth line marks the end of the `DO LOOP UNTIL` loop. This loop stops looping only when the value of `NoSwaps` equals 0. This occurs only if the list is completely sorted.

13. The twenty-sixth through twenty-ninth lines print the final sorted array on the screen.

14. The thirtieth line tells the computer that this is the end of the program.

For sorting small lists, the bubble sort algorithm is fairly fast, but it is extremely slow when a large number of items need to be sorted. Even worse, the bubble sort algorithm takes a long time to sort if one or more low values are near the end of the array, which means the bubble sort algorithm has to run multiple times.

Shell Sort

One problem with insertion sort and bubble sort algorithms is that they often have to move an item from the far end of a list to the front, an especially serious drawback for the bubble sort algorithm. The shell sort algorithm presents a simple solution to make sorting faster.

The shell sort algorithm works by the principle of "divide and conquer." Instead of trying to sort an entire list at a time, the shell sort algorithm divides a larger list into multiple smaller lists. After it sorts these smaller lists, it combines them into a final sorted list.

The shell sort algorithm doesn't actually do any sorting; it works with an existing sorting algorithm (such as insert sort or bubble sort) to speed up the overall sorting process.

Basically, the shell sort works like this:

1. It divides a long list into multiple smaller lists. (Figure 19-3 shows a list divided into three smaller lists. In this case, the shell sort algorithm is taking every third item in the list to create three separate smaller lists.)

2. It sorts each smaller list using an algorithm such as insertion sort or bubble sort. In the example shown in Figure 19-3, the first mini-list contains the numbers 15 and 29, which don't need to be sorted. The second mini-list contains the numbers 16 and 4, so their positions are sorted. The third mini-list contains just the number 78.

3. It smashes all the smaller lists back into a large list. In Figure 19-3, note that the numbers 4 and 16 have been sorted.

4. It divides the long list into multiple smaller lists again, but into fewer smaller lists than in Step 1. In Figure 19-3, the shell sort algorithm divides the list into two small lists, taking every second item to create two smaller lists.

5. It repeats Steps 2 through 4 (if necessary) until a single sorted list remains. Note that after the numbers 16 and 78 get sorted, the entire list is completely sorted.

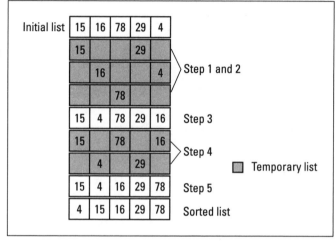

Figure 19-3:
The shell sort algorithm breaks a large list into smaller lists and then sorts those smaller lists.

To see how the shell sort algorithm works, run the following program. This program uses shell sort to initially sort items, and then it uses the bubble sort method to actually sort the items in the list:

```
CLS
MaxSize = 5
DIM MyArray(MaxSize) AS INTEGER
RANDOMIZE TIMER
FOR I = 1 TO MaxSize
   MyArray(I) = INT(RND * 100) + 1
   PRINT MyArray(I);
NEXT I
PRINT "(Initial array)"

X = MaxSize \ 2
DO WHILE X > 0
   Limit = MaxSize - X
   DO
     Switch = 0
     FOR K = 0 TO Limit
       IF MyArray(K) > MyArray(K + X) THEN
         SWAP MyArray(K), MyArray(K + X)
       END IF
```

```
      Switch = K
      NEXT K
      Limit = Switch - X
   LOOP WHILE Switch <> 0

   FOR I = 1 TO MaxSize
      PRINT MyArray(I);
   NEXT I
   PRINT

   X = X \ 2
LOOP

FOR I = 1 TO MaxSize
   PRINT MyArray(I);
NEXT I
PRINT "(Sorted array)"
END
```

Press F8 to see how the computer runs each line in the program, and then press F4 to see what it displays on the screen.

A typical output for this program look like this:

```
94  17  70  90  62 (Initial array)
62  17  70  90  94
17  62  70  90  94
17  62  70  90  94 (Sorted array)
```

The first time that the program runs, the shell sort algorithm compares the numbers stored in locations 1, 3, and 5 of the array (94, 70, and 62, respectively). After sorting this list, it sorts the numbers in locations 2 and 4 of the array (17 and 90). Then it sorts the entire list.

To see how the shell sort program works in detail, examine the program line by line as follows:

1. The first through ninth lines clear the screen, create a variable called MaxSize equal to 5, create an array called MyArray to hold five integers, generate a random number based on the current time, create a random number between 1 and 100, store it in the array called MyArray, and then print the array on the screen along with the string, "(Initial array)".

2. The tenth line creates a variable called X and divides the total size of the list by 2 using integer division. In this case, MaxSize \ 2 = 2. The value of X tells the shell sort algorithm to divide the long list into two smaller lists.

3. The eleventh line starts a DO WHILE LOOP loop that continues as long as the value of X is greater than 0.

4. The twelfth line creates a variable called `Limit` and sets its value to `MaxSize - X`. The first time this line runs, the value of `Limit` is 5 - 2, or 3.

5. The thirteenth line is the start of a `DO LOOP WHILE` loop that continues looping until the value of a variable called `Switch` is no longer 0.

6. The fourteenth line creates a variable called `Switch` and sets its value to 0.

7. The fifteenth line starts a `FOR NEXT` loop.

8. The sixteenth through eighteenth lines compare two numbers stored in the array and switch their positions if necessary using the `SWAP` command, which is the bubble sort algorithm.

9. The nineteenth line sets the value of `Switch` to the value of K.

10. The twentieth line sets the value of `Limit` to `Switch - X`.

11. The twenty-first line marks the end of the `DO LOOP WHILE` loop.

12. The twenty-second through twenty-fifth lines print the partially sorted array on the screen.

13. The twenty-sixth line divides `X` by 2 using integer division. This tells the shell sort algorithm how many smaller lists into which to divide the larger list.

14. The twenty-seventh line marks the end of the `DO LOOP WHILE` loop.

15. The twenty-eighth through thirty-first lines print the final sorted array on the screen.

16. The thirty-second line tells the computer that this is the end of the program.

Quicksort

One of the more popular sorting algorithms is called Quicksort. The Quicksort method works by picking a number from the middle of the list and then sorting the remaining numbers to the left or right of the previously picked number, as shown in Figure 19-4.

After dividing the initial list in half, the Quicksort algorithm repetitively divides each portion of the list in half again, choosing a randomly picked number from each list. After the Quicksort algorithm divides a long list into a bunch of smaller ones and sorts each small list, it then combines all the small lists back into a single long list that is sorted.

Figure 19-4:
The
Quicksort
algorithm
repeatedly
divides a
larger list
into small
lists based
on a number
chosen from
the middle
of the list.

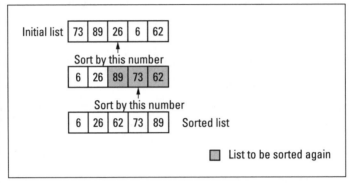

Figure 19-4:
The
Quicksort
algorithm
repeatedly
divides a
larger list
into small
lists based
on a number
chosen from
the middle
of the list.

The Quicksort method works like this:

1. It picks a number from the middle of the list and uses that number to divide the long list in half. All numbers less than the randomly picked number appear to the left, and all numbers greater than the randomly picked number appear to the right.

2. It repeats Step 1 for each half of the list divided by a randomly picked number until all items are sorted in a bunch of smaller lists.

3. It smashes all the smaller lists back into a large list.

Because the Quicksort algorithm repeats the same steps for smaller and smaller lists, it uses a technique called *recursion*. Recursion simply means that a subprogram repeatedly runs itself.

Because the Quicksort algorithm needs to use recursion, the actual Quicksort algorithm must be stored in a separate subprogram. Thus, the complete Quicksort program consists of a main program and a subprogram, as in the following example:

```
DECLARE SUB QSort (NumArray%(), Start%, Finish%)
CLS
MaxSize% = 5
DIM MyArray(MaxSize%) AS INTEGER
RANDOMIZE TIMER
FOR I = 1 TO MaxSize%
   MyArray(I) = INT(RND * 100) + 1
   PRINT MyArray(I);
NEXT I
PRINT "(Initial array)"

QSort MyArray(), 1, MaxSize%
```

```
FOR I = 1 TO MaxSize%
   PRINT MyArray(I);
NEXT I
PRINT "(Sorted array)"
END
```

The main portion of the Quicksort program works as follows:

1. The first line declares a subprogram called Qsort, which accepts three items: an array of integers (called NumArray) and two additional integers (called Start and Finish). The Start variable represents the position of the beginning of the list, and the Finish variable represents the end of the list.

2. The second through tenth lines create an array of five random integers and print the array on the screen for you to see.

3. The eleventh line calls the QSort subprogram by giving it the data stored in MyArray along with the front of the list (1) and the maximum size of the list (MaxSize).

4. The twelfth through fifteenth lines print the final sorted array on the screen.

5. The sixteenth line tells the computer that this is the end of the program.

The subprogram called QSort looks like this:

```
SUB QSort (NumArray%(), Start%, Finish%)
 I% = Start%
 J% = Finish%
 X% = NumArray%((I% + J%) \ 2)

 DO
  DO WHILE NumArray%(I%) < X%
    I% = I% + 1
  LOOP

  DO WHILE NumArray%(J%) > X%
    J% = J% - 1
  LOOP

  IF I% <= J% THEN
   SWAP NumArray%(I%), NumArray%(J%)
   I% = I% + 1
   J% = J% - 1
  END IF
 LOOP UNTIL I% > J%

  FOR K = 1 TO Finish%
    PRINT NumArray%(K);
  NEXT K
  PRINT
```

```
IF J% > Start% THEN
   QSort NumArray%(), Start%, J%
END IF
IF I% < Finish% THEN
   QSort NumArray%(), I%, Finish%
END IF
END SUB
```

The QSort subprogram works as follows:

1. The first line defines the name of the subprogram (QSort) and the data that it needs, which includes an array of integers (NumArray) and two additional integers (called Start and Finish).

2. The second and third lines create two variables (I and J) that are set to the same value as the Start and Finish variables. The subprogram needs the variables I and J because their values change when the sub-program runs, but values of Start and Finish remain the same.

3. The fourth line creates a variable called X that divides the size of NumArray in half and stores this value as an integer.

4. The fifth line starts a DO LOOP UNTIL loop that runs until the value of I is greater than the value of J.

5. The sixth through eighth lines increase the value of I by 1 as long as the number stored in the NumArray is less than the value of X.

6. The ninth through eleventh lines decrease the value of J by 1 as long as the number stored in the NumArray is greater than the value of X. Here, the program is trying to determine which numbers in the list are less than or greater than the number picked in the middle of the list in the fourth line.

7. The twelfth through sixteenth lines compare the numbers in the list and move them to the left or right of the number chosen in the fourth line.

8. The seventeenth line marks the end of the DO LOOP UNTIL loop that started in the fifth line.

9. The eighteenth through twenty-first lines print the partially sorted array on the screen.

10. The twenty-second through twenty-seventh lines run the QSort subpro-gram over and over (recursively), each time feeding it a smaller array of numbers.

11. The twenty-eighth line marks the end of the subprogram.

A typical output for this program looks like this:

```
27 62  5   79  14 (Initial array)
 5 62 27   79  14
 5 14 27   79  62
 5 14 27   62  79
 5 14 27   62  79 (Sorted array)
```

The first time that the program runs, the Quicksort algorithm chooses the third number (5) in the array. Then it sorts the remaining numbers depending on whether they are less than or greater than 5. Because they are all greater than 5, they get stored to the right of the array. Out of the four remaining numbers to the right of 5, the program picks the number 27 and sorts this smaller list, depending on whether the numbers are less than or greater than 27.

Now a third smaller list remains consisting of 79 and 62. This short list gets sorted and then combined with all the other small lists to make up the entire sorted list.

Picking a Sorting Algorithm

The insertion sort, bubble sort, shell sort, and Quicksort algorithms show you the variety of methods that programs can use to sort data. Naturally, computer scientists keep inventing additional sorting algorithms with their own advantages and disadvantages, so choose your sorting algorithms carefully. Pick the right sorting algorithm and your program can run quickly. Pick the wrong sorting algorithm and your program may seem unbearably slow to the user.

As a general rule, insertion sort is best for small lists, bubble sort is best for lists that are already almost sorted, and Quicksort is usually fastest for everyday use. To speed up either insertion sort or bubble sort, consider combining the shell sort algorithm with either insertion sort or bubble sort.

Chapter 20

Searching

· ·

In This Chapter

▶ Performing a sequential search
▶ Performing a binary search
▶ Hashing
▶ Picking a searching algorithm

· ·

Searching for data is the second most common activity (after sorting data) necessary for creating many types of programs. For example, a program that stores names and addresses needs to sort data and then use a search algorithm to find the data that you want (such as looking for all people who live in Los Angeles and who have last names that begin with the letter "M").

To make searching easier, programs usually sort the data first before trying to search it. For more information about sorting, see Chapter 19.

An *algorithm* is just a fancy way of giving the computer specific types of instructions to accomplish a task. Choosing the right sorting and searching algorithms can make your program run quickly and efficiently. Choose the wrong sorting and searching algorithms and your program may run sluggishly, even for small amounts of data.

Searching Sequentially

A sequential search examines every possible item in a data structure (such as an array or linked list) until it finds what it's looking for. This is like looking for a your car keys in your apartment by going through room by room, looking in every conceivable location until you find your car keys. Although such a sequential search will eventually find your car keys (provided that they were in your apartment in the first place), it may take a long time.

For small lists, a sequential search is simple to use and fast. But when you need to search large amounts of data, the sequential search gets bogged down rapidly. Imagine the futility of trying to find your car keys somewhere in the city of New York. That's the type of task that a sequential search must face when searching through huge amounts of data.

A sequential search can start at either the beginning or the end of a list. It then proceeds to examine every item in the list until it finds the one item that it's searching for. Then it stops. To see how a sequential search works, try running the following QBASIC program:

```
CLS
MaxSize = 5
DIM MyArray(MaxSize) AS INTEGER
RANDOMIZE TIMER
MyArray(1) = INT(RND * 10) + 1
PRINT MyArray(1);
FOR I = 2 TO MaxSize
   MyArray(I) = MyArray(I - 1) + INT(RND * 10) + 1
   PRINT MyArray(I);
NEXT I
PRINT

INPUT "Which number do you want to find"; FindMe

FoundIt = 0
FOR J = 1 TO MaxSize
   PRINT "Checking array location"; J
   IF MyArray(J) = FindMe THEN
     FoundIt = 1
     EXIT FOR
   END IF
NEXT J

IF FoundIt = 1 THEN
   PRINT "Found it!"
ELSE
   PRINT "The number you want is not in the list."
END IF

END
```

This program works as follows:

1. The first through third lines clear the screen, create a variable called MaxSize, set the value of MaxSize to 5, and define an array called MyArray that can hold five (the value of MaxSize) integers.

2. The fourth through eleventh lines create a random number and store it in MyArray. Each additional random number is slightly larger than the previous one to create a sorted array of five integers. Then this group of lines prints the complete array on the screen for you to examine.

3. The twelfth line asks the user to type the number to find, which gets stored in the `FindMe` variable.

4. The thirteenth line creates a variable called `FoundIt` and sets its value to 0.

5. The fourteenth through twentieth lines start searching in `MyArray` for the number stored in the `FindMe` variable and print each array location that is checked.

6. The fifteenth through nineteenth lines print the message, "Found it!" if the program has found the number; if the program has not found the number, it prints "The number that you want is not in the list."

7. The sixteenth line marks the end of the program.

One advantage of a sequential search is that it can be used on both sorted and unsorted lists.

Performing a Binary Search

A sequential search starts from the beginning of a list and keeps trudging through the entire list from start to finish until it finds what it's looking for. But if a list is already sorted, you can shorten the search by using a *binary search*. (See Chapter 19 for more information about sorting data.)

A binary search divides a long (previously sorted) list in half. If the list to be sorted contains 10 numbers arranged from smallest (on the left) to largest (on the right), the computer looks to see which half of the list (five numbers on the left and five numbers on the right) contains the number for which it is searching.

Figure 20-1 shows a binary search trying to find the number 37 in a list containing 10 numbers. First, the binary search algorithm cuts the long list in half and examines the number in the middle of the list. Because the list contains 10 numbers, the binary search examines the fifth number in the list. In this case, the middle (fifth) number is 30, which tells the binary search algorithm that the number it wants (37) must be in the right half of the list.

Then the binary search takes the right half of the list (consisting of five numbers) and cuts this list in half, which points to the third number in the list (59). Because 59 is larger than 37 (the number it's trying to find), the binary search algorithm determines that the number 37 must be in the left side of this part of the list.

The left part of this list contains just two numbers, 37 and 45. With two items in a list, the binary search algorithm needs to look at only the first number in this list, which happens to be 37. Fortunately, 37 is the number that the binary search originally was looking for, and the search is over.

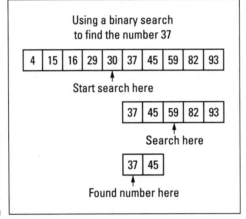

Figure 20-1:
A binary
search
keeps
cutting a list
in half until
it finds
what it's
looking for.

To see how the binary search algorithm works, try the following program:

```
CLS
MaxSize = 5
DIM MyArray(MaxSize) AS INTEGER
RANDOMIZE TIMER
MyArray(1) = INT(RND * 10) + 1
PRINT MyArray(1);
FOR I = 2 TO MaxSize
  MyArray(I) = MyArray(I - 1) + INT(RND * 10) + 1
  PRINT MyArray(I);
NEXT I
PRINT

INPUT "Which number do you want to find"; FindMe

Left = 1
Right = MaxSize
DO
  Half = (Left + Right) \ 2
  IF FindMe < MyArray(Half) THEN
    Right = Half - 1
  ELSE
    Left = Half + 1
  END IF
LOOP UNTIL (FindMe = MyArray(Half) OR Left > Right)
IF FindMe = MyArray(Half) THEN
  PRINT "Found it in location"; Half
ELSE
  PRINT "The number you want is not in the list."
END IF
END
```

You can press F8 to see how each line in the program works. Then press F4 to see what the line displays on the screen.

The binary search program works as follows:

1. The first through third lines clear the screen, create a variable called MaxSize, set the value of MaxSize to five, and define an array called MyArray that can hold five (the value of MaxSize) integers.

2. The fourth through eleventh lines create a random number and store it in MyArray. Each additional random number is slightly larger than the previous one to create a sorted array of five integers. Then this group of lines prints the complete array on the screen for you to examine.

3. The twelfth line asks the user to type the number to find, which gets stored in the FindMe variable.

4. The thirteenth line creates a variable named Left and sets its value to 1.

5. The fourteenth line creates a variable named Right and sets its value to MaxSize, the maximum size of the array.

6. The fifteenth line is the start of a DO LOOP UNTIL loop that repeats until the binary search finds the FindMe number in the array or until it has searched the entire array and can't find the FindMe number.

7. The sixteenth line creates a variable called Half that divides the list in half, using integer division. (Remember that when you divide an odd number, integer division drops all fractions, so 5 \ 2 equals 2.)

8. The seventeenth through twenty-first lines look for the FindMe number in the left half of the array. If the FindMe number is less than the item stored in the middle of the array, the Right variable is set to Half - 1. Otherwise, the value of the Left variable is set to Half + 1. By lowering the value of the Right variable and increasing the value of the Left variable, the program can keep track when it has searched all numbers in the array without finding the number that it's looking for. The moment that the Left variable becomes greater than the Right variable, the program knows that the number it is searching for is not stored anywhere in the array.

9. The twenty-second line marks the end of the DO LOOP UNTIL loop that continues until the FindMe number is found or until the program has determined that the FindMe number does not exist in the array.

10. The twenty-third through twenty-seventh lines print the message "Found it in location," followed by the array position. If the number is not found in the array, the program prints, "The number that you want is not in the list."

11. The twenty-fourth line marks the end of the program.

The binary search algorithm can work only on a sorted list.

Hashing

Finding something is always easier when you know where you stored it last. That's why finding your car keys is easier when they're hanging on a hook by the front door than when you have to search the entire house because you can't remember where you may have put them.

Hashing works on a similar principle. When you want to store an item, hashing first calculates a numeric value (called a *hash function*) that identifies that item. Then the program uses this numeric value to store the item in a specific location in a data structure (such as an array or a linked list). Now, instead of having to search an entire array or linked list to find a single item, the program just needs to look in the specific location using the hash function.

For example, suppose that you wanted to store an integer in an array. If you stored the integer anywhere in the array, you would have to search the entire array to find that number again. But if you used hashing, the task would be much simpler. First, calculate a hash function using the following formula:

```
HashFunction = Number to store MOD 5
```

MOD is a special QBASIC division command that tells the computer to divide a number and return the remainder. For example, 26 MOD 5 would return the value of 1.

This formula tells the computer to take the number that you want to store, divide it by five, and use the remaining value as the hash function. So if you want to store the number 26, the hash function would be 1 (26 / 5 = 5 with a remainder of 1).

No matter what number you choose to store, the hash function calculates one of the following five values — 0, 1, 2, 3, or 4. You can create an array and use the hash function to determine the exact position at which to store an item in the array. Because the hash function of the number 26 equals 1, you could store this integer in array location number 1, as shown in Figure 20-2.

The value of the hash function determines where to store the item in a data structure.

Figure 20-2:
Hashing
calculates a
value to
determine
where to
store data
initially and
where to
find data
later on.

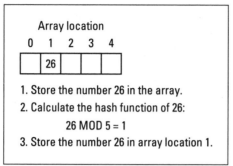

Array location

0 1 2 3 4

| | 26 | | | |

1. Store the number 26 in the array.
2. Calculate the hash function of 26:

    26 MOD 5 = 1

3. Store the number 26 in array location 1.

When you want to find the number 26 in the array again, hashing calculates the same hash function (which calculates to 1), telling the program to look for the number 26 in the first array location. Because hashing doesn't require searching every item in a list, hashing can be faster than sequential and binary searching, especially for long lists of data.

Dealing with collisions

Ideally, a hash function should calculate a unique value. But a hash function will probably calculate the same value for different items. For example, calculating a hash function using MOD 5 (dividing a number by 5 and using the remainder as the hash function) returns a value of 2 for the numbers 7 and 32.

If you're storing large numbers of items, more than one item will likely share the same hash function. When two items share the same hash function, programmers say that a *collision* has occurred. To handle collisions, you need to create a data structure that can store multiple items with the same hash function. Figure 20-3 shows two data structures to handle collisions: a two-dimensional array and a one-dimensional array of linked lists. (Chapter 15 contains information about creating and using two-dimensional arrays. Chapter 17 contains information about linked lists. Remember that QBASIC can't create linked lists, but other languages — such as C/C++, Pascal, and Java — can create linked lists.)

In Figure 20-3, the numbers 7 and 32 share the same hash function (which is 2). Because the number 7 is in array element number 2 (which represents the hash function 2), the number 32 must be stored beneath the number 7 underneath the same hash function of 2. Both a two-dimensional array and an array of linked lists allows the program to store multiple numbers underneath the same hash function location of 2.

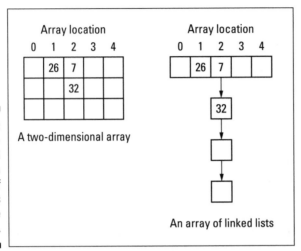

Figure 20-3:
A two-dimensional array or an array of linked lists can handle collisions.

Ideally, you want to use a data structure that can expand or shrink to handle items sharing identical hash functions.

Searching with a hash function

After you store items in a data structure using hashing, you can search for any of those items by calculating a hash function for the item that you want to find. Then you look for the item in the data structure where items sharing the same hash function are stored.

If every item has a unique hash function, the hash function can pinpoint the exact location of an item extremely quickly. Even if multiple items share the same hash function (refer to Figure 20-2), hashing now limits the search to a smaller list of items with identical hash functions. As a result, hashing usually can search faster than sequential or binary searching.

The following QBASIC program creates five random integers (such as 41, 50, 57, 75, 67) and stores them in a two-dimensional array, as shown in Figure 20-4.

```
CLS
MaxSize = 5
RANDOMIZE TIMER
DIM MyArray(0 TO MaxSize - 1, 0 TO MaxSize - 1) AS INTEGER

FOR I = 0 TO MaxSize - 1          ' Vertical
  FOR J = 0 TO MaxSize - 1        ' Horizontal
    MyArray(I, J) = 0
  NEXT J
```

```
NEXT I

Count = 0
FOR J = 0 TO MaxSize - 1
  StopNow = 0
  StoreMe = INT(RND * 100) + 1
  HashValue = StoreMe MOD 5
  DO UNTIL StopNow = 1
    IF MyArray(Count, HashValue) = 0 THEN
      MyArray(Count, HashValue) = StoreMe
      StopNow = 1
    ELSE
      Count = Count + 1
    END IF
  LOOP

  PRINT StoreMe;
NEXT J

PRINT
PRINT

FOR I = 0 TO MaxSize - 1          ' Vertical
  FOR J = 0 TO MaxSize - 1        ' Horizontal
    PRINT MyArray(I, J);
  NEXT J
  PRINT
NEXT I

END
```

Figure 20-4:
A two-dimensional array can store values organized by a hash function.

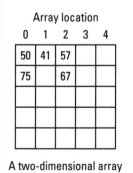

A two-dimensional array

The preceding program uses hashing to store five random numbers in a two-dimensional array as follows:

1. The first through fourth lines clear the screen, prepare to create random numbers based on the computer clock, and define a two-dimensional array named `MyArray` that can hold integers.

2. The fifth through ninth lines fill `MyArray` with zeroes. Note that the `I` variable defines the row number and the `J` variable defines the column numbers in Figure 20-4.

3. The tenth line creates a variable named `Count` and sets its value to zero.

4. The eleventh line starts a `FOR NEXT` loop that starts the hash algorithm to store an integer in the two-dimensional array.

5. The twelfth line creates a variable named `StopNow` and sets its value to zero.

6. The thirteenth line creates a random number from 1 to 100 and stores it in a variable named `StoreMe`.

7. The fourteenth line calculates a hash function and stores it in the variable named `HashValue`. The `HashValue` will always be one of five numbers: 0, 1, 2, 3, or 4.

8. The fifteenth line starts a `DO UNTIL LOOP` loop that tries to determine where to store the `StoreMe` number in `MyArray`.

9. The sixteenth through twenty-first lines try to store the `StoreMe` number in the first row (represented by the `Count` variable) of `MyArray` in the column represented by the value of `HashValue`. If a number is already in the array location, these instructions try to store the number in the next row down until they succeed in finding an empty spot in the array.

10. The twenty-second line ends the `DO UNTIL LOOP` loop that started in the fifteenth line.

11. The twenty-third line prints the five random numbers that the program created.

12. The twenty-fourth line represents the end of the `FOR NEXT` loop that started in the eleventh line.

13. The twenty-fifth and twenty-sixth lines add two blank lines.

14. The twenty-seventh through thirty-second lines print the entire array so that you can see how hashing has sorted the five random numbers that the program has created.

15. The thirty-third line marks the end of the program.

Picking a Searching Algorithm

Sequential searching is the easiest search method to implement and is the fastest for small lists, but for larger lists, sequential searching takes too long. For general use, binary searching is usually faster than sequential searching. The main drawback is that binary searching works only on data that has already been sorted.

Hashing is best for large amounts of data, but it is more complicated to implement because you need to calculate a hash function to store each item in a specific location in a data structure. Then you have the additional problem of dealing with collisions (when two items share the same hash function).

As a general rule, use sequential searching for small lists or unsorted lists; binary searching for larger, sorted lists; and hashing if you don't mind calculating hash functions for each item.

Chapter 21

Optimizing Your Code

· ·

In This Chapter

▶ Choosing the right data structure

▶ Choosing the right algorithm

▶ Fine-tuning the source code

▶ Using a faster language

▶ Optimizing your compiler

· ·

*G*etting a program to work correctly is often a miracle in itself. But after you get a program to work and have eliminated as many bugs as possible, the next question is whether to use (or release) the program right away or take some time to optimize it.

Optimization tries to meet the following three goals (without introducing bugs into the program in the process):

- ✔ Make the program faster
- ✔ Make the program smaller
- ✔ Make the program require less memory to run

The price that you pay for optimization is the additional time needed to examine and optimize your program, the potential of making a program less readable and harder to modify later on, and the risk of turning a slow, large, working program into a fast, small, nonworking, bug-ridden program.

As a general rule, the new version (such as version 1.0 or version 4.0) of any program is rushed out the door just to grab market share. Within a few months, companies usually release slightly modified versions (such as version 1.01 or version 4.1), which fix some bugs (and usually introduce some new ones as well) and optimize the program in some way. In the commercial software market, optimization is usually a luxury, which is why so many programs are referred to as *bloatware*, because they require globs of memory and hard disk space.

Choosing the Right Data Structure

Every program needs to store data, so you need to choose the right data structure for holding information in your program. An array may be easy to create, but you must know the number of items that the array needs to hold ahead of time. Make an array too small and your program runs out of space to store additional data, possibly crashing your program. Make an array too large and you risk allocating space for storage you don't need, which can cause your program to gobble up more memory than necessary.

For example, if you create a large two-dimensional array but store only a small number of items in it, you waste a large amount of space. If you replace the two-dimensional array with a graph, no space is wasted (although you now have the problem of writing additional instructions to create and manage a graph, which is much harder to create and manage than a two-dimensional array).

More important, the data structure that you choose can affect the efficiency of the sorting and searching algorithms in your program. Rather than sort items in an array, a sorting algorithm would run much faster rearranging pointers in a linked list.

To learn more about different types of data structures, see Chapters 15 through 18. To learn more about pointers and linked lists, see Chapter 17.

Choosing the Right Algorithm

An algorithm tells the computer how to accomplish a specific task. For example, think about all the different ways you could tell your friends to get to your house from downtown. You could tell them to take the highway, which would be easier but may take longer. Or you could tell them to take a variety of side streets that would ultimately make the trip shorter but make your directions harder to follow.

Deciding which set of directions to give to someone is much like deciding which algorithm to use in your program. For example, if you must sort a list containing 30,000 names, the bubble sort algorithm sorts that list much slower than the Quicksort algorithm. (See Chapter 19 for explanations on the bubble sort and Quicksort algorithms.) After you sort 30,000 names, using a sequential search algorithm to find a name would be much slower than using a binary search algorithm. (See Chapter 20 for explanations on sequential and binary search algorithms.)

For another example of choosing the right algorithm, think of a video game that displays the top-ten highest scores. Before anyone has played the game, the top-ten highest scores are all zero. The first time that a person plays the game, the video game lists that person's score in the top ten. Each time someone plays the game again, the video game must sort the scores to display the highest to the lowest ten scores.

For this video game example, the insertion sort algorithm would be most efficient. When the video game has two scores, the insertion sort algorithm sorts those two scores from highest to lowest. The third time someone plays the video game, the insertion sort algorithm compares the third score to the previous two scores and inserts the third score in its correct place. Each additional time someone plays the video game, the insertion sort algorithm compares the new score with the previous high scores to determine where to insert it in the top-ten list of scores.

If you use a bubble sort algorithm to sort the top-ten scores, the bubble sort algorithm would need to examine the list multiple times and compare each score with its neighbor — taking more time than the insert sort algorithm as a result. In this particular case, you can see how the insert sort algorithm would be more efficient than the bubble sort algorithm.

As you write your own programs, remember that different algorithms are available for you to use to accomplish identical tasks for your program. Then choose the algorithm that runs the fastest for your program.

Fine-Tuning the Source Code

If you've chosen data structures and algorithms with care, you can still optimize your program by fine-tuning the source code. This means rewriting portions of your program to make it run faster or require less memory.

Ideally, you should use the techniques described in the following sections while writing your original source code. Then you don't need to take the time to apply these techniques during a fine-tuning stage.

Put the condition most likely to be false first

When you use the AND operator, you combine two or more conditions like this:

```
IF (Boolean expression 1) AND (Boolean expression 2) THEN
   ' Follow one or more instructions listed here
END IF
```

This `IF THEN` statement runs only after the computer takes time to verify that both `Boolean expression 1` and `Boolean expression 2` are true. If either one of these Boolean expressions is false, the instructions inside the `IF THEN` statement don't run.

So when you use the `AND` operator, put the expression most likely to be false in the first part of the `AND` operation. For example, if `Boolean expression 1` is false, the computer doesn't bother checking to see whether `Boolean expression 2` is true because one false Boolean expression always makes the entire `AND` operation false.

The moment that the computer determines that the first Boolean expression in an `AND` operation is false, it doesn't check the second Boolean expression, thus saving time and helping make your program run just a little bit faster.

Put the conditions most likely to be true first

The `IF THEN ELSEIF` and `SELECT CASE` statements often need to check several conditions to make a decision, as the following code shows:

```
IF (Boolean expression 1) THEN
  ' Follow one or more instructions listed here
ELSEIF (Boolean expression 2) THEN
  ' Follow one or more instructions listed here
END IF
```

In this `IF THEN ELSEIF` statement, the computer first checks to see whether `Boolean expression 1` is true. If not, it checks to see whether `Boolean expression 2` is true.

But what if `Boolean expression 1` is false most of the time and `Boolean expression 2` is true most of the time? Then the program wastes time always checking `Boolean expression 1` (which is usually false) before it can get to `Boolean expression 2` (which is usually true).

To keep your program from wasting time checking a Boolean expression that's usually false, put the Boolean expression most likely to be true at the front and the Boolean expression least likely to be true at the end of the `IF THEN ELSEIF` statement, like this:

```
IF (Boolean expression 2) THEN
  ' Follow one or more instructions listed here
ELSEIF (Boolean expression 1) THEN
  ' Follow one or more instructions listed here
END IF
```

By placing the Boolean expression most likely to be true at the beginning, you save the computer from wasting time checking one or more additional Boolean expressions that are usually going to be false anyway.

This technique also works for SELECT CASE statements, as in the following example:

```
SELECT CASE Variable
CASE Value1
  ' Follow these instructions if the Variable = Value1
CASE Value2
  ' Follow these instructions if the Variable = Value2
END SELECT
```

SELECT CASE statements check to see whether a variable equals one value (such as Value1). If you put the values most likely to match the SELECT CASE variable up front, you avoid forcing the computer to check a long list of values that are least likely to match anyway.

Although the technique of putting the conditions most likely to be true first may seem trivial, every little bit of time you save can add up to make a faster and more responsive program.

Don't run a FOR NEXT loop needlessly

Loops can gobble up time, so make sure that you choose the right loop. For example, if you're using a sequential search to find an item in an array, you could use a FOR NEXT loop. The FOR NEXT loop can count to make the computer check every position in the array to look for a specific item.

The FOR NEXT loop runs a specific number of times. What do you think happens if it finds the item that it's looking for on the first try? The FOR NEXT loop doesn't care; it continues looping a fixed number of times anyway, thereby wasting time.

When you use a FOR NEXT loop, make sure that you absolutely need the program to loop a fixed number of times; otherwise, use the EXIT FOR command to exit the FOR NEXT loop as soon as possible.

The following QBASIC example uses the EXIT FOR command to exit from the FOR NEXT loop at the moment that it finds what it is looking for. Without the EXIT FOR command, the FOR NEXT loop would always repeat itself 30 times, regardless of whether or not it needed to loop all 30 times, as the following code shows:

```
FoundIt = 0
FOR J = 1 TO 30
  PRINT "Checking array location"; J
  IF MyArray(J) = FindMe THEN
    FoundIt = 1
    EXIT FOR
  END IF
NEXT J
```

Clean out your loops

All instructions that you cram inside a loop must absolutely be placed inside the loop. If you put an instruction inside a loop that serves no purpose in the loop, you force the computer to keep running that instruction repeatedly, thereby slowing down your loop and ultimately your program as well.

For example, consider the following loop:

```
FOR J = 1 TO 5000
  I = 0
  IF MyArray(J) = 55 THEN
    PRINT MyArray(J)
  END IF
NEXT J
```

The preceding FOR NEXT loop repeats itself 5000 times, but the I = 0 instruction is never used inside the FOR NEXT loop. The computer is forced to run the I = 0 instruction 5000 times for no reason. To avoid this problem, simply remove the I = 0 instruction from the loop, like this:

```
I = 0
FOR J = 1 TO 5000
  IF MyArray(J) = 55 THEN
    PRINT MyArray(J)
  END IF
NEXT J
```

In the programming world, *nesting* occurs when you cram one type of control or loop structure inside another one. In the preceding QBASIC program example, an IF THEN statement is nested inside a FOR NEXT loop.

Be especially wary of nested loops. When you nest one loop inside the other, the inner loop runs more often than the outer loop. By ridding the inner loop of any instructions that don't need to be inside that loop, you avoid forcing the computer to repeat an instruction needlessly.

TECHNICAL STUFF

Why C/C++ programs can be hard to understand

Programs written in C/C++ usually run faster and more efficiently than identical programs written in other languages, such as Pascal or BASIC. But C/C++ has developed a well-deserved reputation for creating cryptic code. One reason for this is that C/C++ allows a variety of shortcuts that can make your program run faster but at the sacrifice of readability.

For example, rather than type **x = x + 5** or **y = y – 23**, C/C++ enables you to use shortcuts, as in the following examples:

```
x += 5;     /* equivalent to x =
    x + 5 */

y -= 23;    /* equivalent to y =
    y - 23 */
```

C/C++ also includes something called a prefix or postfix operator that can increment or decrement a variable by one. The following are examples of postfix operators:

```
x++;        /* equivalent to x =
    x + 1 */

y--;        /* equivalent to y =
    y - 1 */
```

The prefix operators that are equivalent to the preceding postfix operators are as follows:

```
++x;        /* equivalent to x =
    x + 1 */

--y;        /* equivalent to y =
    y - 1 */
```

If you think they look and act alike, you're almost right. The big difference occurs when you combine postfix or prefix operators into a formula, like this:

```
x = y + z++
```

The preceding formula is actually equivalent to the following two instructions:

```
x = y + z
z = z + 1
```

You could use the following prefix operator instead:

```
a = b + --c
```

This is equivalent to the following two instructions:

```
c = c - 1
a = b + c
```

C/C++ even offers a strange shortcut for an IF ELSE statement that uses a combination of a question mark and a colon, like this:

```
printf("This number is bigger =
    %d\n", (x > y) ? x : y);
```

This is equivalent to the following normal-looking IF ELSE statement:

```
if (x > y)
  printf("This number is bigger
    = %d\n", x);
else
  printf("This number is bigger
    = %d\n", y);
```

The shorter, more cryptic version of the IF ELSE statement may take up less space and run faster, but it's harder to understand at first glance. When using shortcuts, be aware of how they can make your program harder to read.

Use the correct data types

To save memory, use the correct data types. For example, declare your variables as integers (as in DIM Num AS INTEGER) rather than as long integers (as in DIM Num AS LONG). Long integers can range in value from -2,147,483,648 to 2,147,483,647; ordinary integers can range in value only from -32,768 to 32,767.

However, a long integer variable gobbles up more memory if you need to stuff a really large number into it, such as 2,147,483,647. If your variables never need to hold such a large number, a smaller data type (such as an integer) works just as well and requires less memory.

Use built-in commands whenever possible

Nearly every programming language includes special built-in commands that run faster than equivalent commands that you type yourself. For example, if you have a variable (called MyNumber) that you want to increment by 1, you could use the following command:

```
MyNumber = MyNumber + 1
```

Nothing is wrong with this command, but other languages offer shortcuts for incrementing a variable by 1. In C/C++, you can use a shortcut like this:

```
mynumber++
```

If you want to increment a variable in Delphi (which is based on the Pascal language), you can use the following bit of code:

```
Inc(MyNumber)
```

If you use built-in commands, you risk making your code more cryptic and harder to understand. That's because not all programmers know all the built-in commands (shortcuts) that a particular language may offer. When a programmer encounters a built-in command, he or she may not understand how that particular command actually works.

Using a Faster Language

The fastest possible language in which you can write a program is machine code, followed by assembly language and C/C++, with the other languages (such as Pascal and BASIC) trailing slightly behind. If you want to speed up your program, consider switching to a different programming language.

To help them identify which parts of their program are used most often, programmers use a special program called a *profiler*. You use a profiler to optimize the part of your program that is used most often and make your program run faster.

Many programmers use a simpler language such as Visual Basic to develop a prototype program that they can show to a client and to design the user interface. After you create a prototype program, you have two choices. Your first choice is to dump the entire prototype program and rewrite the whole thing from scratch using a faster language, such as C/C++. Naturally, this can take a long time and doesn't guarantee that the program works right (but at least it should look good). Your second choice is to use the prototype of the program as the basis for your actual working program. But instead of writing the entire program in a single language, you can write the most often used parts of the program in a faster language.

When you use two or more languages to create a single program, you can take advantage of each language's strengths. The drawback of this strategy is trying to make two or three different programming languages cooperate with one another.

Many people create a program using a simple language, such as Visual Basic, and then with each revision, they gradually rewrite parts of the program in a faster language, such as C/C++ or assembly language. The entire program may have started in one language, but eventually it is completely rewritten in a different language.

Optimizing Your Compiler

As an alternative to using a faster language, you can use a faster compiler. If you put the identical program through different compilers, each compiler creates the same program, but one compiler's program may run faster than another compiler's program. Unfortunately, if you write a program in C++ for one compiler (such as Microsoft Visual C++), the program may not run at all in another C++ compiler (such as Borland C++ Builder) without extensive modifications.

To give you more control over your program, most compilers offer options for changing the way that the compiler works. You can change these options to fine-tune your compiler for your particular program, as shown in Figure 21-1.

Make sure that you know what you're doing before you change any of your compiler optimization settings. Most of these optimization settings can make your program run faster but at the expense of turning off the compiler's built-in error-checking feature, which can help you spot bugs in your program. If you turn off your compiler's error-checking capabilities, your program runs faster, but it may crash when an innocent user runs it.

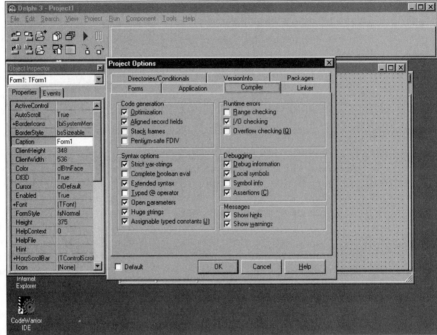

Figure 21-1:
Setting
compiler
optimization
options in
Delphi.

The whole point of programming is to create a working program. When you get a program that works, you can worry about optimizing it to make it faster and smaller. If you can't get your program to work, keep in mind that no one wants an optimized program that runs fast but doesn't do anything useful.

Part VI
Internet Programming

In this part . . .

Programming a computer used to mean running a set of instructions on a single computer. If another computer wanted to run the same program, you had to make a copy of the program and then run each copy on a different computer.

But with the rapid spread of the Internet, a new variation of programming has appeared. Instead of writing a single program to run on a single computer, you can write a single program that can run on a variety of different computers across the Internet. Theoretically, what you create on your computer can be seen by another computer located anywhere in the world.

This part of the book introduces you to the wonderful world of Internet programming languages. Programs written in Internet languages exist as source code on a single computer. When another computer accesses this source code, that computer runs the program and interprets the results.

The most common Internet programming language is called HTML, which is a special language for designing Web pages. If you've ever wanted to create your own Web pages, this is the place to start.

Chapter 22

Playing with HTML

● ●

In This Chapter

▶ Understanding the basics of HTML

▶ Using tags to define text

▶ Using tag attributes

▶ Making lists

▶ Creating hyperlinks

▶ Using graphics

▶ Creating a user interface

● ●

*P*eople have used the Internet to exchange messages and files with one another for years. In the beginning, using the Internet required that you type the right commands and allowed you to see only plain text on a screen staring back at you. In 1992, physicists at CERN, a Swiss research institute for studying particle physics, invented the World Wide Web.

The goal of the World Wide Web (which is where that odd www abbreviation comes from in most Web site addresses, such as www.dummies.com) was to provide a way to share information among researchers. Initially, the World Wide Web consisted solely of text, but eventually people tacked on a friendly graphical interface to make the World Wide Web easier to use. The idea is much like the way that Microsoft Windows originally helped make MS-DOS easier to use.

Because the Internet consisted of a variety of computers, programmers had to make the graphical interface of the World Wide Web a standard that could run on any computer. Every computer can understand ASCII codes, so programmers created an ASCII-based language dubbed *HyperText Markup Language*, or *HTML*.

To create a Web site, you type HTML codes and store them in an ASCII file, which any computer can read. When another computer wants to view your Web site, it uses a special program called a browser that translates the HTML code into a pretty graphical interface.

Why should I learn HTML codes?

Good question. Using a dedicated Web-page creation program such as Microsoft FrontPage, you can type and draw your Web page without once using (much less understanding) HTML codes. Other programs, such as WordPerfect, Microsoft PowerPoint, Quattro Pro, and Microsoft Access can also create Web pages out of ordinary data, sparing you from the complexities of writing and editing HTML code.

But consider these two good reasons to learn HTML. First, Web-page creation programs can help you create Web pages quickly and easily, but they aren't always flexible. If you want to modify your Web page, a Web-page creation program may not always let you do it. But if you know HTML codes, you can modify the HTML

files that make up your Web pages and tweak the pages to act and look exactly the way you want.

Second, knowing HTML codes can help you learn how other people have created special effects on their Web pages. For example, if you find a particularly interesting Web page that uses a bizarre color or displays a strange effect that you'd like to duplicate on your own page, you can view the HTML code of that other Web page to see how it works. (In Microsoft Internet Explorer, choose View⇨ Source. In Netscape Navigator, choose View⇨Page Source.) Then you can use the secrets you learn from other people's Web pages to enhance your own pages.

One of the first (and most popular) Web browsers was called Mosaic, which appeared in 1993. Both Netscape Navigator and Microsoft Internet Explorer are based on Mosaic, so if you'd rather use this other browser, you can download it from www.ncsa.uiuc.edu/SDG/Software/Mosaic.

HTML provides the foundation for a Web page designing language that every computer can understand. In an attempt to make fancier Web pages, new standards for HTML appear regularly along with variations of HTML with odd acronyms, such as DHTML. Although each new version of the HTML standard offers more features, not all computers and browsers support all HTML versions. As long as you stick to standard HTML codes, your Web pages can be viewed by anyone using any computer.

Grasping the Basics of HTML

HTML code defines the way that text and graphics appear in a browser. A Web page actually consists of HTML code stored in an ASCII file, usually with the .HTM or .HTML file extension. HTML code consists of something called *tags*, which appear in brackets. Most (but not all) tags appear in pairs, where the first tag defines the start of something and the second tag defines the end of something, such as defining italic text or a heading, as in this example:

```
<I>This text appears in italics.</I>
```

Ending tags always use a slash character, such as </I> or </BODY>.

You can enclose tags within other tags, as in the following line:

```
<B>This <I>text</I> appears in bold.</B>
```

The preceding two tags display the entire line in bold and display the word text in both bold and italics, which looks like this:

```
This text appears in bold.
```

Tags act like containers for holding text. Think of tags as marking the beginning and ending of a container. Make sure that you don't mix up your tags, or you may get unpredictable formatting of text, as in the following example:

```
<B>This <I>text appears</B> in bold. </I>
```

Ideally, you want tags to be completely located inside the beginning and ending of other tags, as shown in Figure 22-1.

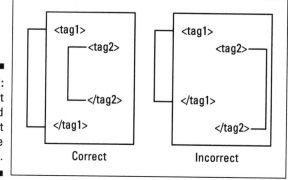

Figure 22-1: The correct and incorrect way to use HTML tags.

HTML codes can look cryptic when crammed together, so feel free to use plenty of blank lines and spaces to make your HTML code look halfway readable. Remember that when a browser interprets your HTML code into a Web page, it ignores blank lines or spaces.

You can write HTML code in any text editor, such as the Windows Notepad or even the QBASIC editor. Just remember to save your file with the .HTM file extension. After you've created a file using HTML codes, you can load that file into your browser by choosing File⇨Open.

The most important HTML tags

The following are the first HTML tags that every Web page needs:

```
<HTML>

</HTML>
```

These two tags simply define a blank Web page. Anything that appears inside these two tags appears in the Web page. Nothing should appear before the `<HTML>` tag or after the `</HTML>` tag. If anything does appear in these locations, it won't appear when viewed in a Web browser.

Creating a header and title

Next you need to define anything that you want to appear on the header (the top) of your Web page using the `<HEAD>` tag, which looks like this:

```
<HTML>
<HEAD>
</HEAD>
</HTML>
```

The most common item to place between the `<HEAD>` and `</HEAD>` tags is a title. If someone decides to bookmark your Web page, the title is the text that gets stored in that person's bookmark list. Without a title, the user's bookmark list will contain the actual filename, which can be cryptic and confusing. After all, what's easier to read in a bookmark listing? An actual Web page name, such as "Web Site Containing American Nuclear Secrets" or a filename, such as NK1999.HTM?

To define a title for your Web page, shove the title tags between the header tags, like this:

```
<HTML>
<HEAD>
  <TITLE>Document title</TITLE>
</HEAD>
</HTML>
```

A Web page needs only one title.

Defining the bulk of your Web page

After you define a header and title for your Web page, you need to define the remainder of your page using the `<BODY>` and `</BODY>` tags, like this:

```
<HTML>
<HEAD>
  <TITLE>Document title</TITLE>
</HEAD>

<BODY>

</BODY>
</HTML>
```

Adding comments

In QBASIC and other programming languages, you can insert comments that explain what your program is doing, when you last changed the program, and who last modified the program. When you're writing HTML code, you can also add comments to your Web pages.

Comments don't appear in a browser; they appear only when you're viewing the HTML code. A comment must appear inside these brackets:

```
<!-- This is a comment. Your mother is ugly. -->
```

The `<!--` marks the beginning of the comment tag and the `-->` marks the end of the comment tag.

Anything that appears between the comment tags does not appear in a browser. Comments are for your own use only.

Defining Text with Tags

The basic HTML tags define your Web page as a whole, but you need to add text to provide something useful for viewers to read. HTML provides special tags for creating the following elements:

- **Headings** separate sections of text and categorize blocks of text under a single topic (similar to the way that headings in this chapter separate and categorize text).

- **Paragraphs** are blocks of text consisting of one or more sentences.

✔ **Quotes** are similar to paragraphs but are indented and surrounded by more space than ordinary paragraphs.

✔ **Text emphasis** displays text in a certain format or style to highlight the text.

Making a heading

HTML lets you choose from six heading styles. Heading 1 signifies the most important heading, and Heading 6 signifies the least important heading. Figure 22-2 shows an example of each type of heading.

To create one of the six headings, use one of the following HTML tags:

```
<H1>Heading 1</H1>
<H2>Heading 2</H2>
<H3>Heading 3</H3>
<H4>Heading 4</H4>
<H5>Heading 5</H5>
<H6>Heading 6</H6>
```

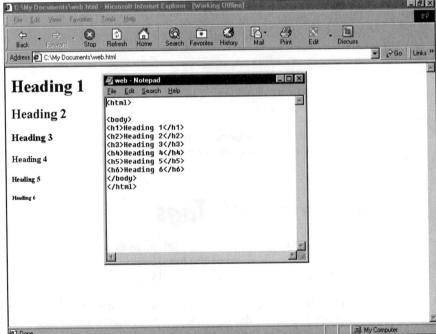

Figure 22-2:
The six types of headings that you can create with HTML tags.

Usually, you want at least two subheadings under each heading. For example, you would want two or three Heading 2s under a single Heading 1. Or you would want two or three Heading 6s under a single Heading 5.

Defining a paragraph

A paragraph is a chunk of text separated from the surrounding text by a blank line (just like the paragraphs you see on this page). To define the start of a paragraph, you use the <P> tag, and to define the end of the paragraph, you use the </P> tag, like this:

```
<P>
This text is considered a paragraph.
</P>
```

When you type text inside a pair of paragraph tags, the entire paragraph can exist on a single line, extending from the left margin of the screen to beyond the right margin of the screen. The paragraph tags automatically take care of displaying text within the margins of the screen.

To make your paragraph text easier to read, you may want to press Enter to make paragraph lines appear on multiple lines instead of on a single line.

If you want to insert a line break in the middle of a paragraph, you can use a special line break tag — the <BR> tag. Unlike other tags, the line break tag appears by itself. Figure 22-3 shows how the paragraph tag <P> and the line break tag <BR> can create a blank line between paragraphs.

Adding emphasis to text

Paragraph tags can separate your text into paragraphs (automatically inserting blank lines before and after the paragraph), and block quotes can indent your text. But you may want to highlight specific words or phrases. To do that, you can use the following pairs of HTML tags:

- <B> and </B> displays text in bold.
- <I> and </I> displays text in italics.
- <U> and </U> displays text underlined.
- <TT> and </TT> displays text as if it were printed from a typewriter.
- <HR> displays a horizontal line. (Note that the <HR> tag is another tag that doesn't appear in pairs.)

Figure 22-4 shows a Web page that uses all these special ways to emphasize text within a browser.

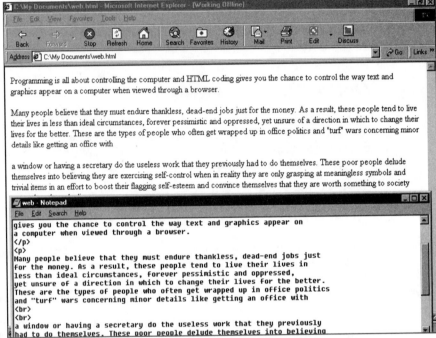

Figure 22-3:
How a
paragraph
looks when
displayed in
a browser.

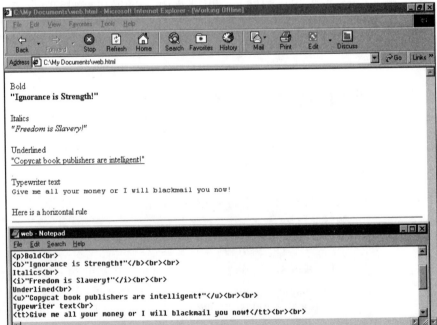

Figure 22-4:
Displaying
text with
special
emphasis
on certain
words and
phrases.

Using Tag Attributes

To truly enhance the appearance of your text, you can use attributes. An *attribute* is a special command that you bury inside an HTML tag. An attribute modifies the appearance of any text defined by that tag. The following are some common attributes:

- ✔ ALIGN sets paragraph or heading text aligned to right, center, or left.
- ✔ BGCOLOR changes the background color of a Web page.
- ✔ TEXT changes the color of text.
- ✔ LINK changes the color of hyperlinks.
- ✔ VLINK changes the color of hyperlinks that the user has already visited.

Aligning text

Headings and paragraphs normally appear left-aligned, but you can also make them right-aligned or center-aligned by using the ALIGN attribute inside the first heading or paragraph tag, as in the following example:

```
<P ALIGN="center">
This text appears centered.
</P>
```

To align text to the right or left, use the word right or left with the ALIGN attribute, like this:

```
<H1 ALIGN="right">
This text appears right-aligned.
</H1>
```

Playing with colors

To define the background and text colors, you have to set the BGCOLOR and TEXT attributes to a six-digit number that represents the RGB (Red-Green-Blue) value. An RGB value defines how much red, green, and blue appears. By altering the amount of red, green, or blue, you can create a variety of different colors such as purple, white, orange, yellow, and so on. The following code is just one example:

```
<BODY BGCOLOR="FFFFFF">        (white background)
<BODY TEXT="000000">          (black text)
```

RGB colors are defined by hexadecimal numbers, which range from 0 to F (0, 1, 2, 3, 4, 5, 6, 7, 8, 9, A, B, C, D, E, F). A zero (0) represents the absence of a color, while an F represents the maximum amount of a color. You can vary the values for red, blue, and green to create other colors.

The first two digits in the BGCOLOR and TEXT attributes represent the amount of red (R), the second two digits represent the amount of green (G), and the last two digits represent the amount of blue (B) displayed. If you want a red background, use this command:

```
<BODY BGCOLOR="FF0000">
```

For a green background, use this command:

```
<BODY BGCOLOR="00FF00">
```

And for a blue background, use this command:

```
<BODY BGCOLOR="0000FF">
```

Coloring your hyperlinks

You may also want to adjust the colors for your hyperlinks. Most Web pages display hyperlinks in a bright color to make them obvious. After the user has visited a hyperlink, that hyperlink can change colors to show the user that he has already been to that Web page. To change colors for your hyperlinks, use these tags:

```
<BODY LINK="#hexadecimal_here">
<BODY VLINK="#hexadecimal_here">
```

The LINK attribute defines the color to display a hyperlink. The VLINK attribute defines the color to display a hyperlink that the user has already visited.

Making a List

Creating a Web page to inform people about something is like creating an attention-grabbing television advertisement. In both cases, you want to show the viewer as much information as possible in an attractive and easily digestible way. Many people find large chunks of text intimidating and hard to read, so consider separating your text into lists.

HTML provides three types of lists (and I'm using a list to show you those lists):

> ✔ **Unordered lists** display text with bullets in front of each line, such as the list of which this text is a part.
>
> ✔ **Ordered lists** number each line of text.
>
> ✔ **Definition lists** indent each line of text.

Unordered lists

To create an unordered list, you need to use two types of HTML tags. The first HTML tags are ⟨UL⟩ and ⟨/UL⟩, which define the unordered list. The second tag, ⟨LI⟩ (which stands for List Item), marks each bulleted item. Here is an example:

```
<UL>
<LI>Take out the trash.
<LI>Develop a nuclear weapon.
<LI>Borrow an expensive appliance from the neighbor.
</UL>
```

The ⟨LI⟩ tag doesn't have an ending tag. You use ⟨LI⟩ by itself.

You can also create a nested unordered list like this:

```
<UL>
<LI>Take out the trash.
<LI>Develop a nuclear weapon.
  <UL>
  <LI>Steal secrets from the United States.
  <LI>Bomb our own embassy.
  <LI>Export more MSG to our enemies.
  </UL>
<LI>Borrow an expensive appliance from the neighbor.
</UL>
```

Figure 22-5 shows how the preceding HTML code creates a nested, unordered list. Note that the nested unordered list uses unique bullets to differentiate it from the outer unordered list.

Ordered lists

While an unordered list displays items with bullets, an ordered list displays items with a number. The first list item is number 1, the second is number 2, and so on.

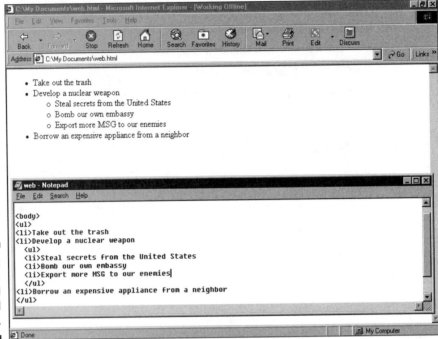

Figure 22-5:
Creating a
nested
unordered
list.

To create an ordered list, use the HTML tags <OL> and </OL> to define the ordered list. Then use the <LI> tag to mark each numbered item. Here is an example:

```
<OL>
<LI>Turn left at the traffic light.
<LI>Drive five blocks.
<LI>Throw a rotten egg at the front door.
</OL>
```

You can also create a nested ordered list like this:

```
<OL>
<LI>Turn left at the traffic light.
<LI>Drive five blocks.
  <OL>
  <LI>Go past a burned down house.
  <LI>Drive through the next three traffic lights.
  <LI>Look for the house with toilet paper in the trees.
  </OL>
<LI>Throw a rotten egg at the front door.
</OL>
```

Figure 22-6 shows a nested, ordered list. Note that the nested ordered list uses different numbering from the outer ordered list.

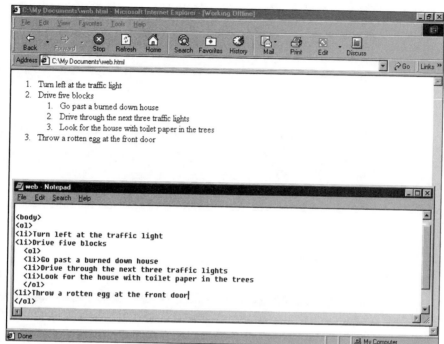

Figure 22-6:
A nested
ordered list.

You can nest ordered and unordered lists inside one another, instead of nesting two unordered lists or two ordered lists.

Definition lists

Definition lists got their name because they are often used in glossaries where one line lists a term and a second line lists the definition of that term. To create a definition list, you need to use three types of HTML tags:

- **The** `<DL>` **and** `</DL>` **tags** define the start and end of a definition list.

- **The** `<DT>` **tag** displays a line of text such as a single word or term.

- **The** `<DD>` **tag** displays a definition for the word or term defined by the preceding `<DT>` tag.

To see how to create a definition list, look at the following code and then take a look at Figure 22-7, which shows how the following HTML code looks in a browser:

```
<DL>
<DT>Cat
<DD>An animal that enslaves its owners.
<DT>Flashlight
<DD>A case for holding dead batteries.
</DL>
```

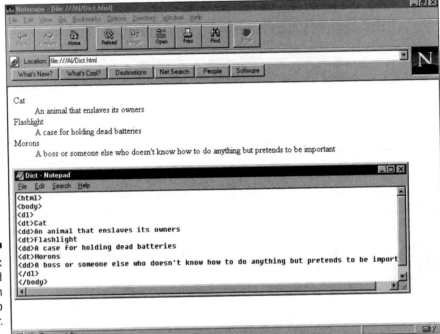

Figure 22-7:
A finished
definition
list in a Web
browser.

Creating Hyperlinks

Every good Web page needs two items: information (usually text) that
provides some useful content, and hyperlinks that link your Web page to
a related Web page. A Web page usually offers two types of hyperlinks:

- ✔ **External hyperlinks** are links to other Web pages that are typically
  located on another computer (and often in another geographical
  location).

- ✔ **Internal hyperlinks** are links to different pages of your Web site or to a
  different part of the same Web page.

To create a hyperlink, you have to use a pair of anchor tags, such as <A> and </A>. Inside the first anchor tag, you have to specify either an external or internal hyperlink. Between the two anchor tags, you type the text or graphics that act as the hyperlink.

Making external hyperlinks

When defining an external hyperlink, the HREF (which stands for Hypertext REFerence) attribute defines two items:

- **The external hyperlink address** appears in a form similar to http://www.someaddress.com.
- **The text or graphic that acts as the hyperlink** is what the user clicks to jump to the external hyperlink.

To use the HREF attribute, you have to put it inside the first anchor tag, as shown in the following example:

```
<A HREF="http://www.dummies.com">Dummies Web page</A>
```

In this example, the words Dummies Web page are the hyperlink. Clicking the hyperlink takes users to the www.dummies.com Web site.

External hyperlinks are completely out of your control, so if a Web site to which you link goes down, your Web page's hyperlink will lead viewers to a dead end.

Making internal hyperlinks

To make a hyperlink to another Web page on your own site, use the HREF attribute, but instead of listing another Web site address, just type the filename of the Web page to which you want to link, as in the following example:

```
<A HREF="index.html">Index</A>
```

This creates a hyperlink of the word Index. When users click on this hyperlink, their browsers display the Web page stored in the index.html file.

Linking to a specific spot on a Web page

One problem with linking to another Web page is that the user may have to scroll down the page to find specific information. To avoid this problem, you can create a hyperlink to a specific spot on a Web page, such as the middle or the bottom of the Web page. That way, the hyperlink directs the viewer to the exact information you want displayed.

Creating a hyperlink that connects to a particular spot on another Web page is a two-step process:

1. **Create an anchor in the spot on the Web page on which you want a hyperlink to display.**

   For example, if you want a hyperlink to direct a viewer to the bottom of a Web page, you place an anchor at the bottom of that particular page.

2. **Create a hyperlink that directs a viewer to an anchor previously defined.**

To create an anchor, you have to use the NAME attribute, like this:

```
<A NAME="TOC">Table of Contents</A>
```

This example displays the text Table of Contents on the Web page and assigns it the name "TOC". After you create an anchor, the next step is to create a hyperlink that points to that particular anchor.

Anchors are case-sensitive, which means that an anchor named TOC is considered completely different from an anchor named toc. If you forget this difference, your anchors won't work at all.

To make a hyperlink point to a predefined anchor, use the HREF attribute and include the Web site address, the Web page filename, and the anchor name, like this:

```
<A HREF="index.html#TOC">Go to Page One</A>
```

The preceding code displays the hyperlink Go to Page One on the screen. When the user clicks this hyperlink, the browser jumps to the index.html filename and displays the anchor defined by the name "TOC". In this case, the browser displays the Table of Contents at the top of the page, regardless of whether the words Table of Contents appear in the middle or at the bottom of the Web page.

Displaying Graphics

Just displaying text on a Web page can get pretty boring, so HTML enables you to display graphic images on your Web pages to make everything look prettier. Graphics can appear as part of the Web page or in the background.

The only picture files you can use for Web pages are GIF (Graphical Interchange Format) and JPG (also spelled JPEG, which stands for Joint Photographic Experts Group) files.

Putting a picture on a Web page

To display a picture on a Web page, you have to use the image tag <IMG> and the source (SRC) attribute to tell the computer the specific filename of the graphic image that you want to display. Here is an example:

```
<IMG SRC="filename.gif">
```

To give you greater control over the placement of a picture in relation to any text that appears next to the picture, you can use the ALIGN attribute. This attribute defines whether text appears at the top, at the bottom, or to either side of the image:

```
<IMG SRC="filename.gif" ALIGN=middle>
```

Figure 22-8 shows examples of text aligned with graphic images in a browser.

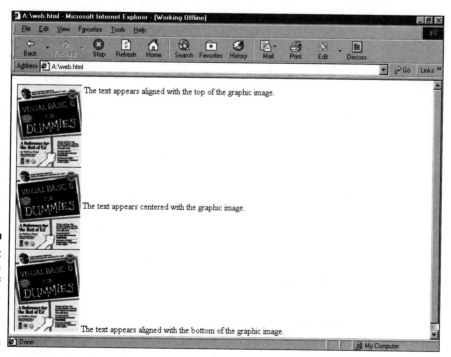

Figure 22-8: The three positions of text aligned with graphic images.

Adding a background picture

In addition to adding colors to a Web page, you may also want to display a picture in the background. To add a picture to a Web page, use the BACKGROUND attribute inside the BODY tag, as in the following example:

```
<BODY BACKGROUND ="filename.GIF">
```

Creating a User Interface on a Form

Although you could use HTML to display text on the screen, you may want to create something more flexible called a *form*. A form enables you to display text boxes, command buttons, and checkboxes on the screen. To define a form, you use the <FORM> and </FORM> tags sandwiched between the <BODY> and </BODY> tags:

```
<HTML>

<BODY>
<FORM>
</FORM>
</BODY>
</HTML>
```

Make sure that you sandwich the <FORM> and </FORM> tags inside the <BODY> and </BODY> tags; otherwise, your form won't appear on the screen.

Of course, the <FORM> and </FORM> tags simply define a form, so you still have to add your user interface items on the form, as shown in Figure 22-9. The following are some common user interface items that you may want to include on a form:

- ✔ **Text boxes** are boxes in which users can type data.
- ✔ **Buttons** are command buttons that users can click on.
- ✔ **Checkboxes** are boxes that users can check or clear to choose or remove an option.
- ✔ **Radio buttons** are buttons that users can check or clear to choose an option. Only one radio button can be checked at a time.

Handling events

Every user interface element can respond to the user. Any time the user does something to a user interface item, such as clicking on a command button, this is called an *event*.

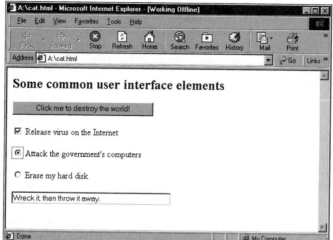

Figure 22-9:
Common
user
interface
elements
that you can
display on
a form.

When an event occurs on a specific user interface item, such as a command button, your form can respond by displaying text, opening a window, and so on. The following are some common events:

- onAbort occurs when the user stops loading an image, either by clicking on a link or clicking the Stop button.

- onBlur occurs when an item, such as a text box or command button, loses focus. This usually occurs when the user clicks on another item.

- onChange occurs when the contents of an item, such as a text box, change.

- onClick occurs when the user clicks on a specific item, such as a radio button or a command button.

- onFocus occurs when the user clicks on an object or highlights an object by using the Tab key.

- onMouseOut occurs when the mouse pointer no longer appears over a certain item.

- onMouseOver occurs when the mouse pointer moves over a certain item.

- onSelect occurs when the user selects text within a text box.

Events are linked to a specific user interface item, such as a command button or checkbox. A single user interface item can respond to more than one type of event.

Creating a text box

A text box can display text and allow the user to type text. To create a text box, type the following command inside the <FORM> and </FORM> tags:

```
<INPUT
   TYPE=text
   NAME="textboxName"
   VALUE="Text inside the text box"
   SIZE=integer
   [onBlur="command"]
   [onChange="command"]
   [onFocus="command"]
   [onSelect="command"]>
```

The TYPE=text command tells the computer to create a text box on the screen. The NAME command assigns any name that you choose to represent your text box. The VALUE command displays text inside your text box. The SIZE command defines how many characters the text box can display without scrolling.

A text box can respond to four different events: onBlur, onChange, onFocus, and onSelect. The following shows how to create a text box that displays the message, "Ow! You click too hard!" when you click inside the text box:

```
<HTML>
<BODY>

<FORM>

<INPUT
   TYPE=text
   NAME="textboxName"
   VALUE="This appears inside the text box"
   SIZE=30
   onFocus="textboxName.value='Ow! You click too hard!'
">

</FORM>

</BODY>
</HTML>
```

Note the use of single and double quotation marks following the onFocus event. The double quotation marks enclose the entire command that you want the computer to follow when the onFocus event occurs. Any command inside the double quotation marks must use single quotation marks, or the entire command will not work.

Creating a command button

A command button displays a button that the user can click to perform a specific action. To create a command button, use the following code inside the `<FORM>` and `</FORM>` tags:

```
<INPUT
   TYPE=button
   NAME="buttonName"
   VALUE="Text that appears on the button"
   [onBlur="handlerText"]
   [onClick="handlerText"]
   [onFocus="handlerText"]>
```

The `TYPE=button` command creates a command button on the screen. The `NAME` command assigns a name to represent your command button. The `VALUE` command displays the text that appears inside the command button, such as `OK` or `Click Me`.

Command buttons can respond to three different events: `onBlur`, `onClick`, and `onFocus`. The following shows how to create two command buttons — one that opens a window to display the Web page stored in a file called index.html, and one that closes the window:

```
<html>

<body>

<form>
<input
 type=button
 name="open"
 value="Open window"
 onClick="mywindow=window.open('index.html')">

<input
 type=button
 name="close"
 value="Close window"
 onClick="mywindow.close()">

</form>

</body>
</html>
```

Notice that the command defined by the `onClick` event uses double quotation marks to enclose the entire command. Anything that appears inside must use single quotation marks or the entire command will not work.

Creating a checkbox

Checkboxes display options that the user can choose by clicking in the checkbox to add or remove a check mark. To make a checkbox, put the following command inside the `<FORM>` and `</FORM>` tags:

```
<INPUT
   TYPE=checkbox
   NAME="checkboxName"
   VALUE="checkboxValue"
   [CHECKED]
   [onBlur="handlerText"]
   [onClick="handlerText"]
   [onFocus="handlerText"]>
   textToDisplay
```

The `TYPE=checkbox` command creates a checkbox on the screen. The `NAME` command assigns a name to represent that checkbox. The `VALUE` command specifies a number or string that the checkbox represents if the user chooses it. The `CHECKED` command displays a check mark in the checkbox. The `textToDisplay` variable represents any text that you want to display next to the checkbox.

A checkbox can respond to three different events: `onBlur`, `onClick`, and `onFocus`. The following creates three checkboxes:

```
<html>

<body>

<h2>Where do you want your computer to go today?</h2>

<form>

<input
  type = checkbox
  name="check1"
  value=99
  onClick="litterbox.value='Throw the computer in the
           trash.'">
  In the trash can

<br>
<br>

<input
  type = checkbox
  name="check2"
  value=99
```

```
 onClick="litterbox.value='Toss the computer outside.'">
 Out the window

<br>
<br>

<input
 type = checkbox
 name="check3"
 value=99
 onClick="litterbox.value='Wreck it, and then throw it
          away.'">
 Smash it to pieces

<br>
<br>

<input
 type = text
 name="litterbox"
 value=""
 size = 40>

</form>

</body>
</html>
```

When you click on a checkbox, a message appears in a text box underneath, as shown in Figure 22-10.

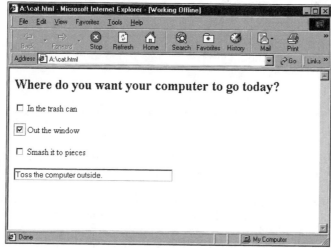

Figure 22-10:
Creating
three
checkboxes.

When you type text to appear next to a checkbox, you don't need to enclose it in quotation marks. If you do enclose the text inside quotation marks, the quotation marks appear on the screen as well.

Creating a radio button

A radio button works much like a checkbox, except that only one radio button can be chosen at any given time. For example, radio buttons are designed to let users answer questions for which only one answer is possible, as in the following example:

```
What is your current marital status?
```

To answer this question, you would have radio buttons for the following three responses:

- ✔ Single
- ✔ Married
- ✔ Divorced

The user can choose only one of the responses. If the user clicks the Single radio button, changes his mind, and then clicks the Divorced radio button, a dot appears in the Divorced radio button to show that it is chosen and the Single radio button becomes empty to show that it is no longer chosen.

```
<INPUT
   TYPE=radio
   NAME="radioName"
   VALUE="buttonValue"
   [CHECKED]
   [onBlur="handlerText"]
   [onClick="handlerText"]
   [onFocus="handlerText"]>
   textToDisplay
```

The TYPE=radio command creates a radio button on the screen. The NAME command assigns a name to represent that radio button.

If you want only one radio button to appear chosen within a group of radio buttons, you have to give all radio buttons exactly the same name.

The VALUE command specifies a number or string that the radio button represents if the user chooses it. The CHECKED command displays the radio button as chosen when it first appears on the screen. The textToDisplay variable represents any text that you want to appear next to the radio button.

A radio button can respond to three different events: `onBlur`, `onClick`, and `onFocus`. The following shows how to create three radio buttons. When you click on a radio button, a message appears in a text box below the button:

```
<html>

<body>

<h2>Where do you want your computer to go today?</h2>

<form>

<input
 type = radio
 name="group1"
 value=99
 onClick="litterbox.value='Throw the computer in the
          trash.'">
 In the trash can

<br>
<br>

<input
 type = radio
 name="group1"
 value=99
 onClick="litterbox.value='Toss the computer outside.'">
 Out the window

<br>
<br>

<input
 type = radio
 name="group1"
 value=99
 onClick="litterbox.value='Wreck it, and then throw it
          away.'">
 Smash it to pieces

<br>
<br>

<input
 type = text
 name="litterbox"
 value=""
 size = 40>

</form>

</body>
</html>
```

Notice that all radio buttons in the preceding example share the same name, which is `"group1"`. If two radio buttons have different names, both radio buttons can be chosen without affecting the other radio button. The main reason to give two different names to groups of radio buttons is so that you can display two or more separate groups of radio buttons that offer options that are completely unrelated to one another.

Deciding to Use Additional HTML Features

The basic HTML codes explained in previous sections of this chapter provide the fundamental elements that you need to know to create and edit simple Web pages. But newer versions of HTML offer additional features for creating tables, displaying fonts, or dividing a Web page into frames.

Frames allow you to divide a Web browser screen into two or more parts, where each part (frame) can display a different Web page or a different part of the same Web page.

Although these features may seem useful and fun, keep in mind that they don't always work with all versions of browsers. If you want to ensure that your Web page can be viewed by all users, stick with the basic HTML tags described in this chapter.

If you want to use newer HTML features like frames, consider making two versions of your Web page: a framed version and a non-framed version. That way, people with older browsers that can't display frames can still view your Web site, and people with newer browsers can take advantage of frames or other advanced features that you include on your Web pages.

Chapter 23

Making Interactive Web Pages with JavaScript

*H*TML code can produce pretty — but ultimately static — pages that resemble billboards or magazine advertisements. Although these Web pages are functional, many people want to take full advantage of the computer and create mini-programs on their Web pages. That way, the Web page can display a button and allow the user to click it to produce a result.

HTML codes by themselves can't create such interactive Web pages, so programmers have resorted to using specialized Web-page programming languages, such as JavaScript and VBScript. If you write miniature programs in either JavaScript or VBScript in your HTML code, you can create Web pages that can interact with users through dialog boxes, list boxes, and command buttons.

Despite the name similarities, JavaScript bears only a superficial resemblance to Java. JavaScript uses simple commands, and JavaScript programs can run only inside a browser. Java uses more complicated commands and can create separate applications.

To practice writing JavaScript programs, use a text editor (such as the Windows Notepad or the QBASIC editor) and save your files with the .html file extension. Then load your browser, choose File⇨Open, and choose the file that you just saved with the .html file extension to see how your browser interprets your JavaScript programs.

Netscape created JavaScript, and to compete against JavaScript, Microsoft created a similar language dubbed VBScript. VBScript isn't as popular as JavaScript, but it is still easy to use because it's based on the Visual Basic language (and to a certain extent, QBASIC). Just remember that any time you write a JavaScript or VBScript program in your Web page, the program may not run on an older version of a browser.

The Basics of JavaScript

To define the start and end of a JavaScript program, you use just two tags, which look similar to HTML tags. Here is an example:

```
<script language = "JavaScript">

</script>
```

You can insert a JavaScript program between the `<BODY>` and `</BODY>` HTML tags, as in the following example:

```
<HTML>
<HEAD>
  <TITLE>Document title</TITLE>
</HEAD>

<BODY>

<script language = "JavaScript">

</script>

</BODY>
</HTML>
```

Because older browsers may not understand JavaScript commands, you should insert two additional lines immediately after the `<script>` tag and immediately before the `</script>` tag, like this:

```
<script language = "JavaScript">
<!--

//-->
</script>
```

The middle two lines tell older browsers to treat any JavaScript commands as comments, essentially making the browser ignore JavaScript altogether. Newer browsers that can understand JavaScript simply run the JavaScript commands.

Objects and JavaScript

JavaScript is based on objects. (See Chapter 18 for more about objects.) Objects include three characteristics: properties, methods, and events.

Properties define the appearance of the object, such as its color. Methods define actions that you can make the object do. One of the most common objects is a `document` object, and its most common method is the `write` command. Events are occurrences that the object can respond to, such as a mouse clicking on an object.

You can still use JavaScript without knowing much about objects, but knowing how objects work can help you better understand JavaScript. For now, just keep in mind that JavaScript is based on objects, so when you see strange JavaScript commands — such as `document.write("Hello, there!")` — you'll be able to recognize that this command is telling a `document` object to write something on the screen.

As an alternative to typing JavaScript code directly into an HTML file, you can store your JavaScript code in a separate file and then specify where to find that file by using the `SRC` attribute, as in the following example:

```
<script language = "JavaScript" SRC="program.js">
<!--

//-->
</script>
```

This example tells the computer to store the JavaScript program in a file called PROGRAM.JS.

Displaying text

JavaScript includes the following simple command for printing text on the screen:

```
document.write("Text to be printed here.")
```

If you want to get fancy, you can include ordinary HTML tags inside the parentheses to format the text. For example, to display text in boldface, just shove in the HTML bold tag, as in the following example:

```
document.write("<B>", "This appears bold.", "</B>")
```

The `document.write` command can also smash strings together by using the plus (+) sign, like this:

```
document.write("<B>", "This appears bold.", "</B>" + " And
            this appears as normal text.")
```

The preceding command creates the following display:

```
This appears bold. And this appears as normal text.
```

Creating variables

In the `document.write` example in the previous section, the plus sign (+) was used to link strings and variables that represent strings. In JavaScript, you can declare a variable by using the magical `var` command, like this:

```
var variablename
```

In JavaScript, you don't need to declare a variable data type; you just declare a variable name. Then you can set a variable to represent a string and use the plus sign (+) to link a string to a variable representing a string, like this:

```
<script language = "JavaScript">
var mymessage
mymessage = "A goldfish."
document.write("What animal has a near death experience every
            time you flush the toilet? Answer: " + mymessage)
</script>
```

This JavaScript program tells the computer to do the following:

1. The first line tells the computer, "Anything you see within the `<script>` tags is a JavaScript program.

2. The second line creates a variable called `mymessage`.

3. The third line assigns the string `"A goldfish"` to the `mymessage` variable.

4. The fourth line writes the string, `"What animal has a near death experience every time you flush the toilet? Answer: A goldfish."`

5. The fifth line tells the computer that this is the end of the JavaScript program.

Making dialog boxes

The `document.write` command can come in handy for displaying text on the screen. But JavaScript can go much further than displaying text by creating dialog boxes. JavaScript can create the following types of dialog boxes:

- An alert dialog box
- A confirmation dialog box
- A prompt dialog box

Making an alert dialog box

One type of dialog box that programs use fairly often is an *alert dialog box.* An alert dialog box usually pops up on the screen to alert the user that something important has just happened or is about to happen, as shown in Figure 23-1. To make this alert dialog box, use the following `alert` command:

```
alert("Nuclear meltdown has occurred. Time to evacuate!")
```

The `alert` command displays a dialog box that stays visible on the screen until the user clicks the OK button to make it go away.

Making a confirmation dialog box

A confirmation dialog box displays a message and gives the user a choice of two buttons — OK and Cancel. If the user clicks OK, the value of the `confirm` command is true. If the user clicks Cancel, the value of the `confirm` command is false. The following program creates a confirmation dialog box that looks like the one shown in Figure 23-2:

```
if (confirm("Do you want to erase your hard drive now?"))
  document.write("Now erasing your hard drive.")
else
  document.write("Then wait until Windows crashes, and that
          will erase your hard drive for you.")
```

Figure 23-2:
A
confirmation
dialog box
gives the
user a
choice.

If the user clicks the OK button, the program displays the string, `"Now eras-ing your hard drive."`. If the user clicks the Cancel button, the program displays the string, `"Then wait until Windows crashes, and that will erase your hard drive for you."`.

Making a prompt dialog box

To prod the user into typing some data into the computer, many programs use a prompt dialog box, like the one shown in Figure 23-3. A prompt dialog box asks the user for input by using the `prompt` command, like this:

```
prompt("How many times has your computer crashed on you
          today?")
```

If you want to provide a default value that the user can choose without typing anything (as shown in the dialog box in Figure 23-3), you can add the default value after the message text, as in the following code:

```
prompt("How many times has your computer crashed on you
          today?", 98)
```

Figure 23-3:
Displaying a
prompt
dialog box
with a
default
value of 98.

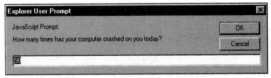

If you don't define a default value, the prompt dialog box simply displays the word `Undefined`.

Because the prompt dialog box asks the user for input, you need to create a variable to hold the data that the user types into the prompt dialog box. After creating a variable, you have to set the variable equal to the prompt command, as in the following example:

```
<script language = "JavaScript">
var userdata
userdata = prompt("How many times has your computer crashed
          on you today?", 98)
document.write("This is what the user typed in = ", userdata)
</script>
```

This JavaScript program tells the computer to do the following:

1. The first line tells the computer, "Anything you see within the `<script>` tags is a JavaScript program."

2. The second line creates a variable called `userdata`.

3. The third line displays a prompt dialog box with the message, "How many times has your computer crashed on you today?" In the text box, it displays a default value of 98. Any data that appears in the text box when the user clicks the OK button gets stored in the `userdata` variable.

4. The fourth line prints, `"This is what the user typed in = "` on the screen, followed by the data stored in the `userdata` variable.

5. The fifth line tells the computer that this is the end of the JavaScript program.

Playing with Functions

Rather than create one massive JavaScript program, you can create subprograms known as *functions*.

A function consists of four parts:

- **The function keyword:** This identifies your function as a legitimate JavaScript subprogram.

- **A function name:** This is the name that your JavaScript uses to "call" the function and make it run. In the following example, the function name is `square`:

```
function square(number) {
   return number * number
}
```

✔ **A list of arguments (data) that the function requires:** The data can be numbers or strings, but items must be separated by commas. In the example under the preceding bulleted item, the only data that the function requires is a number.

✔ **Curly brackets enclosing the function instructions:** The instructions trapped inside the curly brackets tell the function how to work. In the preceding example, the function accepts a number, multiplies that number by itself, and returns the value of this multiplication.

A typical function may look like this:

```
function FunctionName(Data) {
  // one or more instructions
}
```

To create a function, you have to choose a function name, what type of data the function needs, and how the function works. For example, the following function called `square` accepts a single number and multiplies it by itself:

```
function square(number) {
  return number * number
}
```

If you don't want the function to return a value, omit the `return` keyword.

To see how functions can work in a real-life JavaScript program, type the following code into an editor (such as Windows Notepad) and save it with the .html file extension:

```
<html>

<body>

<script language = "JavaScript">
<!--

function square (number) {
  return number * number
}
function printbig (headlevel, headtext) {
  document.write("<H", headlevel, ">", headtext, "</H",
          headlevel, ">")
}

var myvalue, longstring
myvalue = prompt ("How many times has your computer crashed
          on you today?", 98)
```

```
longstring = " This is how many more times your computer will
          crash = " + square(myvalue)
printbig (2, longstring)

//-->
</script>
</body>
</html>
```

Starting with the line that begins with the script tag <script>, this JavaScript program tells the computer to do the following:

1. The first line tells the computer, "Anything you see within the <script> tags is a JavaScript program.

2. The second line defines the entire JavaScript program as a comment for older browsers that don't understand JavaScript.

3. The third line defines a function called square, which accepts one chunk of data that gets stored in a variable called number.

4. The fourth line tells the square function to multiply the number stored in the variable called number and to return the multiplication result to the main JavaScript program.

5. The fifth line marks the end of the JavaScript function called square.

6. The sixth line defines a function called printbig, which accepts two chunks of data that get stored in variables called headlevel and headtext.

7. The seventh line creates an HTML tag for defining a heading level and for displaying text in that heading level.

8. The eighth line marks the end of the JavaScript function called printbig.

9. The ninth line creates two variables called myvalue and longstring.

10. The tenth line displays a prompt dialog box that displays, "How many times has your computer crashed on you today?" For a default value, the prompt dialog box displays the number 98. When the user clicks the OK button, the value displayed in the prompt dialog box gets stored in the myvalue variable.

11. The eleventh line calls the square function with the value stored in the myvalue variable. It takes this result and tacks it on to the end of the string, "This is how many more times your computer will crash = ". Then it assigns the entire string, plus the value of square(myvalue), to the variable called longstring.

    The twelfth line calls the printbig function and feeds it the number 2 and the data stored in the longstring variable. In this case, the printbig function creates a heading 2 and displays the text stored in the longstring variable as a heading 2 on the screen.

Opening and Closing a Window

Although your browser may normally display only one window at a time, you can open two or more windows on the screen to display different Web pages. (Web sites often open a second window to display an advertisement.)

Opening a window

To open a window, sandwich the open command between the <SCRIPT> and </SCRIPT> tags, as in the following example:

```
<script language = "JavaScript" SRC="program.js">
<!--
  WindowName = window.open(web page or address)
//-->
</script>
```

You can also use the window.open command with a user interface item such as a button. I tell you more about using commands with user interface items in Chapter 22.

You have to define the WindowName, which can be any name you want. You also have to define what the window displays. If you want the window to display a specific Web page, you have to type the filename of that Web page, as in this example:

```
MyWindow = window.open("index.html")
```

This command opens a new window called MyWindow and displays the Web page stored in a file called index.html. If you want the window to display a Web site, you have to type the Web site address, like this:

```
MyWindow = window.open("http://www.dummies.com")
```

Defining a window's appearance

To give you more control over a window's appearance, you can define the size and appearance of a window. When you define a window's appearance, you have to give the window a second name followed by any attributes that you want, as in this example:

```
MyWindow = window.open("index.html", "secondname",
          "toolbar=no, resizable=yes")
```

This opens a window that displays the index.html Web page. This window does not have toolbars, but you can resize the window. The second name of the window (in this example, called "secondname") is used if you want to refer to this window from another window, such as through a hyperlink.

Attributes can modify the appearance of a window, such as adding a toolbar and a menu bar. The following list explains these attributes that you can define for any window that you open:

- toolbar[=yes|no]|[=1|0] displays a toolbar at the top of the window with buttons such as Back, Forward, and Stop.
- location[=yes|no]|[=1|0] creates a text box displaying the current Web page or Web address.
- directories[=yes|no]|[=1|0] displays directory buttons at the top of the window.
- status[=yes|no]|[=1|0] displays a status bar at the bottom of the window.
- menubar[=yes|no]|[=1|0] displays pull-down menus at the top of the window.
- scrollbars[=yes|no]|[=1|0] creates horizontal and vertical scroll-bars if the document is larger than the window dimensions.
- resizable[=yes|no]|[=1|0] allows the user to resize the window.
- width=pixels specifies the width of the window measured in pixels.
- height=pixels specifies the height of the window measured in pixels.

For example, if you want to open a window but hide the toolbar, you can set the toolbar attribute to either yes/no or 0/1 like this:

```
MyWindow = window.open("index.html", "secondname",
          "toolbar=no")
```

Or like this:

```
MyWindow = window.open("index.html", "secondname",
          "toolbar=0")
```

Closing a window

After you open a window, you may want to close it. To close a window, you have to use the close command, as in the following example:

```
WindowName.close()
```

This command closes a window identified as `WindowName`. If you want to close a window called `adWindow`, you use the following command:

```
adWindow.close()
```

The name of the window used with the `close` command is the same name used to open the window. You open a window with the following command:

```
WeirdStuff = window.open("index.html")
```

You close the window with the following command:

```
WeirdStuff.close()
```

To learn more about JavaScript from the friendly folks at Netscape who created it, visit
`home.netscape.com/eng/mozilla/3.0/handbook/javascript`.

JavaScript is a full-blown programming language, far too complex to cover completely in this chapter. For more information about JavaScript, pick up a copy of *JavaScript For Dummies,* 2nd Edition, by Emily A. Vander Veer (IDG Books Worldwide, Inc.).

Chapter 24

Using Java Applets in Web Pages

In This Chapter

▶ Understanding how Java applets work

▶ Adding a Java applet to a Web page

▶ Finding free Java applets

*J*ava can create two types of programs: full-blown applications (such as word processors or Web browsers) and smaller applets that can run only when viewed through a browser. (This chapter is concerned only with using Java to write applets, rather than complete applications.)

When you write applets in Java, you can add more sophisticated features to your Web pages. (If you'd rather not write your own Java applets, you can always use applets that someone else has written for you, as long as you trust that the applet works correctly.)

Writing Java applets can get extremely detailed and time-consuming, depending on how much work you want to put into your applet. For specific instructions on how to write programs in Java, pick up a copy of *Java Programming For Dummies* by Donald J. Koosis and David Koosis (IDG Books Worldwide, Inc.).

How Java Applets Work

A Java applet is a miniature program written in the Java programming language. Unlike QBASIC (which is an interpreter that runs programs in memory) or C++ (which compiles programs into machine code), Java applets get converted from source code into a special byte code format.

Byte code format is a special file format unique to Java programs. Some Java compilers, such as Symantec's Visual Café, can compile Java programs into byte code format or directly into machine code format.

Java versus JavaScript

Both Java and JavaScript allow you to create interactive Web pages that ordinary HTML code can't offer. But when should you use Java, and when should you use JavaScript?

JavaScript is easier than Java to learn and use, so it's a much faster method for creating interactive Web pages. On the other hand, Java is a much more powerful and flexible programming language that enables you to create features that would be cumbersome, difficult, or impossible to duplicate in JavaScript.

As a general rule, use JavaScript for short, simple tasks, and use Java for more complicated tasks. Of course, you can use both JavaScript and Java together on the same Web page to get the best of both worlds.

If you'd rather not learn the complexities of Java, stick with JavaScript. If you don't mind the steep learning curve of Java, learn Java and rest assured that Java programming skills likely will remain lucrative for many years to come.

The source code of a Java program is stored in an ASCII file with the file extension of .java, such as Virus.java. When you compile a Java program into byte code format, you create a separate file with the file extension of .class, such as Virus.class.

Because computers understand only machine code, no computer in the world knows how to run a Java program saved in byte code format. If you want to run a Java program stored in byte code format, you have to use a special (and free) program called a Java Virtual Machine (VM). (Chances are good that if you have a browser such as Internet Explorer or Netscape Navigator, you already have a copy of the Java VM on your computer.)

Java programs can run on any computer that has a copy of the Java VM, including Windows, the Macintosh, and UNIX. If you compile your Java programs into byte code format, you can run them on a variety of computers and operating systems without any modifications whatsoever.

To show you what a Java applet looks like (don't worry about understanding how the code actually works), here's a simple Java applet that displays the message, "Stop staring at me!" on the screen:

```
import java.awt.*;
import java.applet.Applet;

public class TrivialApplet extends Applet
{
        Font f = new Font("TimesRoman", Font.BOLD, 24);
```

```
        public void init() {
          repaint();
        }

        public void paint( Graphics g ) {
          g.setFont(f);
          g.setColor(Color.blue);
          g.drawString( "Stop staring at me!", 15, 75 );
        }
      }
```

Figure 24-1 shows the output of the preceding Java program.

You can type a Java program using any text editor (such as QBASIC's editor or the Windows Notepad). To compile your Java program into byte code format, you need to use a Java compiler, such as the free Sun Microsystems (java.sun.com) Java compiler or a commercial Java compiler such as JBuilder from Borland (www.borland.com) or CodeWarrior (www.metrowerks.com) from Metrowerks.

Limiting the power of Java applets

Java applets are miniature programs, which means that they have the potential to erase files or mess up your computer if someone writes a virus or Trojan Horse in Java. To prevent malicious Java applets from attacking your computer, Java restricts Java applets from performing certain tasks such as deleting files, reading the contents of a hard disk, renaming files, creating directories, or running any external programs.

Naturally, since Java's introduction, people have found numerous holes in Java's defenses.

Although none of these weaknesses has yet allowed a malicious hacker to exploit these holes and threaten the world, these flaws do serve to remind programmers that Java presents opportunities to attack your computer, given enough creativity and persistence on the part of a malicious Java programmer.

Generally, you don't have to worry about someone writing a virus or Trojan Horse as a Java applet, but don't be surprised if it does occur one day.

If Java is free, why buy a Java compiler?

In an effort to make Java as widespread and universal as possible, Sun Microsystems provides a free Java compiler, source code, and tools that you can download for free from the Sun Microsystems Java Web site (java.sun.com). But if you can get a free Java compiler, why should you buy a commercial Java compiler?

First, the Sun Microsystems Java compiler provides the bare necessities for writing and compiling a Java program. Using the free Sun Microsystems Java compiler is a lot like walking from New York to Los Angeles: You could do it, but paying extra to take a plane would be easier, faster, and more convenient.

Second, a commercial Java compiler offers additional benefits that the free Sun

Microsystems Java compiler can't offer. For example, JBuilder (from Borland) allows you to graphically design your Java program's user interface and appearance so that you don't have to write Java code to create the user interface yourself. Visual Café from Symantec offers a true compiler that can convert a Java program into either byte code format (for running on different computers) or into machine code format (optimized for running on computers using Microsoft Windows).

If you want to toy with Java, use the free Java compiler from Sun Microsystems. But if you plan to use Java commercially, you'll save yourself a lot of time by using a commercial Java compiler.

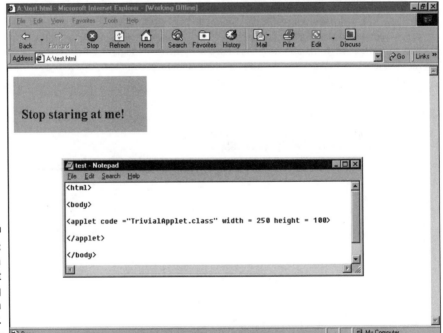

Figure 24-1:
A Java applet running inside a browser.

Adding a Java Applet to a Web Page

When you have a Java applet compiled into byte code format, you're ready to use HTML tags to run that Java applet on a Web page. Adding a Java applet to a Web page involves using two tags, sandwiched between the `<BODY>` and `</BODY>` tags:

```
<APPLET CODE = "JavaAppletName">
Text to display if the Java applet can't run
</APPLET>
```

The `JavaAppletName` variable is the actual name of the Java applet that you want to run. If you want to run a Java applet named `Message.class`, the HTML applet tag would look like this:

```
<APPLET CODE = "Message.class">
Text to display if the Java applet can't run
</APPLET>
```

One or more lines of text can be sandwiched between the `<APPLET>` and `</APPLET>` tags. This text appears only if the Java applet can't run within a particular browser. So rather than display a blank image on the screen, the text appears in order to explain to the user that the Java applet can't run.

Defining the size of a Java applet window

For additional fun, you can define the size of the area that your Java applet appears in by using the `WIDTH` and `HEIGHT` commands, as in the following example:

```
<APPLET CODE = "Message.class" WIDTH = 250 HEIGHT = 100>
Text to display if the Java applet can't run
</APPLET>
```

This example defines a width of 250 pixels and a height of 100 pixels for the applet.

A pixel is a small dot that lights up on your screen. The more pixels your monitor can display (such as 1024 by 768 pixels), the sharper your screen's image is. Every character or graphic image that you see on your screen is made up of multiple pixels.

If you don't define a large enough area for your Java applet, part of it may appear cut off when displayed in a browser.

Aligning the location of a Java applet window

When an applet appears on a Web page, you may want to use the `ALIGN` command to define how text appears next to the applet. You can use the following three `ALIGN` commands:

- `ALIGN=TOP` aligns the text with the top of the applet.
- `ALIGN=MIDDLE` aligns the text in the middle of the applet.
- `ALIGN=BOTTOM` aligns the text with the bottom of the applet.

Figure 24-2 shows how text appears when aligned with an applet in three ways.

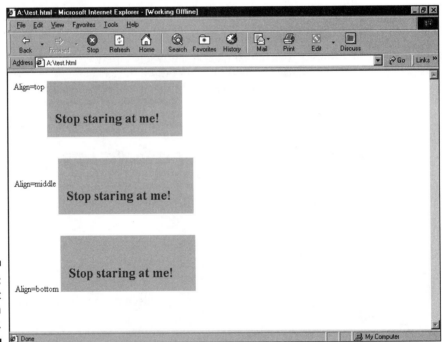

Figure 24-2:
Aligning text with an applet.

Defining space around a Java applet

To keep your text from appearing too close to an applet on a Web page, you can define the amount of horizontal and vertical space to put between the applet and the text. Use the following HSPACE and VSPACE commands to define this spacing:

```
<APPLET CODE = "Message.class" WIDTH = 250 HEIGHT = 100
        VSPACE = 25 HSPACE = 15>
Text to display if the Java applet can't run
</APPLET>
```

The preceding code defines a vertical space of 25 pixels between text and the applet and a horizontal space of 15 pixels between text and the applet. See Figure 24-3 for another example of HSPACE and VSPACE values.

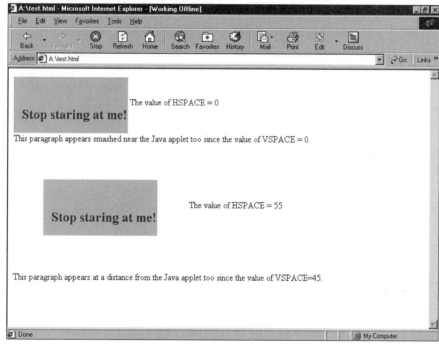

Figure 24-3:
Using
HSPACE
and
VSPACE to
keep text at
a distance
from a Java
applet.

Finding Free Java Applets

If you want to write your own Java applets, you have to spend some time studying Java programming. Java can be a challenging language for beginners to master on their own. Until you master Java (or instead of mastering Java), you may prefer to use Java applets written by other people.

You can paste other people's ready-made applets into your Web pages. Or if the source code is available, you can modify the applet and recompile it yourself, which often helps you understand the Java code more quickly.

To find a list of Web sites that offer Java applets, visit your favorite Internet search engine, such as Hotbot (www.hotbot.com) or Excite (www.excite.com), and search for the string "Java applet." Or you can visit Yahoo! (www.yahoo.com) and click the links labeled <u>Computers and Internet</u>, <u>Programming Languages</u>, <u>Java</u>, and <u>Applet</u>. These links take you to a list of dozens of Web sites where you can download free Java applets and source code.

Part VII
The Part of Tens

The 5th Wave — By Rich Tennant

"Well, this is festive—a miniature intranet amidst a swirl of Java applets."

In this part . . .

After you know the fundamentals of programming, most books, classes, and schools push you out the door and force you to figure out something to do with your programming skills. But this book won't leave you without any directions on where to go with your skills. This part of the book provides ideas for applying and profiting from your programming abilities.

As a programmer, you have unique skills, so don't settle for an ordinary job in an ordinary company doing ordinary work that ultimately gives you an ordinary (and boring) life. Instead, browse through this part of the book and see all the different ways people are using their programming skills at fun, exciting, and unusual jobs that you could get, too. This part also provides guidance for helping you buy your next language compiler, and it offers some tips for playing games to sharpen your programming skills.

Chapter 25

Ten Cool Programming Careers

*A*sk most high school or college guidance counselors what you can do with your programming skills, and they'll likely steer you in the direction of sterile job titles like programmer analyst or data entry operator.

To help stimulate your imagination, this chapter lists some unusual programming jobs that you may want to consider so that you can actually have fun with your life and your job at the same time.

Game Programming

Of all the programming topics in the world, none is more popular than game programming. Besides the obvious job of designing computer games (and getting paid to do it), game programming offers a wide variety of related jobs that can be just as much fun as game designing but don't get as much publicity.

Most computer games are designed by teams. One team may design the game rules, another team does the actual programming, another creates the graphic backgrounds and animation, and still another gets paid to play the latest games to look for bugs and offer suggestions for making the games more exciting (and hence, more profitable for the publisher).

To get involved in professional game programming, you obviously need to have a love for computer games. If you want to write computer games, learn C/C++ and a little bit of assembly language because games need to be as small and as fast as possible. Metrowerks (`www.metrowerks.com`) sells special versions of its CodeWarrior compiler for writing computer games in C/C++ for Sony PlayStation and Nintendo game consoles.

If you'd rather exercise your graphic skills, you have to learn animation, which means studying a lot of math (used to calculate the best ways to make objects move around the screen).

To get started writing your own games, consider using a game engine — a special program that provides instructions to tell the computer how to move animated objects around on the screen. You spend your time designing your game, not worrying about the details of controlling animated characters on the screen.

For a free game engine that runs on Windows, Linux, and the Macintosh, download the Crystal Space game engine from the official Crystal Space Web site (`crystal.linuxgames.com`). Using Crystal Space (and other game engines), you can create 3D triangle mesh sprites with frame animation or transparent and semi-transparent textures for creating see-through water surfaces and windows.

If none of this makes any sense to you, imagine trying to create a game and being forced to learn all these technical terms and how to program them yourself. That's why many people use game engines to help them make new games. Without a game engine, making a game can be as complicated as making your own word processor just so you can write a letter.

To find out more about game programming, visit one of the following Web sites and get started on your new career as a professional game programmer today!

- **Computer Game Developer's Association** (`www.cgda.org`) is the grand-daddy of computer gaming organizations that promotes and protects the computer gaming industry as well as provides conferences to bring computer gaming professionals together.

- **Game Developer** (`www.gdmag.com`) is a special online magazine devoted exclusively to covering the latest game programming techniques and game programming industry news.

- **Game Programmer** (`gameprogrammer.com`) is a Web site that provides information and links to the multitude of game programming resources all over the Internet.

- **DigiPen** (`www.digipen.edu`) is the site of one of the first schools (with close ties to Nintendo) devoted to training game programming professionals and awarding them with real college degrees.

✔ **GameJobs** (www.gamejobs.com) is a site that provides information, tips, and contacts to help you find a job in the computer gaming industry.

Creating Computer Animation

Computer animation isn't just for creating animated characters to shoot or blow up in video games. Programmers also use computer animation in virtual reality, training simulators, and Hollywood special effects (when blowing up a computer-animated building is easier than building a mock-up of an existing building).

Computer animation can range from creating life-like images for TV and movies, to creating multimedia presentations for business, to making cartoons and animated films. If you like to draw but want to become more than just an artist, combine your knowledge of graphics with programming and help design new graphics animation programs, create virtual reality simulators, or work on the next Hollywood blockbuster's special effects.

To learn more about the wonderfully weird world of computer animation, browse through these Web sites and see what sparks your imagination:

✔ **Pixar Animation Studios** (www.pixar.com) is a leading Hollywood animation studio responsible for animating movies like *Toy Story* and *A Bug's Life*.

✔ **MIT Animation and Graphics Club** (web.mit.edu/magc/www) is an MIT club dedicated to the production of animated short films using computer and traditional animation techniques.

✔ **Internet Animation Festival** (la.digitalcity.com/animation/index.html) grants awards (similar to the Academy Awards) for the best computer animation short films.

✔ **Animation Magazine** (www.animag.com) provides news and information for the entire animation industry.

✔ **National Centre for Computer Animation** (ncca.bournemouth.ac.uk) is the United Kingdom's leading research and training institution for computer animation and digital media.

✔ **Computer Graphics World Online** (www.cgw.com) is a magazine covering all the tools, news, and conferences that professional computer graphics artists may need to know about.

Making (And Breaking) Encryption

Ever since nations decided to play the game of war and send their people into battle for their own personal political reasons, armies have used secret codes to communicate with their commanders without revealing information to their enemies.

Because war is not likely to disappear anytime soon, every country in the world will continue to develop encryption techniques for creating codes and breaking the codes of others. If the world of James Bond, espionage, and cloak and dagger spies appeals to your sense of adventure, consider a career in encryption.

Encryption is the art of converting plain text information into unreadable garbage (which often resembles tax forms or legal documents) so that no one but your intended recipient can read it. Then by using a secret password or code phrase, the recipient of your encrypted message can unscramble and read it.

The art of encrypting data involves plenty of math (usually focused on prime numbers). If you plan to pursue a career in encryption, earn some graduate degrees in advanced mathematics and practice your C/C++ programming skills. Then get a job working for the military, a defense contractor, a software encryption publisher, or a security agency such as the National Security Agency (www.nsa.gov).

The National Security Agency (open to U.S. citizens only) is the premier code-making and code-breaking agency in the world, housing the most supercomputers in one location. If you know programming, advanced math, or any foreign language, you can use your abilities to read intercepted messages, track enemy submarine acoustic signatures in the Atlantic Ocean, or search through databases to spot the movements and operations of international terrorists.

If you find encryption fascinating but would rather not help your country prepare for war, consider putting your encryption skills to use in the international banking and financial world, where encryption protects electronic transactions worth billions of dollars every day.

For more information about encryption, visit one of the following Web sites. Many of these sites offer C/C++ source code to various encryption algorithms, so you can practice both your programming and encryption skills at the same time.

> ✔ **CypherNet** (www.cypher.net) is a grass-roots organization dedicated to helping individuals use encryption to protect themselves against their own governments.

- ✔ **Central Intelligence Agency** (www.odci.gov/cia) is the most famous intelligence agency in the world, responsible for spying on other countries.

- ✔ **North American Cryptography Archives** (www.cryptography.org) offers plenty of encryption programs and encryption algorithm source code to help you learn as much as possible about encryption.

- ✔ **International PGP Home Page** (www.pgpi.com) is the home of the most famous personal encryption program in the world, Pretty Good Privacy (PGP).

- ✔ **RSA** (www.rsa.com), which is named after the first names of its founders, Rivest, Shamir, and Adleman, is the number-one encryption company providing encryption technology for many programs that rely on the Internet.

Internet Programming

Many Internet-based companies are popping up because Internet-based companies currently can watch their stock prices soar without ever having to make a profit. With so much activity revolving around the Internet, the increasing demand for Internet programmers is no surprise. The job security is high.

To get involved in this field, spend some time mastering the intricacies of HTML so that you know the basics of designing Web pages. (A little bit of training in graphic design and layout won't hurt either.)

Although HTML can create pretty Web pages, companies really want to take advantage of the Internet to sell products online. To make interactive Web sites, programmers use a variety of languages, including Java, JavaScript, VBScript, Perl, and Python.

To get started in Internet programming, teach yourself HTML; start playing around with an Internet programming language (such as VBScript); sharpen your Windows NT, Linux, or UNIX operating system skills; learn more about accessing databases using SQL; and play with Web servers such as Apache (which often comes free with Linux).

(Coincidentally, IDG Books Worldwide, Inc. publishes many books about the preceding topics, including Java and Linux. To learn more about these books, visit www.dummies.com.)

Visit one of the following Web sites to see how quickly you can start working (and earning a lot of money) in an Internet programming position:

- ✔ **Cool Web Jobs** (www.coolwebjobs.co.uk) lists various Internet programming jobs, along with advice to help you find the best job for you.

- ✔ **Web Jobs USA** (www.webjobsusa.com) is dedicated to helping Internet professionals find jobs practicing their Web page and Internet programming skills.

- ✔ **Java Jobs** (javajobs.com) provides tutorials, training, and Java-related job listings.

Fighting Computer Viruses

Every month, malicious programmers release hundreds of new computer viruses into the wild. Fortunately, many of these computer viruses have bugs that keep them from working properly: They don't spread, they're too easy to detect, they don't do anything other than take up space, and so on.

Still, every year a few new computer viruses manage to cause immense headaches to computer users throughout the world. One of the first of these super-viruses was the Michaelangelo virus, which tries to wipe out your hard disk on March 6 of every year.

Although most virus writers create viruses for their own amusement and entertainment, a small minority actively write destructive viruses as an intellectual challenge. Because malicious programmers, such as virus writers, will always be around, programmers who can create and update anti-virus programs can always find work.

To learn more about computer viruses, study assembly language. Most viruses and anti-virus programs use assembly language to create small, fast programs that can directly access the actual computer hardware. To learn more about different anti-virus companies and what type of positions they have available, visit any of the following Web sites:

- ✔ **Network Associates** (www.nai.com) publishes the popular VirusScan anti-virus program.

- ✔ **Symantec** (www.symantec.com) publishes the popular Norton AntiVirus program.

- ✔ **Data Fellows** (www.datafellows.com) publishes the well-regarded F-Prot anti-virus program.

Hacking for Hire

Hackers are often extremely skilled (or extremely patient) people who enjoy the technical challenge of breaking into computers. Although breaking into computers is technically illegal, your chances of getting caught increase immensely the moment that you start causing damage.

Rather than risk getting thrown in jail because you can't resist playing around with computers, consider the alternative challenge of trying to outwit the hackers themselves. As a computer security expert, you can work for the government to help track down malicious hackers, or you can work for a corporation and keep hackers out of a company's computers.

By working as a "good" hacker, you get to face all the technical challenges of hacking while getting paid. Plus, you get to experience the thrill of working on the side of law enforcement agencies to track down hackers around the world.

To learn more about using your hacking skills on the side of law enforcement, visit the following Web sites:

- **Federal Bureau of Investigation** (www.fbi.gov) is the agency in charge of United States law enforcement on a national level, including investigating and prosecuting computer hackers.

- **Ethical Hackers Against Pedophilia** (www.ehap.org) is a volunteer organization that pledges to use its hacking skills to track down and stop pedophiles on the Internet.

- **AntiOnline** (www.antionline.com) provides news and hacking tools, along with a network of computers on which hackers can safely and legally expand their skills.

- **2600** (www.2600.com) is a quarterly hacker magazine that provides hacking-related articles and information.

- **Hacker News Network** (www.hnn.com) provides the latest news about computer hacking.

Participating in an Open Source Project

To get a job, you need job experience, but you can't get job experience unless you have a job. Given this paradox, the most reliable way to solve the problem is to demonstrate your abilities by working for free.

To get valuable programming experience that will impress big companies, consider participating in an open source project. The whole idea behind an open source project is to get programmers to contribute to the development of a single project, such as the Linux operating system or the GNOME user interface for Linux.

Working on an open source project not only gives you instant credibility (provided that you actually contribute something useful), but it also gives you valuable experience in working with a real-life programming project. While other programmers may get shuffled into entry-level positions working on boring projects that nobody really cares about, you'll get to work on something that can give you pride and a sense of accomplishment.

The prestige of contributing to an open source project can later help you find a better-paying job, or it can be an amusing hobby. Either way, open source projects give you a chance to prove to the world what you can actually accomplish with your programming skills.

To get involved with an open source project, visit one of the following Web sites and start programming:

- ✔ **Open Source** (www.opensource.org) provides news and information about the value of open source projects.
- ✔ **Free Software Foundation** (www.fsf.org) has information about open source projects and the GNU C compiler, in particular.
- ✔ **Perl** (www.perl.com) is the home page of the Perl programming language, which is quickly becoming the most popular programming language for the Internet.
- ✔ **Apple Open Source** (www.publicsource.apple.com) is the place for information on Apple Computer's open source operating system projects.
- ✔ **GNOME project** (www.gnome.org) guides the development of the GNOME interface, which aims to put a friendly graphical user interface on Linux.
- ✔ **Mozilla** (www.mozilla.org) is the open source project for Netscape Navigator, the second most popular Web browser in the universe.
- ✔ **Linux** (www.linux.org) is the premier UNIX-clone operating system that has even Microsoft worried.

Niche Market Programming

One problem with programming classes is that they teach you how to write programs, but they don't teach you how to put your skills to practical use. Most companies use computers, so try to combine your knowledge of programming with another field.

For example, who is better qualified to design and write medical software than a programmer with a medical background (or a medical professional with a programming background)? Sports fanatics have combined programming skills with enthusiasm for sports to design horse race handicapping software, health professionals have designed nutrition and diet software, and lawyers have created special legal software.

Practically every field has unique needs that general-purpose software (like spreadsheets or databases) can't solve. That's why programmers are hired to develop custom software.

Best of all, niche markets are so small that you never have to worry about monolithic companies like Microsoft competing against you and wiping out your business. In addition, only a handful of programmers can even possibly write programs for certain niche markets (how many programmers have experience in hotel management?), which means that you'll have less competition and a market practically begging for your software.

If you've ever wanted to take advantage of your previous job experience and combine it with your new programming skills, consider developing a program that solves a specific problem in a niche market. Who knows? With your programming skills, you could find new opportunities in a field that might have seemed like a dead end.

Teaching Others about Computers

Become an expert in any field, and you can teach others your unique skills. In addition to the obvious teaching positions in schools, training others to use popular programs such as Microsoft Word, Lotus Notes, or C++ programming is a lucrative business.

Training professionals travel around the world, conducting classes for corporations who want to train their workers to use a variety of programs in hopes that they'll become more productive. As a trainer, you get to see the world, meet people, and see for yourself how many different ways Holiday Inns can design the inside of a hotel room.

If you like dealing with people, enjoy travelling, and love sharing your knowledge of computers with others, this may be the perfect position for you.

Selling Your Own Software

There's no better way to go into business for yourself than to develop and sell your own software. Unlike restaurants or bookstores, you don't need a large amount of space or an extensive inventory. You simply write a program, and sell it electronically over the Internet.

The most popular way to test-market a program is through shareware distribution: You give away copies of your software, and ask that people send you money if they find it useful. To encourage more people to send money, your program must be useful and work reliably.

Despite the seemingly bizarre business logic of giving away your product and trusting that people will actually pay you for it, many shareware authors have earned hundreds (and sometimes millions) of dollars for their programs over the years. (One of the most successful shareware programs is WinZip, which you can download at www.winzip.com.) Distributing programs as shareware can make you rich or earn you a little bit of extra spending money.

If you've ever wanted to start your own business but didn't want to take out a loan, starting a shareware business is the easiest and cheapest solution. All it takes is a good idea, some decent programming skills, and a little bit of marketing know-how to launch your business.

If your program doesn't appeal to the average computer user, try selling it to a niche market instead. In addition to niche markets for stock brokers, law enforcement agencies, or restaurant owners, niche markets also target specific computers, such as the Palm III or Windows CE.

You can turn your programming skills into your own business with the right computer program. And if you like programming, what other job lets you stay home all day, play around with your computer, and still get paid for it in a business all your own?

Chapter 26

Ten Additional Programming Resources

. . . .

In This Chapter

▶ Commercial compilers

▶ Shareware and freeware compilers

▶ Proprietary languages

▶ Mail-order houses

▶ Sources for source code

▶ Join a user group

▶ Usenet newsgroups

▶ Core War

▶ Battling robots

▶ Lego Mindstorms

. . . .

*I*f QBASIC is your first foray into the wonderfully wacky world of computer programming, you may be curious about where to go from here. Although you can continue practicing your programming skills with QBASIC, you won't be able to develop any programs that you can sell commercially. Even worse, you won't be able to sell any of your QBASIC programs to run on computers that use Windows, Linux, or the Macintosh operating system.

Browse through this chapter to discover the other programming languages that you can choose next. If you're serious about programming as a career, the next logical choice is to learn C, C++, or Java. Of course, this means learning the arcane syntax of C, C++, or Java, so you may want to consider a simpler (but still powerful) alternative such as Visual Basic.

Then again, why limit yourself to C, C++, Java, or any version of BASIC when you can choose from literally hundreds of different programming languages with oddball names like Modula-2, LISP, LOGO, Scheme, Prolog, ICON, APL, COBOL, FORTRAN, Ada, and Perl.

Because programming can often get frustrating and downright troublesome, this chapter also includes resources where you can find additional help from real-life people — for example, at computer user groups in your area or Usenet newsgroups on the Internet.

To save you money, this chapter also points you to mail-order houses where you can find a wide variety of programming tools at steep discounts. If you get tired of practicing programming, this chapter also directs you to various programming games that you can play to sharpen your programming skills and have fun at the same time.

Just remember that no matter what language you use or where you find additional programming help, ultimately your own skills determine whether your programming project gets done on time and works or is so buggy and unreliable that it gets abandoned.

Trying Commercial Compilers

The most important tool for any programmer is a language compiler. (See Chapter 4 for information on what a compiler does and why you would want one.) Although you can find plenty of free language compilers, most programmers rely on commercial compilers that offer support and regular updates. Most commercial compilers cost several hundred dollars (which doesn't matter if your company is paying for them), but you can often buy special beginner or standard editions of compilers that cost much less (typically ranging in price from $50 to $150).

Windows 95/98/NT/2000 programming

Like it or not, Microsoft Windows is the dominant operating system on the planet (although Linux is quickly gaining momentum). If you plan to write a program to sell to people, the largest and most profitable market is the Windows market.

The standard language for writing Windows programs is Visual C++, produced by the friendly folks at Microsoft (www.microsoft.com). Despite the addition of the term "Visual," Visual C++ is a fairly complicated C/C++ programming environment that even professional programmers have trouble mastering. Still, if you want to write Windows programs, you can't go wrong by picking up a copy of Visual C++.

Many people don't want to devote half their lives to learning the cryptic structure of C/C++ or the equally mystifying internal routines of the Windows operating system, so many programmers choose the second most popular programming tool: Visual Basic.

Unlike Visual C++, Visual Basic is actually easy to learn and enables you to design the appearance of your program visually. With Visual Basic, you can design the appearance of windows, buttons, dialog boxes, and menus, and then write BASIC code to make the whole thing actually do something useful. If you want to preserve your knowledge of QBASIC, learning Visual Basic is the next logical step in any programmer's quest to dominate the programming world.

Because of the growing popularity of Java, you may want to take a look at Symantec's (`www.symantec.com`) Visual Café, one of the first and fastest Java programming environments for Windows. Unlike other Java competitors, Visual Café includes a true compiler to convert your Java programs into machine language so that your Java programs will run fast in Windows.

A close competitor to Visual Café is JBuilder by Borland (`www.borland.com`). Borland has a long history of providing quality programming tools. You can find more third-party books that discuss JBuilder (such as *JBuilder For Dummies*) than discuss Visual Café.

Borland also sells two other popular rapid-application development tools called C++Builder and Delphi. Unlike Microsoft's Visual C++, C++Builder is a true rapid-application development tool that enables you to design your program's user interface in the same manner as Visual Basic. After you've completed the user interface, you just write C++ code to make the program actually work.

A rapid-application development (RAD) tool allows you to build the user interface quickly. (For more information about RAD tools, see Chapter 2.)

If you find C++ too confusing to learn and want something a bit more powerful than Visual Basic, consider another Borland alternative — Delphi. Like Visual Basic and C++Builder, Delphi allows you to visually design the user interface and then make the whole thing work by writing commands using the Pascal programming language.

Despite Delphi's second-class status (as a result of the Pascal language rapidly falling out of favor in the programming community), it has the reputation of letting you create programs in as little time as Visual Basic, but your programs run nearly as quickly as programs created in Visual C++. (In case you're wondering, Visual Basic programs tend to run slowly, and Visual C++ programs tend to be hard to create.)

To help you choose the best compiler for your needs, Table 26-1 lists several popular Windows compilers.

Table 26-1	Popular Windows Compilers	
Compiler Name	*Language Used*	*Web Site*
Visual C++	C, C++	www.microsoft.com
Visual Basic	BASIC	www.microsoft.com
Visual Café	Java	www.symantec.com
JBuilder	Java	www.borland.com
C++Builder	C, C++	www.borland.com
Delphi	Pascal	www.borland.com

Macintosh and PalmPilot programming

The Macintosh has a reputation for being one of the easiest computers in the world to use — and one of the hardest to program. Fortunately, the latest Macintosh programming tools have made Macintosh programming much easier.

The premier Macintosh programming tool is CodeWarrior (which is often credited with saving the Macintosh because it was the only reliable programming tool available at one time). CodeWarrior, created by Metrowerks (www.metrowerks.com), enables you to write programs in four different languages: C, C++, Java, and Pascal. So rather than buy four separate compilers, you have everything you need in one package.

Best of all, Metrowerks sells special versions of CodeWarrior so that you can write programs for Windows (both Windows 95/98/NT/2000 and Windows CE), Solaris, Linux, Sony PlayStation game consoles, Nintendo game consoles, and the most popular handheld computer in the world, the PalmPilot. If you plan to write programs for the Macintosh, the PalmPilot, or game consoles such as Nintendo or Sony PlayStation, CodeWarrior should be your first (and probably only) choice.

Of course, CodeWarrior doesn't support BASIC, so if you want to program a Macintosh using BASIC, you have three choices: Future Basic, Visual MacStandard Basic, and RealBasic.

Future Basic (www.staz.com) closely resembles QBASIC but can compile your programs into machine language so that you can sell and distribute your programs to anyone who owns a Macintosh.

Windows CE programming

Microsoft has created a stripped-down version of Windows called Windows CE, which is used in handheld and palm-size computers. Unfortunately, programs written for Windows 95/98/NT/2000 can't run on Windows CE. If you want to write programs for Windows CE, you have to use a special Windows CE compiler.

Microsoft developed Windows CE, so naturally Microsoft offers Windows CE programming toolkits for both Visual C++ and Visual Basic. The main drawback of using these two compilers is that you need to buy both a copy of Visual C++ (or Visual Basic) and its accompanying Windows CE toolkit. That means paying close to $495 for Visual C++ (or Visual Basic), plus another $195 for the Visual C++ (or Visual Basic) Windows CE toolkit.

Unfortunately, to write a Windows CE program using Visual C++ or Visual Basic, you need a computer running Windows 95/98/NT/2000 because you can't write Visual Basic or Visual C++ programs directly on a Windows CE handheld or palm-size computer.

Two programming languages that do enable you to write Windows CE programs directly on your Windows CE handheld or palm-size computer are Pocket C (www.orbworks.com) and NSBASIC (www.nsbasic.com). Pocket C uses a stripped-down version of the C programming language, and NSBASIC uses a stripped-down version of the BASIC programming language. Pocket C and NSBASIC aren't quite as powerful as Visual C++ and Visual Basic, but they allow you to create commercial-quality programs directly on a Windows CE computer.

Both Visual MacStandard Basic (www.zcurve.com) and RealBasic (www.realbasic.com) resemble Visual Basic. As with Visual Basic, you can design the user interface of your program and then write BASIC code to make your program work.

RealBasic even goes one step further and allows you to convert Visual Basic source code to run on the Macintosh. If you have any Visual Basic programs that you need to turn into Macintosh programs, you can do it with RealBasic.

Of course, converting Visual Basic programs into RealBasic won't be 100 percent accurate, which means you may have to modify the programs slightly. So if you really need to create both Macintosh and Windows programs, write your program in RealBasic and let RealBasic turn it into Macintosh and Windows programs at the same time.

Table 26-2 lists the most popular Macintosh compilers for writing programs for the Mac.

Table 26-2	Popular Macintosh Compilers	
Compiler Name	*Language Used*	*Web Site*
CodeWarrior	C, C++, Java, Pascal	www.metrowerks.com
RealBasic	BASIC	www.realbasic.com
Visual Mac-Standard Basic	BASIC	www.zcurve.com
Future Basic	BASIC	www.stazsoftware.com

Linux programming

If any operating system can break the Microsoft stranglehold on the personal computer market, Linux looks like the best choice. Linux is surging in popularity, and many companies and programmers are quickly porting their programs to run under Linux.

Several commercial vendors have promised Linux versions of their compilers (such as CodeWarrior and JBuilder), but you may be pleased to know that Linux has a rich assortment of language compilers that you can use for free.

Depending on your version of Linux (RedHat, Caldera, SUSE, or Debian, for example), you may already have a language compiler such as GNU C (a C language compiler) or EGCS (a C++ compiler).

Even though Linux doesn't offer as many applications as Windows or the Macintosh, plenty of Linux compilers are available for a variety of languages, including Ada, Pascal, FORTRAN, and BASIC. To find a Linux compiler, visit the Linux Applications and Utilities Web site at www.hongik.com/linux.

Testing the Shareware and Freeware Compilers

Choosing a programming language can often be as emotional and subjective as choosing someone to marry. Rather than buy a handful of commercial compilers only to find out that you don't like any of them or the programming languages they use, take some time to download a shareware or freeware compiler instead.

When you test shareware or freeware compilers, you can practice using different programming languages such as C++ or Java. When you find a programming language that you like, consider buying the shareware or a similar commercial compiler. For a list of free compilers for a variety of different programming languages, visit the Catalog of Free Compilers and Interpreters Web page at www.idiom.com/free-compilers.

BASIC compilers

If you love QBASIC and don't want to give it up, visit PowerBasic (www.powerbasic.com) and download its FirstBasic or PowerBasic shareware compilers that can convert your QBASIC programs into actual MS-DOS programs. If you want to convert your QBASIC programs into Windows programs, try the PowerBasic for Windows shareware compiler.

For another way to leverage your QBASIC programming skills in the Windows development market, take a look at Liberty BASIC (world.std.com/~carlg/basic.html), which bills itself as "QBASIC for Windows." (Oddly enough, Liberty BASIC was written in a language called SmallTalk, which goes to show you how one language can help you write a compiler or interpreter for another language.)

Because Windows offers the greatest potential market, with Linux catching up rapidly, you can play it safe by trying XBasic (www.basmark.com), which allows you to write Basic programs for Windows 95/98/NT/2000 and Linux, essentially doubling your market.

If you have a Macintosh, download the freeware Chipmunk Basic interpreter (not a compiler) from www.rahul.net/rhn/cbas.page.html. If you're using a Windows CE handheld computer, download the freeware BasiCE interpreter (www.jps.net/deang/basice.htm) so that you can write and run Basic programs under Windows CE.

C/C++ and Java compilers

C and C++ are powerful languages, but they can be intimidating to many people. Rather than spend lots of money buying a commercial C/C++ compiler, spend some time playing with shareware and freeware C/C++ compilers first. For an inexpensive shareware C interpreter/compiler, grab a copy of EiC (www.datagrid.com/~eic).

The most popular C compiler for Linux is the GNU C compiler, so that same compiler has been ported to Windows and renamed the Cygwin compiler (sourceware.cygnus.com/cygwin).

For those who want to tackle Java programming, download the free Java software development kit direct from Sun Microsystems (java.sun.com), the inventors of Java. This bare-bones Java programming tool can help you learn Java. Then when you're ready to create serious applications, you can buy a commercial Java tool, such as JBuilder or Visual Café.

Pascal compilers

Although Pascal has faded in popularity in North America, it's still popular in Europe. For a free Pascal compiler for MS-DOS, Windows, and Linux, download FPK-Pascal from tfdecl.fys.kuleuven.ac.be/~michael/fpc/fpc.html. If you've always wanted to dig into the guts of a compiler, visit the WinPascal Web site (www.bloodshed.nu/winpascal), where you can join an ongoing effort to create and develop a Pascal compiler for Windows.

Oddball language compilers and interpreters

Not everyone likes the idea of following the pack and learning traditional languages like C/C++ or BASIC. For you rebels out there, consider some of the oddball free language compilers or interpreters that give you a chance to play with some obscure programming languages.

Prolog has gained a loyal following as one of the more popular languages with which to learn about artificial intelligence. If you want to understand all the excitement about artificial intelligence languages, and Prolog in particular, download a free copy of Strawberry Prolog from www.dobrev.com.

Back in the early 1980s, the Department of Defense tried to force the Ada programming language into full-scale use for all military projects. Unfortunately for the Pentagon, by the time Ada compilers were available, most of the rest of the world had already switched to C/C++ and left Ada behind. Still, Ada has its supporters, and if you want to experiment with a language that tried to be the best programming language in the world, grab a copy of GNAT Ada from www.gnat.com.

Although BASIC was designed to teach beginners how to program computers, another language called LOGO was specifically designed to teach kids how to program computers. If you want to program Windows using the LOGO language, get a free copy of MSWLogo from Softronics (www.softronix.com).

If you'd like to experiment with the LOGO language on a Macintosh, you can get a copy of a LOGO interpreter called Turtle Tracks (`www.ugcs.caltech. edu/~dazuma/turtle/index.html`). Interestingly enough, Turtle Tracks was written in Java, so if you really feel ambitious, you can modify the Java source code and see how much programming you really know.

To track down other oddball language compilers and interpreters, visit `dir.yahoo.com/Computers_and_Internet/Programming_Languages.`, the Yahoo! programming language Web page You'll find links to more programming languages than you knew existed.

Using a Proprietary Language

Programming languages such as C/C++ and Java have a wide variety of books, magazines, newsletters, source code, and users around the world who can provide help and advice for solving specific problems. Unfortunately, popular programming languages are designed to solve a wide variety of different problems, which means that they usually can't solve any single problem quickly and easily.

As an alternative to popular programming languages, consider using a proprietary programming language. A proprietary programming language may not have the wide range of support that general-purpose languages can offer (such as books or magazines), but they can make programming much easier, especially for beginners.

Proprietary programming languages are usually developed by a single company to perform a specific type of task, such as creating multimedia presentations or artificially intelligent programs. Proprietary programming languages have the following advantages:

 ✔ Proprietary languages are generally easier than popular languages to learn.

 ✔ Proprietary language programs are often smaller and faster to create because the languages are designed to perform a specific task.

Although proprietary programming languages can be easier to learn and allow you to create fancy applications with a minimum amount of programming, they have their own disadvantages, which may make you wary of using them for critical projects:

 ✔ You won't find as much third-party support (such as books or magazines) for proprietary languages as for popular languages.

 ✔ Proprietary languages may run only on certain operating systems (meaning that porting the program to another operating system could be virtually impossible).

- ✔ You're dependent on a single company for support. If the company that made your proprietary language goes out of business, your program may be difficult or next to impossible to update.

- ✔ Buying a proprietary language may be extremely expensive compared to buying general-purpose language compilers.

- ✔ Proprietary language programs often run slower than programs created in a general-purpose language.

HyperCard

One of the most popular (and ultimately most ignored) proprietary programming languages comes from Apple Computer's HyperCard program. HyperCard was originally designed to allow non-programmers to write programs using an index card metaphor.

An entire HyperCard program is meant to resemble a stack of index cards, with one card at a time appearing on the screen. Text and pictures appear on each card, and cards can provide hyperlinks to other cards. By using a simplified programming language called HyperTalk, you could write programs to make your HyperCard stack calculate results or display information.

Although HyperCard is considered the forerunner of hypertext and visual programming (long before the popularity of the World Wide Web and Visual Basic), the HyperCard programs often ran too slowly and were limited to running only on the Macintosh.

Apple Computer no longer gives away free copies of HyperCard with every Macintosh, and the company has pretty much let HyperCard drift further into the background of neglect. Still, HyperCard's latest claim to fame was that it was used to create the best-selling game, Myst, which shows that imagination is ultimately more important than the programming language you choose.

To learn more about HyperCard, visit `www.apple.com`.

MetaCard

In the wake of HyperCard's initial popularity, many companies offered HyperCard-clone programs. Following HyperCard's steady decline into obscurity, most of these HyperCard-clone programs have also died.

One of the few remaining HyperCard clones is MetaCard, which not only runs HyperCard stacks, but also runs them on a variety of different operating systems including the Macintosh, Windows, and UNIX. So if you've written any programs using HyperCard and want to preserve your programs while allowing them to run on different computers, consider using MetaCard (`www.metacard.com`).

KnowledgePro

KnowledgePro is a curious mix of object-oriented programming, hypertext, and artificial intelligence rolled into one. Available for both MS-DOS and Windows, KnowledgePro allows you to use its unique programming language to display windows, text, buttons, and graphics with a minimal number of commands.

After you create a program in KnowledgePro, you can convert it into C++ code and then compile this code into a true machine code program. Thus you get the advantage of creating a program quickly using KnowledgePro, along with the advantage of creating a program that runs quickly.

If you still have no idea how KnowledgePro might be able to help you, visit the company's Web site (www.kgarden.com) to download a trial copy or view the list of users and the applications they've created to see whether KnowledgePro might be right for you.

Clarion

Clarion is a programming language specifically designed for creating database applications. Because Clarion programs are compiled into machine code, they run much faster than similar database programs such as Microsoft Access or Visual FoxPro.

Best of all, Clarion is one of the few languages that allows you to create programs for Windows 3.1, Windows 95/98, Windows NT, and the World Wide Web without any modification whatsoever of your original source code. That way you can sell and distribute your program to as many people as possible. For more information about Clarion, visit www.topspeed.com.

PowerBuilder

One of the more popular database development languages is PowerBuilder, which enables you to visually design a database application with a minimum of coding. Whether you need to share data with big mainframe computers or minicomputers, PowerBuilder could be the product for making your next application. To find out more about PowerBuilder, visit www.sybase.com.

Shopping by Mail Order

You can buy language compilers directly from the publishers, but unless they're offering a special discounted price, you're better off buying from a mail-order house. Mail-order houses sell products at a discount — and they often aren't required to charge you sales tax.

In addition to offering a wide variety of commercial compilers at discounted prices, mail-order houses often stock a variety of programming tools that you may never find anywhere else, such as special programming editors, code analyzers, language utilities to make programming easier, copy-protection kits, and installation programs.

These mail-order houses specialize in programming tools:

- ✔ **Programmer's Paradise** (www.pparadise.com) offers a variety of programming tools for a variety of languages.

- ✔ **ZAC Catalogs** (www.zaccatalog.com) offers utilities, add-ons, and programming toolkits for rapid-application development tools such as Visual Basic, Delphi, and C++Builder.

- ✔ **VBXtras** (www.vbxtras.com) specializes in Visual Basic add-ons and programming aids.

Getting Your Hands on Source Code

Because one of the best ways to learn anything is to learn from someone else, many programmers voluntarily share their source code so that others can benefit from their work. The Linux operating system is the ultimate example of people sharing source code.

If you can get the source code to another program, you can include its features in your own program, thus saving you time. Many companies sell programming utilities (such as miniature word processors, spreadsheets, or graphics-charting programs) that you can paste together into your own programs. As a bonus, some of these companies also include the source code so that you can modify the program for your needs.

To buy the source code to programs that solve fairly complicated problems (such as sending and receiving faxes or encrypting data), visit one of the mail-order houses listed in the "Shopping by Mail Order" section of this chapter.

You can often find the source code to small programs scattered around the Internet for free. These small programs typically solve simple problems, but one of those problems might be exactly what you need.

To find source code for your favorite language, use a search engine to search for the string "C source code." This search string likely will turn up a long list of useless Web sites and an occasional useful Web site that offers source code that you can download for free.

To help narrow your search for source code, try visiting one of these Web sites:

- ✔ **Code Guru** (www.codeguru.com) offers source code snippets to a variety of popular languages, including C/C++, Visual Basic, and Java.

- ✔ **Planet Source Code** (www.planet-source-code.com) provides Visual Basic and Java source code.

- ✔ **Carl & Gary's Visual Basic Page** (www.cgvb.com) is loaded with tons of information and source code exclusively for Visual Basic.

- ✔ **The Delphi Source** (www.doit.com/delphi) features source code just for Delphi programmers.

- ✔ **QBASIC.com** (www.qbasic.com) offers news and source code specifically regarding QBASIC.

- ✔ **ABC: All BASIC Code** (www.basicguru.com/abc) has source code for nearly all varieties of BASIC, including QBASIC, QuickBasic, and Visual Basic.

- ✔ **The JavaScript Source** (javascript.internet.com) offers loads of free source code for programming in JavaScript.

- ✔ **The cprogramming.com site** (www.cprogramming.com) offers lots of source code for C/C++ programmers to use and enjoy.

Joining a Local User Group

Programming can be lonely and difficult in isolation. If you're lucky (or unlucky, depending on your point of view) to live in a big city, you may be able to find a local programming user group.

User groups meet regularly — usually weekly or monthly — and allow programmers to share tips and information with one another concerning their favorite language, such as C/C++, Java, or Delphi.

Many user groups advertise in local computer magazines and newsletters, which you can often find in your favorite computer store. For another way to find a user group in your area, visit the Web site of your favorite compiler company (such as www.microsoft.com or www.borland.com). Company Web sites often list user group meetings in different cities.

Frequenting Usenet Newsgroups

Learning anything can be much easier if you have some friends to help you out. If you don't have any knowledgeable programming friends nearby, use the next best resource — a Usenet newsgroup.

Newsgroups act like electronic bulletin boards where anyone can leave a message asking for help. Complete strangers from all over the world can give you advice or information to answer your question. If you browse through newsgroups long enough, you can often respond to other people's messages and give them some help as well.

Nearly every programming language has a newsgroup where loyal programmers gather and swap tips, tricks, and news. Check out these newsgroups:

- ✔ `comp.lang` is a general-purpose programming newsgroup.
- ✔ `comp.lang.basic` is a newsgroup for BASIC programming enthusiasts.
- ✔ `comp.lang.c` is for C programming fanatics and followers.
- ✔ `comp.lang.c++` allows you to learn C++ from this newsgroup.
- ✔ `comp.lang.delphi` lets you band together with other Delphi programmers.
- ✔ `comp.lang.java.help` is a great place for getting help with programming and using Java.
- ✔ `comp.lang.pascal` covers Pascal programming, including some Delphi programming news and information.

This is just a short list of available programming newsgroups. With a little bit of searching, you can find newsgroups for other programming languages and specific compilers such as Visual Basic, C++Builder, and Visual Café.

Playing Core War

People tend to learn faster and more effectively when they're having fun (which is a lesson that public schools and copycat book publishers still haven't figured out yet). Although writing a program that can calculate a second-order differential equation may improve your programming skills, it may also make you think that programming can be extremely boring.

So to keep you from getting bored and to show you that programming can actually be a lot of fun, play one of many programming games available for free (or for a nominal price). The purpose of programming games is to help sharpen your programming skills. If you want to win, you have to learn to write the smallest, fastest, and most efficient programs — just like in real life.

The granddaddy of all programming games is Core War. In the old days, computers didn't use floppy or hard disks. Instead, they used something called core memory.

The idea behind Core War is to write a program that gets "stored" in the core memory of an imaginary mainframe computer. To play Core War, each player has to write a program using a simplified version of assembly language, dubbed Red Code. Each program must search for enemy programs and erase them from the computer's core memory. The winner is the player whose program is the last surviving program in core memory.

Although Core War is popular, it's not a very visually exciting game to watch. All you see are the various programs stalking one another in core memory and trying to erase the instructions of enemy programs, which often looks no more interesting than watching a visual depiction of your hard disk getting defragmented.

For more information about Core War, visit one of the following sites:

- ✔ www.ecst.csuchico.edu/~pizza/koth
- ✔ www.koth.org
- ✔ ftp.csua.berkeley.edu/pub/corewar

To exchange messages with other Core War fanatics, visit the news:rec.games.corewar newsgroup, where you can learn about the latest Core War tournaments and get started writing your own killer programs.

Programming a Battling Robot

The Core War programming game (covered in the previous section) doesn't have great graphics to hold a player's attention. To satisfy the players' need for visual appeal, rival programming games incorporate more adventurous graphics. And, of course, what could be more appealing than war and gladiatorial combat. Instead of sending human gladiators into an arena to fight to the death, some programming games provide an imaginary arena where battling robots fight to the death.

Each robot has identical capabilities to move, search, and shoot. But the actual actions of each robot are determined by the way each player programs his or her robot. To program a robot, you have to write a miniature program using a simplified version of the C, C++, or Pascal language.

The challenge is not only to write a program that runs correctly, but also to provide your robot with instructions that create an optimum defensive and offensive strategy for surviving, stalking, and killing enemy robots at the same time.

Write a large program that gives your robot limited choices, and your robot will probably get blown up within seconds. Write a small program that runs quickly and provides your robot with enough intelligence to avoid damage while pummeling its opponents as often as possible, and your robot will likely survive any battle.

In addition to providing a more visually appealing way to see whose programming is better, battling robot games also give you a chance to practice writing programs in your favorite language, such as C, C++, or Pascal. When you master how to control a robot using C or Pascal, you'll be able to transfer your robot programming skills to real-life programs.

Most battling robot programs run only on MS-DOS. If that's okay with you, download a free copy of a battling robots game from one of the following Web sites:

- **The C++ Robots game** is at www.gamerz.net/~c++robots.

- **The C-Robots game** is at ftp://oak.oakland.edu/pub/simtelnet/ msdos/c/crobots.zip.

- **The P-Robots game** (for Pascal programming) is at mysteria.com/ pub/pascal.

Toying with Lego Mindstorms

Nearly every kid has had the chance to play with Lego building blocks (and plenty of parents have had the chance to step on a Lego building block in their bare feet). Because so many kids love playing with computers, the fine people controlling the Lego empire decided to combine Legos with computers, and the result is something called Lego Mindstorms (www.legomindstorms.com).

With Lego Mindstorms, you build a robot using Lego bricks, and then you program it using a simplified, graphically oriented programming language. Of course, if you find this simplified programming language too tame, the Lego Mindstorms Web site offers a free software developer's toolkit that allows you to program a Lego robot using Visual Basic. Programming a Lego robot involves pasting together blocks of instructions, similar to snapping together Lego building blocks.

For hardcore programmers who would rather use a language tougher than Visual Basic, visit the LegOS Web site (www.multimania.com/legos) and download tools that allow you to control your Lego Mindstorms robots using assembly language, C, C++, Pascal, or practically any programming language you choose.

With a copy of Lego Mindstorms and any of the available free programming toolkits, you can create your own robots made of Legos and program them to attack one another, chase your dog around the house, or run berserk and protect your house against prowlers. When you practice your programming skills with Lego Mindstorms, you can create almost anything you want within the safe, friendly environment of Legos.

Index

(continued)

IDG BOOKS WORLDWIDE BOOK REGISTRATION